The Rise of Asia

NEW HORIZONS IN INTERNATIONAL BUSINESS

Series Editor: Peter J. Buckley
Centre for International Business,
University of Leeds (CIBUL), UK

The New Horizons in International Business series has established itself as the world's leading forum for the presentation of new ideas in international business research. It offers pre-eminent contributions in the areas of multinational enterprise – including foreign direct investment, business strategy and corporate alliances, global competitive strategies, and entrepreneurship. In short, this series constitutes essential reading for academics, business strategists and policy makers alike.

Titles in the series include:

The Rise of Asia

The 'Flying-Geese' Theory of Tandem Growth and Regional Agglomeration

Terutomo Ozawa

Emeritus Professor of Economics, Colorado State University and Research Associate, Center on Japanese Economy and Business, Columbia Business School, USA

NEW HORIZONS IN INTERNATIONAL BUSINESS

Edward Elgar
Cheltenham, UK • Northampton, MA, USA

Published by
Edward Elgar Publishing Limited
The Lypiatts
15 Lansdown Road
Cheltenham
Glos GL50 2JA
UK

Edward Elgar Publishing, Inc.
William Pratt House
9 Dewey Court
Northampton
Massachusetts 01060
USA

A catalogue record for this book
is available from the British Library

Library of Congress Control Number: 2009922762

Mixed Sources
Product group from well-managed
forests and other controlled sources
www.fsc.org Cert no. SA-COC-1565
© 1996 Forest Stewardship Council

ISBN 978 1 84720 815 6

Printed and bound by MPG Books Group, UK

For all my mentors and friends with gratitude – and to my family with love

Contents

Figures and tables

FIGURES

TABLES

About the author

Terutomo Ozawa received an MBA and a Ph.D. from Columbia University. He is on the editorial advisory board for *Transnational Corporations* (UN journal), on the editorial board for the *Journal of Asian Economics*, and on the editorial board for the *Global Economy Quarterly*. He has written extensively on multinational corporations, structural change, and economic growth. He also has served as a consultant for international organizations such as the OECD, UNCTAD, UNESCAP, UNITAR, the World Bank, the Asian Development Bank, and the Asian Productivity Organization. He was president of the International Trade and Finance Association in 2003.

Abbreviations

ABM	Automated Banking Machine
ADB	Asian Development Bank
ADF	Augmented Dickey–Fuller
APEC	Asia-Pacific Economic Cooperation
ASEAN	Association of Southeast Asian Countries
ATM	Automatic Teller Machine
BOP	Balance of Payments
BOT	Build, Operate, and Transfer
BRIC	Brazil, Russia, India, and China
BT	Biotechnology
CA	Current Account
CDO	Collateralized Debt Obligation
CVRD	Companhia Vale do Rio Doce
DIAE	Division on Investment and Enterprise
ECLAC	Economic Commission on Latin America and the Caribbean
EIBA	European International Business Association
EPZ	Export Processing Zone
Ex-Im	Export Import
FA	Financial Account
FDI	Foreign Direct Investment
FG	Flying-Geese
FRB	Federal Reserve Bank
GDP	Gross Domestic Product
GPS	Global Positioning System
HDTV	High-Definition Television
HPAEs	High-Performing Asian Economies
IAB	Investment Analysis Bureau
ICOR	Incremental Capital-Output Ratio
ICSEAD	International Center for the Study of East Asian Development
IL-IS	Inward-Looking Import Substitution
IPO	Initial Public Offering
IT	Information Technology
IS-EP	Import Substitution-Export Promotion

JETRO	Japan External Trade Organization
JICA	Japanese International Cooperation Agency
LBO	Leveraged Buyout
LNG	Liquid Natural Gas
M&A	Merger & Acquisition
MITI	Ministry of International Trade and Industry
MNC	Multinational Corporation
MPX	Import–Production–Export
NAFTA	North American Free Trade Agreement
NGOs	Non-governmental organizations
NIE	Newly Industrializing Economy
NSF	National Science Foundation
NT	Nanotechnology
OECD	Organization for Economic Cooperation and Development
OECF	Overseas Economic Cooperation Fund
OEM	Original Equipment Manufacturing
OL-EP	Outward-Looking Export Promotion
OPEC	Organization of Petroleum Exporting Countries
PC	Product Cycle
PPP	Purchasing Power Parity
S&E	Science and Engineering
SAFE	State Administration of Foreign Exchange
SAIS	School of Advanced International Studies
SWF	Sovereign Wealth Fund
TPG	Texas Pacific Group
UNCTAD	United Nations Conference on Trade and Development
UNCTC	United Nations Center on Transnational Corporations
UNU	United Nations University
VC	Venture Capital
VECM	Vector Error Correction Model
WEF	World Economic Forum
WIDER	World Institute for Development Economics Research
WIR	World Investment Report
WTO	World Trade Organization
www	World Wide Web

Foreword

Professor Terutomo Ozawa again breaks new ground in reformulating the flying-geese theory of economic development. He follows up on his previous publication, *Institutions, Industrial Upgrading, and Economic Performance in Japan: The 'Flying-Geese' Paradigm of Catch-up Growth* (2005), by shifting from the topic of catch-up economic development in a given individual country to that of 'regionalized growth' in his new book, *The Rise of Asia*. He boldly translates the conventional FG theory of *national* economic development into the realm of *supra-national* regional growth. This focal shift is well mirrored in the subtitles of these two sister monographs: *Catch-up Growth* (in a given economy) for the previous volume and *Tandem Growth* ('interactive growth' within Asia's hierarchy of economies) for the present one.

Ozawa asks why growth has been so successfully regionalized in Asia. He interprets Asia's catch-up as an outcome of what he calls 'US-led growth clustering'. And the forces of such clustering are examined in terms of the economics of flying-geese formation. He makes us rethink how to examine economic development – not so much in separate individual countries as in integrative terms on a regional basis. In other words, what he advocates is a region, not a country, as the basic unit of analysis.

Ozawa's analysis now covers a wide spectrum of phenomena related to regionalized growth. He introduces FG-style stage models for infrastructure development, development finance, and business finance, thereby encompassing both the real- and the money-dimensions of economic growth. The interesting notions of 'stages co-mingling, reconstructing and skipping' and 'time and space compression' capture some salient features of Asia's catch-up growth, FG-style. He thus shows us how extensively the way we 'think in flying-geese terms' – that is, 'think in dialectical, evolutionary, hierarchical, and interactive terms', as he puts it, can be applied to the wide-ranging features of catch-up growth at the regional level. As demonstrated throughout the book, this 'FG way of thinking' takes a long-term, holistic, and dynamic vision, 'connecting the dots' (that is, looking at major economic events/upheavals as concomitant, related phenomena deriving from the common underlying forces of the global economy) rather than taking a reductionist, short-term, and static perspective.

In short, Ozawa's new work marks another significant advance in elaborating and extending – as he does in his own iconoclastic way of interpretation – the original ideas set forth by Professor Kaname Akamatsu of Hitotsubashi University. He thinks outside the box. This thought-provocative book is a must-read, together with the previous one, for anyone who adopts the FG frame of reference for understanding of – and research on – the topic of economic development in an age of ever-deepening integration.

Kiyoshi Kojima
Emeritus Professor of Economics
Hitotsubashi University

Koganei, Tokyo
summer, 2008

Preface and acknowledgements

This book is a sequel to *Institutions, Industrial Upgrading, and Economic Performance in Japan: The 'Flying-Geese' Paradigm of Catch-up Growth* (Edward Elgar, 2005; paperback edition, 2006). In that book, I examined how postwar Japan succeeded in catching up with the advanced West by upgrading its industrial structure through emulative learning. It is a story of great transformation in which a war-devastated Japan was reconstructed and emerged as the world's second largest economy over as short a span as less than three decades. Analysis was focused on the process of catch-up growth in that particular nation, Japan. By contrast, this book looks at Asia as a whole (and as the basic unit of analysis) and examines interactive/emulative growth between the US (the lead goose) and the region's catching-up economies – and among the latter themselves. It explores how emulative learning has spread to other Asian economies that followed in Japan's tracks. But Japan itself has been a great beneficiary of US-led global capitalism, especially during the Cold War. In a nutshell, the present book tells the story of how a cohort of Asian countries led by the US has advanced together, though in a staggered fashion, in structural upgrading and economic growth.

No economic system is perfect – that is, there is *no* first-best system. It always has advantages and drawbacks, boons and banes. For the system to prevail, however, the positive ought to be greater than the negative over the long haul, if not in the short run. It is a matter of whether a particular way of organizing economic activities is second-best, third-best, or even lower best. Capitalism, when combined with democracy, even though far from first-best, has proven far superior to socialism, communism, and authoritarianism in raising the standard of living *and* safeguarding human rights and individual liberty. But capitalism itself can still function in varying degrees in catching-up countries even under an undemocratic regime such as communism (as evidenced in China).

Countries are at different stages of economic growth. Such differences are the source of benefits that *both* the advanced and the less advanced can capitalize on by interacting – and integrating closely – across borders. It is the fortune of our times that the most economically advanced nation that 'leads' the world happens to operate on the principles of market capitalism and democracy. (Just imagine the nightmare of having a communist, totalitarian, or authoritarian country as the hegemon that dictates to the entire world, though we tend to dwell on, and grumble about, the frailties of capitalism and democracy.)

I introduced the notion of 'tandem growth' in a background paper (1994) submitted to UNCTAD in preparation for the *World Investment Report (WIR) 1995*. To my delight, it was soon afterwards picked up in a *Financial Times* article that reviewed the WIR. Tandem growth as a new concept was thus apparently appealing. Until very recently, it had been best illustrated by the pattern of staggered catch-up growth in a string of East Asian economies. The US provided a favorable growth environment in East Asia during the Cold War. Japan's catch-up growth was quickly followed first by the newly industrializing countries (NIEs), which was in turn emulated by the ASEAN-4, and more recently by China and Vietnam. This series of growth has been set in motion under what may be called 'US-led growth clustering'. When economic activities are organized and coordinated within an extended hierarchy of countries, 'economies of hierarchical concatenation' are engendered, benefiting all the constituent countries, but especially those catching up (Ozawa, 1995, 2005).

In this regard, when we study economic development, the fundamental unit of analysis should no longer be so much the nation-state per se but rather *a supra-national regionalized cluster* or *a mega-supra-national region,* such as Europe, North America, East Asia, Latin America, and the like. True, each national economy is still more consciously coordinated and more policy-governed than such a supra-national region. But the private sector is now increasingly integrated on a supra-national basis. The 'flying-geese' theory of tandem growth and regional agglomeration presented in this book is all about this supra-national regional integration of economic activities. In contrast, the conventional 'flying-geese' theory as originally set forth by Kaname Akamatsu largely adopts the nation-state as the basic unit of analysis – that is, to explain how catch-up growth occurs in a particular developing country, albeit in an open-economy context.

Many of the ideas presented here owe much to a host of precious opportunities I have luckily been blessed with, the opportunities to associate – and exchange ideas – with other scholars in the past. The previous 2005 book already acknowledges the heavy intellectual debts I owe to many of them (notably, Professor Kiyoshi Kojima of Hitotsubashi; Professor John H. Dunning of Reading, UK; Professor H. Peter Gray of Rutgers; Professor Jean-Louis Mucchielli of the Sorbonne; Professor Hugh Patrick of Columbia; Professor Colin Dodds of Saint Mary's; Professor Tetsuo Abo of Tokyo University; and Dr Dieter Ernst of the East-West Center, Hawaii). Hence, acknowledgements below are limited to only those who have inspired me specifically in connection with the present study and who were not mentioned previously.

Overdue acknowledgement must be given to Lord and Professor John Eatwell of Cambridge University, UK. After my journal article, 'Government Control over Technology Acquisition and Firms' Entry into New Sectors: The Experience of Japan's Synthetic Industry', was published in the *Cambridge Journal of Economics*, **4** (2), 1980, I was invited to give a talk to the Cambridge Political Economy Society. Then, Professor Eatwell asked me to come back to Cambridge in connection with the special BBC Cambridge TV series on Britain's industrial competitiveness, a program based on his book, *Whatever Happened to Britain? The Economics of Decline* (Duckworth, 1982). (In that book, he used as a reference my 1974 book, *Japan's Technological Challenge to the West, 1950–1974: Motivation and Accomplishment*, MIT Press.) Our interview appeared in two episodes of the TV series.

At that time (in the early 1980s), Japan was in the spotlight. Its rise to industrial power was the hot topic of the day. Japan was clearly on top of the world. Its automobile industry, in particular, was the envy and admiration of the world. And 'Japanization' of British factories was soon to be talked about. Some even speculated about Japan's imminent takeover of the United States as the world's economic leader, hinting that 'Pax Nipponica' would replace 'Pax Americana'. Also, Professor Eatwell organized a conference in 1981 in Moleria, Mexico, where I had the pleasure of getting acquainted with the late Lord Nicholas Kaldor of Cambridge, and Professor Alice Amsden of MIT. In addition, Professor Eatwell invited me again to spend an entire academic year as a visiting scholar in the Faculty of Economics and Politics, Cambridge University, 1982–3. It was my privilege to become acquainted with Professor Geoffrey C. Harcourt and Professor Ajit Singh during my stay. This wonderful sojourn gave me ample time to think about why a particular advanced economy falls into a decline while some, especially in East Asia, can successfully catch up and thrive. It was also a wonderful opportunity for our son, Edwin (then 14 years old), and daughter, Clare (then 8 years old), to be exposed to excellent British education at state schools in Cambridge that emphasized writing essays in take-home assignments as well as classroom exams (not just marking 'checks' on multiple-choice quizzes). They benefited enormously.

Also, I am indebted to Professor Clark W. Reynolds of Stanford, then the director of the Americas Program, for intellectual stimulation when he invited me as a paper presenter to three different conferences on economic development in Latin America held at Stanford in the late 1980s and the early 1990s. We co-authored two book chapters, 'Japanese Investment in Mexico: A New Industrial Nexus?' in Ramon Myers (ed.), *Integrating the World Economy: Japanese Direct Investment in Six Countries during the Late Twentieth Century* (Hoover Institution Press, 1996) and 'La Nueva Conexion Estados Unidos-Mexico-Japan: Interaccion Economica Trilateral e Integracion Regional en la Cuenca del Pacifico', in Alejandro Bejar and John Borrego (eds), *La Insercion de Mexico en la Cuenca del Pacifico* (Universidad Nacional Autonoma de Mexico, 1990). At those conferences organized by Professor Reynolds, I gained valuable under-standing about Latin American economies and also had the honor of meeting Professor Moses Abramovitz, Professor Masahiko Aoki, and Professor W.W. Rostow.

By the good offices of Professor Reynolds, I was then asked by Professor Riordan Roett of Johns Hopkins (SAIS) to present a paper at a confer-ence on Mexican economic development in Mexico City in 1990, and the paper was published as a book chapter, 'The Dynamics of Pacific Rim Industrialization: How Mexico can Join the Asian Flock of the "Flying Geese"', in Riordan Roett (ed.), *Mexico's External Relations in the 1990s* (Lynne Rienner, 1991). (The same chapter was also reproduced in D. Chudnovsky (ed.), *Transnational Corporations and Industrialization*, Vol. 11, UNLTNC, London: Routledge, 1993.) It was at that conference that I met former Mexican finance minister (1982–6) Jesus Silva-Herzog F., who by then had kindly made an arrangement to have my 1988 OECD mono-graph, *Recycling Japan's Surpluses for Developing Countries*, translated into and published in Spanish by the Center for Latin American Monetary Studies. These occasions led me to think of two different regions, Latin America and Asia, on a comparative basis (as reflected in Chapter 6).

I am also grateful to Dr Charles Oman of the OECD's Development Center in Paris for many years' professional association and friendship. Our friendship began in the spring of 1980 when I attended the Center's conference on foreign direct investment at his invitation. He then kept inviting me back to a number of conferences over the next decade and a half and funded a couple of my research projects. Some of them resulted in OECD publications: *Japan's General Trading Companies: Merchants of Economic Development*, (1984, co-authored with Kiyoshi Kojima, and translated into French and Japanese), and *Recycling Japan's Surpluses for Developing Countries*, (1988, also translated into French and Spanish). The former was part of the larger research project organized by Dr Oman for what he called 'the new forms of investment' (a comprehensive phrase describing all non-equity forms: see his pioneering monograph, *New Forms of Investment in Developing Countries*, OECD, 1984). All these research projects at the Center induced me to mull over *how* and *why* Asia was rapidly growing as a region – with cross-border investments of both the old and the new forms as the major driver of catch-up growth.

Dr Oman kindly encouraged our professional acquaintance to evolve into close friendship at the family level. He showed my wife and me around the Loire Valley (with its many great chateaux). In particular, Mrs Monique Oman has so warmly hosted us for dinner at their Paris home numerous times, delighting us with her exquisite recipes and culinary skills. In 1988 when my daughter and I happened to be in Paris, she welcomed us to stay with her parents in Jarnac, and showed us around Cognac, Bordeaux, and La Rochelle. On another occasion, she drove my wife and me to Auvers, the site of Vincent Van Gogh's work in his last days and of his grave. And most recently she kindly took us to their charming country house in Plaizac, an idyllic southern France village near Cognac, for a week-long vacation in the spring of 2007. Our get-together in Japan in the late fall of 1996 was equally memorable. We are very grateful for all the nice things the Omans have done for us so generously.

The consulting work on multinational corporations I have had the good fortune to do over many years for the United Nations has motivated me to analyze the role of foreign direct investment in economic development. Through the kind offices of Professor John Dunning, my work began with the United Nations Center on Transnational Corporations (UNCTC) which had been once located in New York City (1975–92) before it moved to the United Nations Conference on Trade and Development (UNCTAD) in Geneva in 1993. I am thankful to Dr Karl P. Sauvant, former Director of the UNCTAD Division on Investment, Technology and Enterprise Development (DIAE), for inviting me to UNCTC and then to UNCTAD to work on the various issues of the *World Investment Report* (an annual UN publication) on several occasions (1992, 1994, 1997, and 1999). In 2005 he left UNCTAD and became director of the Vale Columbia Center on Sustainable International Investment, Columbia University, New York.

Most recently (in 2007–8) I was again involved in preparing the *World Investment Report 2008*. Chapter 5 of this book (Structural Upgrading, Infrastructure Development, and the Insatiable Quest for Natural Resources) draws on a background paper, 'History Repeats Itself: Evolutionary Structural Change and TNCs' Involvement in Infrastructure Overseas, Flying-geese Style', I submitted to UNCTAD. My involvement with the WIR benefited me intellectually as I was able to learn so much from others at the brain-storming meetings. In this regard, I owe a lot to Ms Anne Miroux, Head of the Investment Analysis Branch, IAB/DIAE/UNCTAD; Professor John H. Dunning of Reading; Professor Peter Buckley of Leeds; Professor Robert Pearce of Reading; Mr Hafiz Mirza, Chief, Development Issues Section, IAB/DIAE; Mr Masataka Fujita, Chief, Investment Trend Section, IAB/DIAE; Mr Torbjorn Fredriksson, Officer-in-charge, Policy Issues Section, IAB/DIAE; and all other staff members. I am especially grateful for Mr Mirza's warm personal hospitality during my stay in Geneva. The same goes for Mr James Zhan, Officer-in-charge, DIAE, with whom I had the pleasure of co-authoring a book, *Business Restructuring in East Asia: Cross-border M&As in the Crisis Period*, Copenhagen Business School Press, 2001.

I am also deeply indebted to Professor Christian Bellak of the University of Economics and Business Administration, Vienna, Austria. He invited me as a speaker at a workshop on the Six Countries Programme on Innovation, held at Parkhotel Schonbrunn, Vienna, May 25–6, 1998. I presented a paper, 'The "Flying-Geese" Paradigm of Technological and Structural Upgrading: What Went Right and What Went Wrong in East Asia', and was thus able to use the conference as a sounding board for my ideas about the theory. Moreover, to my surprise, Professor Bellak kindly organized a special panel session at EIBA's (European International Business Association) annual conference in Oslo, Norway, December 10–13, 2005, a panel on 'The Flying-geese Theory of Growth and International Business' – in recognition of my contribution to the FG theory. There I made a brief presentation titled 'The Quiddity of the Flying-Geese Theory: A Reformulation'.

Another word of gratitude must be added for Dr Eric D. Ramstetter of the International Center for the Study of East Asia Development (ICSEAD) in Kita Kyushu, Japan. In June 2004, I was invited to present a paper titled 'The Division of Labor Revisited: Manufacturing Paradigms, Worker Welfare, and Comparative Advantage Recycling in East Asia', at the Center. This gave me a valuable opportunity to get feedback from the Center's research scholars.

Chapter 4 in this book is based on my paper, 'Asia's Labor-driven Economic Development, Flying-geese Style: An Unprecedented Opportunity for the Poor to Rise?', presented at the United Nations University–World Institute for Development Economic Research (UNU–WIDER) conference on The Impact of Globalization on the Poor in Asia, United Nations University, Tokyo, April 25–6, 2005, and circulated as Discussion Paper No. 40, 2005, APEC Study Center, Columbia University, and also as Research Paper No. 2006/59, UNU–WIDER (copyright UNU–WIDER, 2006). The Appendix to Chapter 4 is based on 'The Dynamics of the "Mature" Product Cycle and Market Recycling, Flying-geese Style: An Empirical Examination and Policy Implications' (co-authored with Harvey Cutler), *Contemporary Economic Policy*, **25** (1), January 2007, 67–78 (copyright the Western Economic Association, 2006), reprinted in part and modified with permission from Blackwell Publishing, Inc.

Chapter 5 is based on 'History Repeats Itself: Evolutionary Structural Change and TNCs' Involvement in Infrastructure Overseas, Flying-geese

Style', a background paper submitted to UNCTAD in preparation for WIR 2008 and posted both as Working Paper No. 261 on the web site of the Center on Japanese Economy and Business, Columbia Business School, and as Discussion Paper No. 58 on the web site of the APEC Study Center, Columbia University, 2008.

Terutomo Ozawa

Fort Collins, CO, USA
at the foot of the beautiful Rockies
July, 2008

PART I

Agenda

1. Is the flying-geese theory passé – or still relevant?

1.1. THE 'FLYING-GEESE (FG)' ANALOGY

Before the Asian crisis broke out in July 1997, the analogy of 'a flying-geese (FG) formation' (*ganko keitai* in Japanese) had been frequently used with enthusiasm to describe the sequential pattern of rapid growth and structural upgrading in East Asia. The popular description went that Japan led the gaggle, followed by the NIEs, which were in turn pursued by the ASEAN-4 and China – all soaring together up the ladder of economic development. This string of 'tandem growth' (Ozawa, 1995, 2005) was once the admiration and envy of the world. The World Bank (1993) even called it 'the East Asian Miracle'. In the wake of financial turmoil, however, such a metaphor lost its power of depiction. After all, the Asian flock fell from the sky disgracefully. Yet, the crisis-stricken quickly rebounded with burgeoning trade surpluses. Together with the galactic rise of China and India, Asia is presently again the center of attention in the world.

The poetic allegory of 'flying-geese formation' was originally introduced in the 1930s by Professor Kaname Akamatsu of Hitotsubashi University, Tokyo, to describe his theory of industrialization in developing countries (inter alia, Akamatsu, 1935, 1937). Although the FG theory was already well known in Japan, it only began to be accepted outside the country after East Asian growth had gotten worldwide attention during the 1970s. Above all, it caught the fancy of policymakers, particularly after Saburo Okita, former Japanese Foreign Minister, had made reference to it at the fourth Pacific Economic Cooperation Conference in Seoul in 1985.

The media soon adopted this catchy phrase and popularized it. For example, observing the Asia Pacific in 1989, *The Economist*, wrote:

> When geese migrate, they fly in a V-formation. The pattern is a favourite analogy of Japanese civil servants for the economic development of East and South-East Asia. Japan leads. Behind it follow the [NIEs]. In the third rank are [ASEAN-4] and coastal China. As with flying geese, the arrangement is purposeful, well-ordered and coordinated.[1]

The analogy has so far been used mostly in a casual way as a shorthand depiction of the staggered growth sequence of a number of closely clustered economies in East Asia. But there has been little reference to theoretical explanations of *why* such tandem growth occurs. For that matter, no analysis has yet been made of *how* the FG formation for economic development was causatively related to, and ultimately culminated in, the Asian financial crisis of 1997–8.

Actually there is another metaphor that is worth mentioning here, the one used in 1996 by Lee Kuan Yew, former Prime Minister of Singapore (1959–90), to describe East Asia's clustered growth. In answering a reporter's question, 'What created the economic success across Asia?' Lee gave the following reply:

> I think the basic underlying reason for the success is the people, who are disciplined, take education seriously – especially mathematics, science and engineering – and have cultural habits of high savings and high investments, always working for the next generation. Then came the rapid spread of this industrialization process. It accelerated with the Plaza Accord in 1985, which pushed up the yen, then forced the Korean won and the Taiwanese dollar and the Singapore dollar up. This forced the relocation of Japanese industries to the newly industrialized economies, from these economies to the rest of Southeast Asia, then China, Vietnam and now Myanmar. This had a cascading effect.[2]

Lee thus employed the cascade metaphor instead. His observation is about the relationships between 'upstream' and 'downstream' countries in the cascade – instead of the 'leader and follower geese' analogy. Yet the essence is the same.[3] What is particularly interesting is that Lee explicitly credited Asian success to: (i) human capital formation (especially in mathematics, science, and engineering), (ii) high savings and high investments, (iii) the rising values of Asian economies' currencies as a factor in industrial migration, and (iv) the sequential relocation of industries first from Japan to the NIEs, and then, from the NIEs to the rest of Asia. In this respect, Lee actually put his finger on some crucial linking mechanisms of the 'cascading' phenomenon of clustered growth (these and other mechanisms are discussed in later chapters).

1.2. RELEVANCY

1.2.1. A Hierarchy Matters: Dynamics of Growth Clustering

Nowadays we hear so often that the FG theory of economic development, though once popular about two decades ago, is a thing of the past and is no longer pertinent as a way of explaining today's Asian economic growth. Yet, when it is elaborated on and reformulated as is done in this book, the

FG model still serves as quite a useful frame of analysis – say, to define the 'ladder of economic development' and examine poverty reduction, infrastructure development, the growth patterns of financial markets, the reverse flow of capital – and even recent soaring commodity prices, as will be seen in the following chapters.

At the outset, however, it is important to keep in mind that the FG paradigm is based on a *hierarchical multi-layered economic structure of inter-country relationships between leaders and followers* – that is, to put it bluntly, between 'unequals'. They are at different stages of industrial development and sophistication. Perhaps this notion of hierarchical relationship, even if a temporary and passing phenomenon, seems to be ideologically offensive to (i) those who staunchly believe in the 'politically correct' idealism of total equality with no basis for hierarchical ranking, or (ii) some pure neoclassical economists who have no interest in political economy and who do not see economic agents and their activities in hierarchical terms.

In the realm of global economic growth, nevertheless, unequal positions, notably in knowledge creation and accumulation, can be a valuable resource for both leaders (path-breakers) and followers (emulators), because they generate *economies of concatenation*. Indeed, it can be argued that the world history of economic development is nothing but a repeated history of industrial leadership and subsequent emulation. The world never grows smoothly and evenly; it grows only in fits and starts; some lead, others follow; they often trade places. Historical accidents and politico-institutional forces trigger chains of cumulative causation, in both directions; sparking economic growth at some times and slowing down or even halting progress at other times. A hierarchy may become steeper or flatter. No particular country, however, can retain its dominant power forever without challenges from other countries or is condemned forever to the bottom of the hierarchy (that is, the pre-industrial state of underdevelopment).

Nowadays it is often said that the FG theory no longer holds, since there is no longer a powerful leader in the global economy. The argument goes that the industrial power of the lead goose, the US, as well as that of the second goose, Japan, has declined relative to other countries, notably the NIEs and BRICs (Brazil, Russia, India, and China), and that the global economy no longer grows top-down in a trickle-down fashion as envisaged by the FG theory of tandem growth. In other words, the post-World War II hierarchy of countries, in which the US was once indisputably the world's strongest and most powerful economy, has eroded to such an extent that no industrial hegemony prevails. True, we no longer live in the global economy where learning and growth opportunities were uni-directionally handed down from more advanced to less advanced countries. Growth stimuli move in both directions. Yet, there still exists a hierarchy of countries, even though it is no longer as steep as it used to be. The world economy has become increasingly homogeneous in many ways; the world has 'flattened'. We are in a period of 'hierarchy leveling' (or 'industrial homogenization') rather than 'hierarchy raising' (or 'industrial heterogenization'). (As will be made clear in Chapter 2, Akamatsu foresaw the alternating periods of heterogeneity and homogeneity in economic structure among countries).

1.2.2.   Misconception No. 1: Japan is the Lead Goose

There are some misconceptions and misunderstanding about the FG paradigm that need to be dispelled. To begin with, the FG paradigm is interpreted in such a way that Japan is looked upon as the lead goose that single-handedly shapes and controls the rest of the Asian flock. *The Economist's* and Lee's observations quoted above are the prime examples. Sure, Japan has been a significant contributor to regional growth, both psychologically (via the 'demonstration effect' as Asia's first economic superpower) and commercially (as a key provider of industrial knowledge and industrial inputs). But its role has actually been as second goose under the aegis of US-led global capitalism. Japan is not quite the hub of Asian growth. All other Asian countries have also strived to catch up directly with the advanced West rather than with Japan. The former has been imparting industrial knowledge and accepting Asian exports more open-mindedly and more willingly than Japan.

In this regard, Pempel (1996/7, p. 16) caustically observes:

> . . . Heading a 'flying V' of Asian economic geese, Japan would pull the region forward with its own successes in industrialization and manufacturing. The other Asian countries would follow Japan's lead and a succession of Asian 'geese' would replicate Japan's developmental experiences, and that of the other 'geese' ahead of them in formation, all moving steadily forward in their levels of manufacturing sophistication.

> . . . Japan, of course, would remain the country destined to lead all regional development and would control all leading technologies and industries, but by following Japan's lead along a common trajectory, other countries would quickly benefit.

> . . . The implicit arrogance of a permanent place at the front of the avian Asian advance seems never to have been challenged by most Japanese advocates of the model . . .

On the contrary, indeed, Japan has been *a follower goose riding on America's long coat-tails*. The FG formation in Asia has been a creation of US-led growth clustering, though Japan no doubt played a key role as the second goose in Asia. The US is truly the lead goose whom Japan eagerly emulated as a latecomer. This point was also made clear in Okita's speech: 'In the Pacific region, . . . the United States developed first as the lead country. Beginning in the late 19th century, Japan began to play catch-up development in the non-durable consumer goods, durable consumer goods, and capital goods sectors in that order' (Okita, 1985, as cited in Kojima, 2003, p. 31).

Moreover, the implied 'permanence' of Japan's position is certainly never guaranteed. The NIEs – and now China in particular – have been swiftly closing the development gap vis-à-vis Japan. This is particularly evident in some specific industries, such as computers, semiconductors, cell phones, and finance. Japan can never keep its emulators behind forever. Eventually, if not immediately, Japan will meet the same fate as Great Britain which was challenged and eventually bested by other Western nations. After World War II, the US has likewise been caught up with, if not yet fully, by Japan and other challengers. No permanence is the essence of FG formation (more on this in Chapter 2).

In short, industrial dynamics across Asia is a reflection of the evolution of modern capitalism that originated in the West and is presently driven largely under American leadership. Asia's economic vicissitude has stemmed from both the growth stimuli and the disequilibrating forces of hegemon-led global capitalism.

1.2.3. Misconception No. 2: A Master Plan

A second misinterpretation, as a corollary of the first, is that 'the arrangement is purposeful, well-ordered and coordinated', as noted in the above-cited quotation from *The Economist*. It implies some sort of a master plan behind the scenes. But Japan has had *no* master plan – for that matter, nor does the United States as the first lead goose. True, individual countries are inevitably engaged in economic policies and strategies. Some use industrial and innovation policies to facilitate their industrial upgrading. Nevertheless, US-led growth clustering itself – as the powerful undercurrent of global growth – is basically driven by market forces, though political motivations and actions are always behind it. It is the logic of capitalism and the reactions of participating countries that shape the seemingly 'purposeful' pattern of tandem growth. In fact, the US itself is often at the mercy of global capitalism, which dramatically and relentlessly alters its own economic structure. There is a rising backlash even in the US against the forces of globalization it has unleashed as its economic leadership in the world is being eroded, its comparatively disadvantaged industries abruptly contract at home, and jobs are offshored.

What is more, the FG formation as seen in Asia is essentially a historical 'accident'. Over many centuries, a myriad of confluent forces have been converging in such a fashion as to advance global capitalism. It emanated most strongly from the Industrial Revolution in England. Such capitalist momentum is currently pushing forward across the Asian Pacific, inducing its economies to advance in tandem growth – and even plunge in tandem crisis as witnessed during the 1997–8 Asian financial débâcle and most recently in the fall of 2008. It is certainly not 'purposeful, well-ordered, and coordinated'. It is, in fact, at the mercy of market whims and subject to 'maniacs, panics, and busts' (Kindleberger, 1996), as will be discussed in Chapter 7.

1.2.4.   Misconception No. 3: The Unique Asian Phenomenon

A third major myth is that the phenomenon of FG formation is something uniquely Asian and unprecedented. It is, however, neither peculiarly Asian nor new. A spread of concatenated industrialization across borders – indeed, a significant FG formation – once occurred throughout the Western world, both the Old and the New World, with Great Britain as the lead goose. The Industrial Revolution in England ushered the world into a modern economy fundamentally built on science and technology, propagating industrialization in the rest of the world. Continental Europe succeeded in industrializing by following Britain's footsteps (Landes, 1969) through commercial contacts and conscious efforts at emulation and learning. France and Belgium and then Germany served as the region's second geese, relaying modern industrial skills and surplus capital to others – and even remote corners of Europe. At that time, individual artisans and technicians possessed superior knowledge, which was transferred abroad through visitations or migration. Prior to the English hegemony, the changing fortunes of Florentine, Venetian, Genoese, and Dutch capitalism (Arrighi, 1994) also attest to the universality of FG formation.

In the New World, the United States emulated and learned from Great Britain at the start of industrialization: 'When the U.S. began to industrialize in the nineteenth century, she was following a path which had been blazed earlier by Great Britain. Much of the technology which was introduced into America during this period was in fact borrowed from that country, with varying degrees of modification' (Rosenberg, 1972, p. 59). To put it more bluntly, 'America started off as a copier' and 'stole British technology' (Thurow, 1985, p. 1). America, however, quickly pioneered, introducing numerous innovations of its own in the area of mass production and mass marketing. In other words, the US proved to be a strong second goose that was capable of eventually taking over the UK as the subsequent lead goose.

On the basis of historical evidence, therefore, it is reasonable to argue that any region can experience a similar phenomenon under a certain set of enabling conditions. At present, however, the Pax Americana has declined because of a diminished lead over the rest of the world, and there are no strong second geese like Japan and the NIEs in any other regions.[4] Interestingly enough, the most noticeable FG formation currently in the making is within China itself. Industries are migrating from the coastal regions into the hinterland of that vast country (Bhalla and Qiu, 2004) – in addition to less-developed adjacent countries such as Vietnam and Cambodia.

1.3. RADELET AND SACHS' INTERPRETATION

Radelet and Sachs (1997) recognize the significance of the FG theory by identifying it as one of the three major doctrines of development strategy:

> . . . the 'flying geese' model, according to which *countries gradually move up in technological development by following in the pattern of countries just ahead of them in the development process.* In this vision, Korea and Taiwan take over leadership in textiles and apparel from Japan as Japan moves into the higher-technology sectors of electronics, transport, and other capital goods. A decade or so later, Korea and Taiwan are able to upgrade to electronics and auto components, while the textile and apparel industries move to Indonesia, Thailand, and Vietnam. . . (emphasis added, p. 52)

The FG model is clearly defined above as a process of sequential catch-up in technological progress, one country following on the heels of more advanced countries up the ladder of 'technological development' – that is, tandem growth emanating from emulation and learning in industrial knowledge.

What *institutional* arrangements are necessary for a developing country to move forward in technological development? Radelet and Sachs explain the distinct institutional arrangements that were each specific to the three major doctrines of development strategy:

> If the paradigmatic institution of the big push was *state ownership of industry* [as exemplified by the Stalinist drive toward rapid industrialization in the 1930s and China's Great Leap Forward of 1958–61], and for import substitution was *private ownership backed by protectionism* [as once seen throughout Latin America's inward-focused development strategy], for flying-geese development it is *the export platform.* The idea behind an export platform

is to create an *enclave economy hospitable to foreign investors and integrated into the global economy, without the problems of infrastructure, security, rule of law, and trade policies that plague the rest of the economy.* Asian governments introduced several variations of the export platform, including export processing zones (EPZs), bonded warehouses, special economic zones, and duty drawback systems. Governments supported these institutions with macroeconomic policies that strengthened the incentives for labor-intensive exports, especially via appropriate exchange rates. (1997, pp. 52–3, emphasis added)

The big push approach was thus pursued in the interests of nationalistic self-reliance under communism and in isolation from the outside world. The import-substitution strategy, too, was carried out in an inward-focused fashion avoiding integration with the global economy as much as possible. Both doctrines proved to be failures. In sharp contrast, the FG doctrine promotes integration with, and capitalization on, the outside world, by means of what Radelet and Sachs call 'capitalist enclaves' (p. 45) that serve as the bootstraps of catch-up development.

The enclaves, notably export processing zones (EPZs) and special economic zones, constitute the *localized pockets of market capitalism*, free from and unencumbered by the regulatory controls and political/bureaucratic constraints that prevail in the rest of the country – so as to be *gradually* and *progressively* integrated into the global economy that is currently molded by US-led capitalism. They are, therefore, attractive to foreign MNCs that can bring in all the necessary productive resources (such as technology, managerial skills, capital goods, and access to export markets) lacking at home. The enclaves are *an institutional innovation* that is pragmatically designed to introduce thorough reforms ('wipe the slate clean', so to speak) only in certain confined localities if such reforms are impractical for the entire economy.[5] The entire institutions cannot be changed overnight, but they can be *partially* modified by creating enclaves.[6]

In short, Radelet and Sachs' interpretation emphasizes the establishment of 'capitalist enclaves' as a starting point for market reforms and integration with the global economy that 'stirs powerful forces for economic growth' (p. 46). However, it leaves unexplained the *causal* factors for technological upgrading and the sequence of technological development. It suffices here to note that in the post-World War II period a series of favorable developments in the Asian Pacific almost serendipitously coalesced into growth agglomeration in the form of de facto regional economic integration. It is a *regional* phenomenon feeding on synergistic interactions within that hierarchically clustered group of economies, a phenomenon that happens to have so far occurred only in the Asia Pacific in the recent past.

1.4.   A 'FLYING-GEESE' WAY OF THINKING

The global economy has seen a host of major events ever since the end of World War II. Among the momentous ones are the quick reconstruction and growth of postwar Japan as the world's second largest economy, the miraculous rise of the NIEs (despite their small size and resource scarcity), the recent rise of BRICs (Brazil, Russia, India, and China), the air and water pollution China now faces (just as Japan did in the 1960s), China's controversial resource diplomacy in some rogue African states (notably Sudan), an impressive reduction in Asian poverty, the rise of sovereign wealth funds, the soaring prices of commodities, and America's subprime mortgage meltdown. On the surface, these events seem to be unrelated happenings. Actually, however, they are interconnected and stem from the same common underlying forces. They are mere symptoms of the evolving global economy driven by US-led capitalism, as will be explored throughout this book.

Is there any economic development theory that can explain all these seemingly discrete events as integral parts of a big picture? Sure, there are a large number of theories on trade, investment, environmental issues, etc. But they are all discrete partial analyses, looking only at individual trees in the forest, so to speak. Here, the FG framework can help us join up the dots to understand the major undercurrent that has been sweeping and shaping the global economy.

1.5.   AGENDA

Our agenda is as follows. Chapter 2 examines and interprets Akamatsu's original ideas that still remain to be elaborated and expanded. The importance of dialectical thinking is emphasized. Chapter 3 presents a stages (FG) model of industrial upgrading (that expands on, and reformulates, one of Akamatsu's three patterns of FG formation) by way of defining what has hitherto casually been called 'the ladder of economic development'. The intermediating factors that enable a catching-up economy to climb up the hierarchy of industrial activities are identified and analyzed. A concept of 'hegemon-led growth clustering' is presented as a new paradigm of regionalized growth and structural transformation. Different regions vary in their capabilities to capitalize on such growth opportunities. 'Stages jumbling' and 'time and space compression' are the accompanying results of the spread of industrial upgrading under US-led growth clustering.

Chapter 4 examines the record of poverty reduction in East Asia. A comparative-advantage-recycling (FG) model of labor-intensive manufacturing, in which comparative advantage in such manufacturing is being relayed from one economy to another down the East Asian hierarchy of countries, captures the core mechanism of poverty alleviation. An appendix to Chapter 4 provides an empirical test of 'market recycling' (or comparative-advantage recycling) in the US import market for a labor-intensive good, TV sets.

Chapter 5 introduces a stages (FG) model of infrastructure development. It explains why any country at the stage of heavy and chemical industrialization engages in an aggressive search for natural resources, as once carried out by the advanced West under colonialism, and recently by Japan during its resource-intensive industrialization of the 1960s and the 1970s. China's voracious appetite for energy and industrial commodities – and their China-driven run-ups in commodity prices – can be equally explained in terms of an FG stages theory. Chapter 6 looks at another developing region, Latin America, and asks the question: What is holding it back from benefiting as much from US-led global capitalism as Asia has done? This helps us understand the critical features, notably the institutional factors, of Asia's catch-up growth on a comparative basis.

The subsequent two chapters direct attention to the erstwhile neglected side of the FG theory, the financial dimension. Chapter 7 is concerned with the open-economy finance of economic development. A new concept, 'borrowed growth', is proposed to examine the benefits and perils of current-account-based finance. Such finance is also explained in terms of a stages (FG) model of development finance that can shed light on the boom-and-bust of economic activity. 'Borrowed growth' is the driving force of US-led growth clustering. Chapter 8 takes up America's role as the leading innovator in financial services by studying the recent growth of private equity (venture capital and leveraged buyout firms) as a prime example. A stages (FG) model of corporate finance serves as the basic framework for analysis in elucidating the stages-differentiated features of corporate finance and the 'perverse' flow of capital from the developing to the advanced world (the 'Lucas-Schulz' paradox).

NOTES

1. 'Together under the Sun: A Survey of the Yen Bloc', *Economist*, July 15, 1989.
2. Andrew Tanzer, 'Ride It! You Can't Fight It!', *Forbes*, August 12, 1996, pp. 46–7.
3. One major difference is that a cascade maintains permanent relations between upstream and downstream positions, whereas a FG formation allows for exchanges in leadership.
4. The potential regions exist, however; they are the Americas, if NAFTA is extended throughout Latin America, and Eastern and Central Europe once they successfully shift to the market system.

5. Radelet and Sachs (1997) hone in on this point:

> If there is anything to the 'Asian miracle,' it is that several governments, benefiting from Japan's early experience and from each other's experience since the 1960s, have been able to create an economic environment for profitable, private investment – almost always with important foreign partners – despite serious shortcomings in overall political and economic conditions. They did so, in most cases, by creating in the midst of weaker economic institutions *a capitalist enclave* that has gradually spread throughout the economy. Put another way, Asia's challenge, so far accomplished, has been to create a virtuous circle, in which *a modern economic sector originally confined to an enclave* has not only expanded through new investments but has fueled a much broader modernization of political and economic institutions . . . global capitalism stirs powerful forces for economic growth even in the face of serious limitations in law, economic structure, and politics. (pp. 45–6, emphasis added).

6. It is interesting to note that the idea of 'a modern economic sector originally confined to an enclave' is now clearly promoted and applied by Sachs to UN-initiated economic development projects in Africa. As part of the UN Millennium Project on poverty reduction Sachs initially set up 12 'research villages' in ten African countries and soon added another 66 villages. These villages are designed as the 'modern sectors' that are provided with 'fertilizer and seed to improve food yield; anti-malarial bed nets; improved water sources; diversification from staple into cash crops; a school feeding programme; deworming for all; and the introduction of new technologies, such as energy-saving stoves and mobile phones' ('African Poverty: The Magnificent Seven', *Economist*, April 29, 2006, pp. 51–2).

PART II

Real-sector growth: industrial upgrading

2. Akamatsu's flying-geese theory – in the rough

2.1. ORIGINAL CONCEPTUALIZATION

2.1.1. Three Patterns of FG Formation

The phrase, 'a wild-geese-flying pattern (*ganko keitai*) of industrial development', was originally coined by Kaname Akamatsu (1897–1974) of Hitotsubashi University, Tokyo, in the mid-1930s. We usually associate this phrase with the image of a regionally clustered group of economies advancing together in leader–follower relations, a pattern of economic development best exemplified by high-performing Asian economies. It is in this particular pattern that the flying-geese theory has become popularized.

Though not widely known, this particular FG pattern is, however, just one of two 'derived' patterns and is not what Akamatsu called '*kihonkei* [the fundamental or basic pattern]'. What he identified as the '*kihonkei ganko keitai* [the fundamental geese-flying pattern]' is related specifically to, and extracted from, the development process of Japan's manufacturing industries. In fact, Akamatsu initially used the phrase 'flying-geese' as a metaphor to describe *a dynamic evolutionary sequence of development by a new modern industry, an industry theretofore nonexistent in Japan, but that only came to be established after national efforts at modernization were launched in 1868.* (Up until then, the Tokugawa feudal regime had ruled Japan for two and a half centuries, withholding itself from contact with the outside world under a so-called '*sakoku* [seclusion]' policy.) Thus, Akamatsu's unit of analysis was originally a *given* modern industry in an economically backward country such as Japan then was – a country that was bent on industrializing by opening up to trade and interacting with, and learning from, the advanced countries. That new approach was a 180-degree turn from seclusion to state-controlled openness.

More specifically, Akamatsu empirically examined the evolutionary development paths of Japan's modern manufacturing industries, such as woolen goods, cotton yarn, cotton cloth, spinning and weaving machines, general machinery, bicycles, and industrial tools over the pre-World War II period (mostly from 1870 to 1939). In each industry study, he detected wave-like, staggered time-series curves of imports, domestic production, and exports in that sequential order (see Figure 2.1). These curves reflected the alternating trend patterns of structural change in which importing in a given industry occurs first, domestic production then ensues (giving birth to a new import-substituting industry at home), and finally exporting takes place – a sequence of import (M)→domestic production (P)→export (X) or the MPX sequence, a pattern that Akamatsu called 'fundamental'.

The analogy of flying-geese formation was introduced for the first time when he published a journal article, '*Wagakuni Yomokogyohin no Boeki Suisei* [The Trend of Japan's Trade in Woolen Goods]' (1935): 'We discover a series of connections from import to production, from production to export . . . We should be able to formulate a wild-geese-flying development of import, production, and export in an industry' (1935, p. 208). And he chose the term 'a wild-geese-flying development' because 'wild geese fly in orderly ranks forming an inverse V, just as airplanes fly in formation. This flying pattern of wild geese is metaphorically applied to the three time-series curves . . .' (1962, p. 9).

In addition to the 'fundamental' pattern of MPX, Akamatsu also identified two others which he called '*fukujikeitai* [secondary or auxiliary patterns]'.[1]

> The wild-geese-flying pattern described above includes three subpatterns. The first basic pattern is the sequence of import–domestic production–export. The second pattern is the sequence from consumer goods to capital goods and from crude and simple articles to complex and refined articles. The third pattern is the alignment from advanced nations to backward nations according to their stages of growth. (1961, p. 208)

While the basic pattern refers to the MPX process of developing a given new industry, the second (a sequence of structural upgrading) reflects evolutionary qualitative changes in the industrial structure of a particular developing country once a given new industry is brought into existence or a process of industrial upgrading over time ('from consumer goods to capital goods' and 'from crude and simple articles to complex and refined articles') at the economy level. The second pattern of qualitative transformation in goods or an industry is made possible by way of the strategic process of MPX. In Akamatsu's interpretation, therefore, it can be considered 'auxiliary' to the fundamental FG pattern.

In contrast, the third pattern (that is, an alignment of countries at different growth stages) goes beyond the intra-country industry level. It is concerned with a *hierarchical* arrangement ('alignment') of countries that exist in the world economy – in terms of their relative positions with respect to how industrialized each country is in comparison with others (that is, countries are aligned at different stages of economic development).

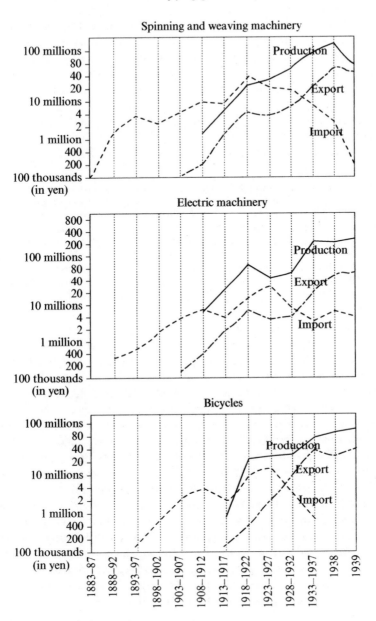

Source: Akamatsu (1962, p. 22).

Figure 2.1 *Flying-geese patterns of industrial development in prewar Japan*

In other words, there are leaders and followers in industrialization. In Akamatsu's own words: '. . . the underdeveloped nations are aligned successively behind the advanced industrial nations *in the order of their different stages of growth in a wild-geese-flying pattern*' (1961, p. 208, emphasis added). The third ('auxiliary') pattern is thus a phenomenon observable within the world's hierarchy of countries.

Akamatsu (1962) then generalized about a catch-up process of industrialization in terms of what he described as the 'following facts with regard to the economic development of less-advanced countries':

> First, for *all* industrial goods there exists a *sequential* order, from import to domestic production and further to export. Secondly, the time for the curves of domestic production and export to go beyond that of import will come earlier in crude goods and later in refined goods, and similarly, earlier in consumer goods, and later in capital goods. Thirdly, the import curve falls in proportion to the rise of the domestic production curve, and it is probable that the export curve will sooner or later begin to fall with respect to crude goods or consumer goods and the domestic production curve of these goods will also decline in the future. (1962, pp. 9–10)

The process of import substitution and subsequent export promotion (that is, the MPX sequence) comes easier – hence occurs 'earlier' – for technologically simple or standardized goods ('crude goods') than for more sophisticated goods ('refined goods') – and for consumer goods than for capital goods, since the former are technically less complex than the latter and therefore comparatively advantaged in developing countries. Also, the preponderance of each sequential activity in a given industry, whether imports, domestic production, or exports, is merely ephemeral as the industry goes through its life-cycle of birth, growth, maturity, and senescence (via import-substituting output growth at home and then export growth for a while until the entire industry eventually loses its vitality). This life-cycle process demonstrates how a developing country can acquire a new industry by emulative learning (or copying/borrowing as the first step to knowledge acquisition) from the advanced countries. And herein lies the significance of the existing hierarchy of countries within which knowledge is transferred from advanced to developing countries. Technological borrowing constitutes an early-stage industrialization strategy; 'a sort of formula for the industrial development of less-advanced countries' (1961, p. 9).

2.1.2.   Dynamic Infant-industry Protection – beyond Import Substitution

Yet the MPX sequence does not occur automatically. It must be consciously promoted at policy level. Here, Akamatsu stressed the role of 'economic nationalism' in building locally owned industry with appropriate government measures (that is, industrial policy). As explained below, such measures represent a dynamic version of infant-industry protection – dynamic because a local industry is intended not only to substitute imports but more importantly to develop into an export industry. Yet, government measures are not meant to replace market forces; industries ought to be fostered along the logic of comparative advantage.

A shift from 'crude' (less value-added) to more 'refined' (higher value-added) industries—and from consumer goods to capital goods is carried out basically by the market mechanism, which economic policy ought to facilitate. With this structural shift, rising income makes consumers' tastes more sophisticated and more demanding in quality and variety, simultaneously enabling them to purchase higher quality (higher valued-added) goods. For a shift toward capital goods from consumer goods, a country must acquire technological capacity, and the size of local demand needs to be large enough to initially justify production of capital goods at home. In its efforts to upgrade industrial activity, however, any developing country as a latecomer enjoys a latecomer's advantage in acquiring technology off the shelf, technology that is already readily available in more advanced countries through the 'international knowledge market', so to speak. And the export focus of the MPX infant-industry strategy makes it possible to overcome the small size of a domestic market.

This catch-up model, then, boils down to a country's *trade-guided* growth strategy by importing not only knowledge but also seeking out markets for exports. It is an outer-focused model of emulative learning and derived economic development, in the sense that a developing country industrializes by learning from advanced countries and capitalizing on the latter's markets. This is the very reason why Akamatsu argued:

> It is impossible to study the economic growth of the developing countries in modern times without considering the *mutual interactions* between these economies and those of the advanced countries. When Western European Capitalism began to expand its production and trade on a worldwide scale, it awakened the less-developed areas of the world to modern economic development. (1962, p. 1, emphasis added)

In essence, economic development is a phenomenon that occurs through interactions within a hierarchy of countries. Here, the spread of capitalism from the advanced West sets the stage for economic development in the developing world. And capitalism is the underlying and enabling force that drives the process of catch-up growth in the developing world, since *it creates the essential markets through which the developing countries are able to obtain industrial knowledge and capital that are required for catch-up growth.* (Capitalism, however, spreads growth unevenly, depending on the social capacities of the host countries.)

Interestingly, what Akamatsu identified as the fundamental pattern (that is, the dynamic infant-industry model of MPX under state guidance and support) is no longer relevant to the present world. Trade liberalization and WTO rules restrict direct government involvement in industrial development. Furthermore, the development process of MPX no longer transpires as these steps now most likely occur simultaneously when foreign MNCs come in and instantly establish local production as a platform for both domestic and export sales. What is most fundamental and relevant is actually a hierarchy of countries – and that of industries – in the global economy: that is, Akamatsu's third and second patterns. *An existing global hierarchy of economies is the vital springboard of interactive growth between the developing and the advanced world, and the relative positions of economies within a hierarchy of industries (that is, on the ladder of economic development) engender a dynamic source of comparative advantages for trade and cross-border investment among the economies.* Thus, the hierarchy of economies emerges as the 'fundamental' pattern – in lieu of the MPX pattern of building a local industry – in our constantly globalizing or internationalizing world.

2.2. INTERACTIONS BETWEEN DEVELOPING AND ADVANCED COUNTRIES

Akamatsu's three patterns of FG formation are functionally interrelated and interactive in transmitting growth stimuli from the advanced world to an initially backward area – and vice versa. In his historical analysis, the United States was once a follower goose during the Pax Britannica, along with Continental European countries. Akamatsu classifies the mutual interrelations into two alternating periods: a period of 'differentiation or heterogenization' that produces 'complementary and co-accelerative relations', and one of 'homogenization or uniformization' that creates 'substitutive/competitive and conflictive' relations.[2] (Here, the notions of 'differentiation' and 'uniformization' are synonymous with those of 'divergence' and 'convergence' in the jargon of present-day development theories.)

In a nutshell, the world economy is supposed to go through the following alternating periods in economic relationship, accompanied by continuous structural evolution on the part of both the leader countries and the follower countries:

- A period of heterogenization/differentiation = complementary and
  (comparative advantage expansion) co-accelerative
  relations

  Trade liberalism in the advanced world

- A period of homogenization/uniformization = substitutive and
  (comparative advantage contraction) conflictive relations
  Trade protectionism in the advanced world

Using these distinctive alternating periods, Akamatsu (1961, 1962) presented a stages model of Asia's engagement (at both commercial and political levels) with the advanced West in the wake of 'the eastward advance of Western European capitalism' (1962, p. 1), a model that can be recapitulated below – with supplementary analyses and additional interpretations.[3]

2.2.1. Stages Model of Interactive Growth

Akamatsu's model can be summarized in terms of four stages:

First stage Cross-border commercial interchange begins after the opening of backward Asia to the world economy. Asia initially exports primary goods to the industrialized West in exchange for consumer products. This leads to a rise in trade because of the heterogenized (differentiated) comparative cost structures between the two regions. At this juncture, Asian countries themselves are not trading so much with each other, since their economic structures are similarly underdeveloped and based mostly on similar primary goods. What little handicraft industry exists in Asia is doomed to be destroyed by imports of Western consumer goods that flood into local markets. (This adverse effect of opening trade is emphasized by other scholars. For example, Myrdal (1957) characterized it as the 'backlash effect' of industrialization.)

Western capital and technology infiltrate Asia to promote the large-scale production of primary goods (for example, raw materials and agricultural goods), as well as to construct railroads, ports, and other infrastructure facilities. This type of *FDI* in resource extraction and related infrastructure helps create and strengthen the host countries' comparative (and absolute) advantage in primary goods. Meanwhile, the import of consumer goods sets in motion an MPX process on the part of the host countries. The resulting expansion of inter-industry trade (exchanging Asia's primary goods for Western manufactures) thus ensues during this early period of heterogenization/differentiation in economic relations, which are 'complementary and co-accelerative' for trade and growth. (Here, the idea of comparative advantage augmentation is hinted at – and will be examined in detail in Chapter 3.)

Second stage   European capital moves into Asia's materials-processing industries (that is, the resource-processing type of FDI). This results in the growth of resource-based industries and exports of processed goods (as a new export). Though to a lesser extent, foreign capital also begins to be invested in consumer goods manufacturing, aimed mainly at local markets, spawning modern manufacturing (M→initial P). However, foreign capital's presence in these industries will soon be challenged by national capital, which is promoted under the host country's MPX infant-industry strategy. As a result, domestic production marks the beginning of a period of homogenization/uniformalization of industrial structures in consumer goods, which leads to 'a narrowing of comparative cost differentials' (1961, p. 197) or a comparative-advantage contraction.

National capital now starts to produce its own consumer goods, thereby replacing *both* imports and those manufactures previously initiated by foreign capital. These domestically produced consumer goods are sold only in the domestic market at first. However, they will sooner or later be exported to overseas markets (the early-to-mature P phase – first, overlapping the late M phase, and then, finally entering the X phase of the MPX sequence in consumer goods). Consequently, so far as a particular type of consumer goods is concerned, a period of complementary and co-accelerative relations morphs into one of 'substitutive and conflictive' relations. Yet, simultaneously, demand for capital goods – and hence new imports – emerges (that is, the early-M phase of the MPX sequence in capital goods). (This stage is what Akamatsu described as a period of 'advanced differentiation' or 'high-degree heterogenization' in trade.)

Third stage   On the whole, manufactured (consumer) goods in general, previously imported, are now all produced by national capital (the full-fledged P phase of the MPX sequence in consumer goods) – hence a period of 'homogenization' in the two regions' structures of consumer goods manufacturing. But the capital goods required by these local industries now need to be imported in exchange for primary exports. There still exists, therefore, a state of 'advanced differentiation' in trade relations because '. . . along with the progress of uniformization of consumer goods industries', 'the capital goods industries in advanced nations, on the other hand, advance still further, and advanced differentiation progresses' (1961, p. 207).

Eventually, industrialization in some Asian country proceeds to a higher stage where it can now export consumer goods (the X phase in consumer goods), if not to the advanced countries, at least to its neighboring countries that are just beginning to open up trade and produce only primary goods: 'At this stage, the developing nation [an early starter] becomes homogeneous with advanced nations with respect to consumer goods industries, but differentiation takes place relative to neighboring nations which she was previously homogeneous as a primary industry nation' (1961, p. 207). In other words, this particular early follower-goose becomes an intermediate advanced economy.

A new type of trade thus develops between the intermediate advanced country and its primary producing neighbors within Asia. This intra-Asian trade derives from heterogenization/differentiation in industrial structures within the region itself. In other words, the MPX sequence of light industry (consumer goods) development has just been completed: 'At this third stage, domestic production, which was initiated by the import of finished goods, develops into export industries' (Akamatsu, 1961, p. 207). Now, the intermediate advanced country starts to produce some capital goods (the early P phase in capital goods). This means that the third stage constitutes the beginning of a period of 'high-degree homogenization' in capital goods.

Fourth stage   Eventually, some early emulators in Asia will succeed in developing vertically integrated manufacturing industries in both final and capital goods (for example, apparel and textile machinery or electric home appliances and related components/parts) and export manufactures (both consumer and capital goods). This is likely to occur in some manufactures, but any catching-up country will continue to go through the MPX process of industrial development in other industries where it is still behind the West. As a consequence, intra-manufacturing process trade (Asia's export of consumer goods to the West in exchange for capital goods) still remains. And intra-industry trade in the form of Asia's low-end goods in return for the West's high-end goods in a particular consumer-good industry – and even in a particular capital good industry – emerges.

As a result of this advanced industrialization in Asia, coupled with rising incomes and wants for 'refined' consumer goods, Asia creates its own demand for resources – that is, for their own exportables at home. This leads to a decline in both primary exports and manufactured imports, resulting in an improvement in Asia's terms of trade. More importantly, furthermore, these developments indicate that the two regions' economic structures are becoming increasingly homogenized, and that their relations are turning substitutive and conflictive. The upshot is that protectionism may arise on the part of the West.

In short, Asia's growth on the whole thus starts to decouple from resource dependence (especially primary exports) and is now built on manufacturing industries and their exports. That is to say, Asia's catch-up finally witnesses the successful denouement of the FG development strategy. Meanwhile, the West itself strives to decouple from resource dependence by way of innovating 'synthetic materials' that can substitute for natural materials (such as dyestuffs, rubber, fibers, and fertilizers). This moderates the West's hunger for natural resources overseas – and its need for colonialism.

> . . . as the old imperialism, which had penetrated into less-advanced countries seeking for materials and provisions as primary products, came to be gradually eliminated by nationalism, advanced countries began to produce artificial materials by means of chemical syntheses and adopted re-agriculturization policies in an effort to lessen their dependency upon less-advanced countries for those materials and provisions. From another angle, it might be said that the advanced countries have attempted to homogenize their industries with the primary industries of less-advanced countries by synthetic industries and re-agriculturization in order to *stave off the pursuit by less-advanced countries through their industrialization.* (1962, p. 8, emphasis added)

It should be pointed out here that the role of innovation in keeping the West's lead is certainly not limited to its efforts to replace natural resources but applies as much – or even more – to the manufacturing sector where new and higher-end products and processes need to be constantly introduced 'to stave off the pursuit' of Asian countries, which are bound to build up manufacturing by emulating. Nevertheless, Western innovations constantly create new opportunities for Asia further to learn and catch up, generating further dynamics of interactive growth.

It should also be noted that Akamatsu qualifies the stages model above with respect to both the simplified classification of manufactures only as consumer and capital goods and the clear-cut demarcation lines used for the above stages of international engagement. As to the goods classification;

> Although reference is made here simply to consumer goods and capital goods, there are many kinds and qualities of consumer goods and capital goods. Accordingly, the sequential phenomenon of 'import–domestic production–export' occurs not only in connection with capital goods following consumer goods, but also in the *progression from crude and simple goods to complex and refined goods.* (1961, p. 208, emphasis added)

In other words, manufactures become differentiated in terms of quality and sophistication, creating new room for trade within the same type of industry or product (that is, intra-industry trade). And concerning the stages delineation, Akamatsu notes: 'These stages, however, overlap each other and cannot be clearly classified nor applied to every developing country in Asia' (1962, p. 2).

As to foreign versus national capital, Akamatsu sees a role for foreign capital in bringing about local production and supplementing national capital that may be in short supply in the early phases of economic development. In his own words,

> . . . national capital alone may not always be sufficient to import machinery and plants, nor is the export of special products enough to cover the import of capital goods. Either of these cases, or a situation in which both existed, could cause difficulties in the international balance of payments. This makes the induction of foreign capital necessary. (1962, p. 7)

Moreover, we know that foreign capital also brings in technology, skills, and access to foreign markets. These are critical inputs that would make it possible for developing countries to build modern industries at home (that is, during a shift from the M to the P phase). Yet Akamatsu emphasized 'economic nationalism', in the sense that nationally controlled – not foreign-controlled – industries are the ultimate goal: 'Economic nationalism tries to utilize foreign capital for its homogeneization with the advanced country's economy while excluding submission to colonialism', and such nationalism 'induces foreign capital voluntarily for its own need' (1962, p. 7). Foreign capital is thus merely a temporary means of development strategy and is to be eventually replaced by national capital.

To recapitulate, Akamatsu sketched out a long span of history involving the evolutionary interrelationships of a developing Asia with the advanced West in terms of a stages model. It demonstrates how developing countries may catch up under global capitalism, through interactions between the advanced and the less developed with the alternating periods of heterogenization (that is, a widening divergence in comparative costs that promotes trade) and uniformization (that is, a convergence in comparative costs that impedes trade). These periods occur as the catching-up countries' economic structures are upgraded through their infant-industry (MPX) strategy (that is, in the present-day context, designed to induce foreign capital and technology to flow in to help create comparative advantages) – and as the advanced (lead goose) countries themselves in turn strive to introduce innovations in order to stay ahead of the catching-up countries. It is a model of trade-driven growth in which the doctrine of dynamic comparative advantage plays the central role. The catching-up countries (follower geese) go through a progression of ratcheting up the ladder of industrial upgrading (the analogy of 'a ladder' will be examined and defined in Chapter 3). It is not a one-shot climb but a step-by-step sequence of continuous advance through emulative learning along the trail of industrialization that has been pioneered and already blazed by the more developed countries. In other words, a development flight map, as it were, is made available by the advanced world (lead geese) for the developing countries (follower geese) to follow.

2.3.   RELATEDNESS TO WESTERN THEORIES OF ECONOMIC DEVELOPMENT

Akamatsu frequently cited the Western literature on economic development and trade, notably the German literature, since he studied in Germany for two years, 1924–6. For example, in his 1961 article published in English, he made extensive references, among others, to Werner Sombart (in German), Friedrich List (in German), N.D. Kondratieff, John A. Hobson, D.H. Robertson, Joseph Schumpeter, R.F. Harrod, W.F. Stolper, and J.R. Hicks. And in his 1962 article, also written in English, references were made to Karl Marx (in German), Gunnar Myrdal, and Albert Hirschman. This section further explores the relation of his work to Western economic thought, especially to more recent examples.

As seen above, Akamatsu's basic three-phase (MPX) model constitutes the core mechanism of catch-up industrialization when an underdeveloped country opens up for trade and capitalizes on the opportunities to interact with the advanced world. Such trade opening initiates and sets in motion a derived process of industrial development in hitherto underdeveloped countries. The MPX process is a strategically controllable activity at policy level, whereas the other two patterns (industrial structural change and a hierarchy of countries aligned at different growth stages) are parametrically given and prearranged for latecomers, who follow in the steps of more advanced countries.

In fact, the basic pattern of MPX is equivalent to a combined contiguous process of import substitution-cum-export promotion (IS-EP), the first part of which is inward-looking in orientation, and the second part of which is outward-looking. These two development strategies were conceptualized and recognized as key concepts in the 1960s (Keesing, 1967) – and have been popularized in the lexicon of development economics (*inter alia*, Balassa, 1980). Furthermore, the MPX process involves a new infant-industry protection strategy – new in the sense that exporting is required and regarded as the ultimate criterion of successful protection. Previously, John Stuart Mill (1848/1909) and Charles Bastable (1887) both defended infant-industry protection on the grounds of substitutability of local production for imports; they considered such protection to have been successfully executed if the cost of domestic production declines to the import price level (Mill's criterion) or if the future gains from a newly fostered local industry outweigh the protection costs (investment in protection) (Bastable's criterion). It is thus clear that Akamatsu's criterion went beyond the M→P phase (that is, the IS-based establishment of a new domestic industry) to the X phase – that is, the new industry also must develop into a competitive export industry.

Interestingly, Akamatsu presented his model of development as an alternative to Ragnar Nurkse's then-dominant theory of a 'big push' (1953). The latter emphasized a deficiency in investment inducement in underdeveloped countries, and therefore, called for a 'big-push' strategy in order to overcome the lack of demand and complementariness. The big push means a massive bundle of synchronized simultaneous investments in a wide range of interrelated industrial activities at home. It is basically a 'balanced growth' approach. It is an all-out cross-sectional approach. In contrast, Akamatsu's approach is an intertemporal, step-by-step strategy of developing domestic (and nationally owned) industries over time by way of opening the economy for imports (so as to let imports detect and create potential local demand for modern industrial goods) – but eventually replacing imports with local production. It is akin to an 'unbalanced growth' approach.

In this regard, the flying-geese theory is also related to, and can be interpreted in terms of, Albert Hirschman's theory of unbalanced growth (1958), which closely fits the sequence of imports→domestic production→exports. The MPX process capitalizes on the backward and forward linkages that are the critical elements of intertemporal growth. Here, the idea of import substitution (that is, imports→domestic production) is based on the notion of backward linkage in demand, since domestic production is induced by imports (whose consumption encourages import-substituting production at home). A shift in domestic production from consumer goods to capital goods is similarly made possible by backward linkages. And the phenomenon of newly created exports (that is, domestic production→export) results from forward linkages in supply (exports as an outlet for domestically produced goods).

Actually, Akamatsu predated Hirschman's (1958) theory of unbalanced growth, a once-well-received theory in the West. Hirschman similarly stressed the key role of imports as a harbinger of a potential domestic market and as an initiator of domestic production when the domestic market reaches a certain threshold in size:

> . . . Some of [domestic investors] have learned . . . to look abroad and to infer from foreign experience where new ventures can be successfully started. But

imports still provide the safest, most incontrovertible proof that *the market is there*. Moreover, they condition the consumer to the product, breaking down his initial resistance. Imports thus reconnoiter and map out the country's demand; they remove uncertainty and reduce selling costs at the same time, thereby bringing perceptibly closer the point at which domestic production can economically be started. This point is of course again determined by the minimum size of plant, as well as by cost and location factors that jointly define the 'domestic production threshold.' (1958, p. 121)

Hirschman continued; 'We have stressed here the "creative" role imports can play in the development process, a role that has been almost entirely overlooked' (pp. 124–5). Obviously, he was unaware of Akamatsu's work published in Japanese much earlier (in the 1930s) that exactly pointed to the 'creative' role of imports.

Both scholars explored at what point in time imports would effectively trigger domestic production (that is, the timing of import substitution). Akamatsu viewed high profitability of imports as an inducement to local entrepreneurs to take up production: 'if [an underdeveloped] nation's imports bring higher profits as compared with domestic industry, this constitutes a discrepancy and attracts domestic capital to the domestic production of imports' (1961, p. 212). By comparison, Hirschman looked at the minimum size of a local market as the threshold for import substitution. In either case, however, imports are considered to be destined to decline as import substitution takes effect. As Hirschman put it, 'the chances of survival of any given commodity flow [or import] toward underdeveloped but developing countries are inversely proportional to its current rate of expansion' (1958, p. 123). Put differently, the more successful the import is, the sooner its demise.

Although Hirschman thus rightly focused on the phenomenon of import-induced production as Akamatsu had done earlier, he examined only the import-domestic production (M→P) segment, and missed out the subsequent P→X nexus of Akamatsu's entire MPX sequence. That is, there is no story in Hirschman's analysis of how import-induced domestic production is to develop into an exporting industry.

True, Hirschman did stress a strategic role for exports, but only as an earner of foreign exchange, which is needed to finance imports – and not as a sequential extension of domestic production of a given import:

. . . underdeveloped countries are often insufficiently aware [of] the strategic role played by exports in economic development. Economic policy of underdeveloped countries often treats exports like a stepchild, either because foreign interests are involved in the production of export commodities under 'enclave' conditions or for revenue reasons. If it is grudgingly recognized that *exports are essential for the financing of imports*, then reference is usually made to the imports of raw materials, machinery, and equipment needed to support productive activities and investments that are already under way. The importance of imports in creating and mapping demands and in paving the way for the next development move is usually disregarded and thus leads to an underestimate of the crucial contribution of exports. In other words, there is no real alternative between export promotion and import substitution. The former may often be the only practical way of achieving the latter. (1958, p. 124)

What he is saying above is that import substitution (that is, domestic production) necessarily requires the 'imports of raw materials, machinery, and equipment needed to support productive activities and investments', whose financing needs to be provided by earnings from exports – hence export promotion is inseparable from import substitution. But this does not mean that export promotion needs to be carried out in the same industry where imports are successfully replaced by domestic production. Other industries that can export are in a position to provide import finance in foreign exchange. In addition to the financing of input imports for a newly created domestic industry, the very initial imports that show local producers a potential domestic market *also* must be financed. The critical role of exports as a foreign exchange earner, therefore, cannot be overemphasized in import-induced industrialization. Hirschman, nevertheless, fails to connect import-substituting production directly to the next stage in which new exports are created out of such domestic production – that is, he did not follow up and go thoroughly over the entire sequence of imports→domestic production→exports.

Surprisingly, on the other hand, Paul Krugman (1984) literally touched on Akamatsu's entire MPX sequence of industrial development by introducing the catchy phrase of 'import protection as export promotion' (though he made no reference to Akamatsu's work). Some major differences exist, however, between Krugman and Akamatsu in conceptualizing the intervening causal mechanism. For Krugman, import protection under monopolistic competition leads to scale economies (increasing returns), which will eventually enable the protected local producers to gain export competitiveness in price. On the other hand, Akamatsu's analysis is framed in terms of comparative-advantage building; only those industries that are potentially capable of attaining comparative advantages are given protection for import substitution. That is to say, the criterion is not the attainment of scale economies but that of comparative advantages. This means that latecomers must first develop unskilled-labor-intensive industries (and not scale-driven capital-intensive industries amenable to increasing returns) that are consistent with their existing factor endowments and technological conditions.

Also, Akamatsu referred to W.W. Rostow's concept of 'take-off', though very briefly: 'The stage at which imported consumer goods come to be produced domestically is the take-off stage in the wild-geese-flying pattern' (1961, p. 209). Rostow is concerned, however, with an economy-wide start of industrialization, at which domestic investments reach a level of self-sustainability and all sorts of industrial activities come into exist-ence. In contrast, Akamatsu's phenomenon of import substitution refers to a *particular* industry – that is, without much consideration of what is happening in the rest of the economy.

2.4. EXTENSION OF THE MPX TO FDI AND REVERSE IMPORTS: THE FULL-CIRCLE SEQUENCE

Interestingly, Akamatsu anticipated a conceptual extension of the MPX sequence to foreign direct investment (FDI) abroad and newly created reverse imports (M*) in his study of Japan's cotton yarn industry. He noticed a persistent decline in Japan's imports of cotton yarn from the peak observed during the period 1878–87 to the bottom during 1908–17, but a sharp rebound of such imports during 1928–37, while at the same time Japan's exports exhibited an exactly opposite trend of decline, as shown in Figure 2.2.

According to Akamatsu, this resurgence of imports and a concurrent drop in exports were caused by (i) the rise of cotton-yarn spinning in coun-tries less advanced than Japan, (ii) Japanese spinning companies' overseas investment in other Asian countries, notably China (Shanghai), which began to produce 'coarse thread cotton yarn', and (iii) Japanese special-ization in more 'fine yarn', while importing coarse yarn from overseas. In other words, there were qualitative changes in yarn production at home and yarn imports. Yet such yarn imports began to decrease before World War II and then disappeared in the postwar period (in the mid-1950s). Akamatsu, however, treated this second wave of imports merely as an aberration from the inevitably declining segment of a long-term import trend pattern and failed to fathom the full implications of outward FDI for the home country's industrial and trade structures.

Nonetheless, Akamatsu's analysis did adumbrate an eventual shift in production away from home to low-wage locations, from which foreign-manufactured goods are imported back – a phenomenon now popularly known as 'outsourcing' or 'offshoring'. That is to say, the MPX sequence now extends to the full circle of M$\rightarrow$P$\rightarrow$X$\rightarrow$outward FDI$\rightarrow$M*. To be fair to Akamatsu, he was not then in a position to fully observe this full-circle phenomenon when FDI flows were still at an inchoate stage as they were in the early postwar period. To paraphrase Krugman, this sequence may

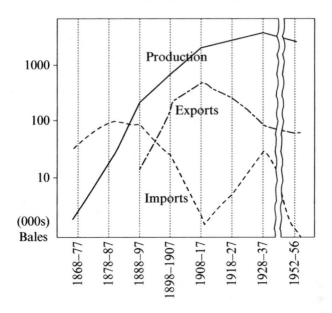

Source: Akamatsu (1962, p. 17).

Figure 2.2 Import, production, and export of Japanese cotton yarn

be paradoxically described as 'import restriction as import promotion'. This is a dynamic evolutionary chain of causalities stemming from a rapid structural transformation of a new (hitherto non-existent) industry transplanted to a catching-up country.

Two other scholars (Kojima, 2006; Yamazawa, 1990) touched on the full-circle (M all the way to M* again) model. Kojima (inter alia, 2006) identifies the MPX phase as a 'catch-up' period and the FDI→M* phase as a 'post-catch-up' period. A full-circle model is also presented in Yamazawa (a student of Kojima) (1990). A catching-up country's new-found ability to make FDI in a particular industry proves that it has completed 'catch up' in that industry, since FDI requires some firm-specific advantages to be a successful overseas investor/producer (Hymer, 1960/1976). It is worth stressing here that in the full-circle model of M→P→X→outward FDI→M*, the initial import, M, is obviously different from the last import, M*, in its role of stimulating economic growth, though exactly the same product may be involved. M serves to develop a domestic market for a particular manufacture, which enables local producers to initiate a new industry at home. On the other hand, M* occurs later on when the home country transplants that same industry abroad as it loses comparative advantage. In other words, the country moves up the ladder of economic development, importing the very goods it once exported.

The P→X phase becomes increasingly two-way interactive in impacting on each other as exports stimulate domestic output, which in turn supports exports by way of the economies of scale and learning. Here, the economies of agglomeration à la Adam Smith or Gunnar Myrdal (cumulative causation) take effect. The good times do not last long, however; domestic production cannot be retained for long in a fast-growing country. The very success of export-driven industrial growth results in higher wages at home, weakening competitiveness. Also, successful exports lead to a currency appreciation that ironically works against exports.

The upshot is an inevitable transition to the X→outward FDI phase. This transition may be triggered (i) by the fact that overseas production becomes more cost-effective due to rising wages and appreciating currency at home, (ii) by the commoditization (standardization) of an export product that was once new and innovative, making it easier for low-wage developing countries to start production themselves, and/or (iii) by protectionism in export markets where local production is induced to be set up as a 'tariff factory'. And the final FDI→M* phase means *reverse or return* imports' of finished, as well as intermediate/capital goods, especially those that are low-end and labor-intensive in nature.

Why is this full-circle model important? We can contend that the model zeroes in on the dynamics of intra-Asian (that is, regionalized) economic integration and growth agglomeration and serves to link up Akamatsu's three patterns of FG formation causatively and more clearly as a unitized (systemic) analytical framework. Chapter 4 will examine the theoretical implications of the full-circle model in connection with the phenomenon of 'comparative-advantage recycling'.

2.5.   FLYING-GEESE THEORY VS. PRODUCT-CYCLE THEORY

Unfortunately, the FG theory is often erroneously interpreted as something homologous to the product-cycle (PC) theory of trade and investment (Vernon, 1966; Hirsch, 1967). Akamatsu's two papers published in English (1961, 1962) helped make the FG theory known overseas, but the Vernon–Hirsch PC theory attracted much greater attention. After all, the PC theory is theoretically more refined and has been tested empirically more frequently than Akamatsu's original FG theory. Consequently, the latter is often treated as a version of the former.[4] And this misfortune has been perpetuated partly because Akamatsu himself and his students, such as Kojima, erroneously identified the FG theory as being a variant of the PC theory.

For example, Kojima actually renamed the FG theory as a 'catching-up product cycle' theory (1978), arguing that the PC theory is constructed from an advanced country's perspective as an innovator, while the FG theory represents a catching-up country's standpoint as a borrower of technology. He also pointed out that the former looks at a single innovative product whose export enjoys an absolute advantage, whereas the latter is concerned with a pattern of international division of labor based on the doctrine of comparative advantage (Kojima, 1975a). Also, Yamazawa (1990) followed this up by similarly conceptualizing the FG model as the theory of 'catching-up product cycle (CPC) development'. What they said in terms of distinguishing the two theories was absolutely correct, but their choice of nomenclature that included the term 'product cycle' was unfortunate, since it failed to treat the FG theory as *sui generis*. In other words, these two theories were interpreted merely as two sides of the *same* coin. Such a nomenclature does an injustice to the FG theory, diluting its uniqueness and importance, even though the FG theory is certainly related to the PC theory.

True, both theories involve the transfer of industrial knowledge from advanced to developing countries. But significant differences need to be recognized. The PC theory deals with changes in the nature of a given technological innovation embodied in a new product or a new production process that is destined to be standardized over a short span of time (as best exemplified in electronics and other research-based, short-product-cycle goods). And it does not consider how an innovating country's factor endowments change; this is in fact treated as given or irrelevant. It is a *micro*-theoretic partial-equilibrium analysis.

The FG theory, on the other hand, concerns the use of an already standardized/mature technology in a developing country's newly created or augmented industry in which it has a comparative advantage. And the technology involved is imported (usually via FDI) from an advanced country, magnifying the extent of comparative advantage. This is what Kojima identifies as 'pro-trade FDI' (1975b). This type of knowledge transfer has a 'comparative-advantage augmentation' effect not only for developing countries but also equally for advanced countries (simply because of the symmetrical effect that magnifies a comparative disadvantage for the latter). But such a new or reinforced comparative advantage in standardized (normally labor-intensive) goods cannot last long as the very importation of modern technology sparks industrial growth, leading to higher wages. In other words, *changes in the factor endowments (capital-labor proportions) ineluctably occur in a rapidly catching-up country, thereby shifting comparative advantages from low value-added to higher value-added industries at home (Akamatsu pattern II) – and from home to lower-wage countries via overseas investment (Akamatsu pattern III).* The FG theory is thus a *macro*-theoretic general equilibrium analysis built on the doctrine of dynamic comparative costs. Its focus is on the *derived* process of industrial development and growth. It deals with the dynamic *structural* changes in the economy.

   Put in technical terms, for the PC theory, a production function for a new product or process changes as a new technology becomes standardized, though the country's factor endowment (capital-labor) ratio remains unchanged (that is, no structural change but only a change in the technical nature of a *given* product). For the FG theory, however, a factor endowment (capital-labor) ratio changes in the wake of technology absorption, though the acquired technology itself is already standardized – hence, its production function remains unchanged. Apart from these technical differences, furthermore, the FG theory is holistic, dealing with global capitalism – and historical, focusing on the structural transformation of the world economy over time. The PC theory stems from a particular stage of growth, a R&D-driven stage in which new products are spawned out of corporate R&D activities, whereas the FG theory covers the entire range of evolutionary industrial transformation (Chapter 3). Indeed, we can claim that the PC theory is an integral part of a big picture depicted by the FG theory, and not the other way round, as will be seen in the following chapters.

2.6.   HEGELIAN DIALECTICS AND EVOLUTIONARY ECONOMICS

While studying in Germany, Akamatsu pursued his interest in Hegelian dialectics and consciously adopted it as a method of thinking in economics: 'My views have been formed mainly through empirical studies of the growth of the Japanese economy, but at the same time they are based upon a method of thinking which I call "synthetic dialectics" which I devised while studying Hegelian philosophy during my studies in Germany' (1961, p. 213). He published a book, *Hegelian Philosophy and Economic Science* (in Japanese; Tokyo, 1931). In fact, he called the FG theory 'a theory of development by discrepancy or contradiction'.

   Indeed, an evolution of economic structure can be presented most appropriately as a *perpetual* sequence of constant changes with contradictions, disequilibria (discrepancies), and transformation, a never-ending process that is stimulated and driven by opposing economic forces and tendencies. At a given point in time, an economic situation may be in transitional chaos or disturbance, but eventually settles down with some stable temporary conditions (which are, however, in turn disturbed by new contradictory forces in an endless state of evolution). Generally speaking, 'dialectic refers to a dynamic tension within a given system and the process by which change occurs on the basis of that tension and resultant conflict' (Young and Arrigo, 1999). More specifically, the German philosopher Georg Wilhelm Friedrich Hegel (1770–1831), in his book *The Science of Logic* (1812/1991), theorized that ideas evolve through a dialectical process – that is, a new idea (namely a thesis) gives rise to its opposite (antithesis), and in the wake of resultant contradictions and tension, a third entity (the synthesis) emerges (Peng and Ames, 2001). This thesis-antithesis-synthesis sequence is of relevance to evolutionary economics. However, these triadic phases are not a *sine qua non* for a dialectic process, since 'It is not so much the number of phases a situation has which makes it dialectical but a *specific relation* of opposition between those phases which generates a succession of other phases' (Hook, 1958, p. 61, original emphasis). A synthesis in turn becomes a thesis in a perpetual flow of events. And contradictions or paradoxical developments are the key features of dialectic change.

It is easy to see how the three FG patterns that Akamatsu conceptualized are framed in Hegelian dialectics. The fundamental FG pattern of MPX reflects the triadic phases of dialectics, as imports represent a *thesis*, domestic production an *antithesis*, and exports a *synthesis*. The import of a particular manufactured good creates a dynamic tension, in the sense that an opportunity for domestic production is created in contradiction to imports. And domestic production results in exporting activity. The two other FG patterns (industrial upgrading and an alignment of countries) are also emblematic of the process of development that inevitably engenders, and reacts to, paradoxical/contradictory short-term outcomes on the heels of the successful MPX sequence.

In dialectical reasoning, a chain of events is driven by disequilibria that produce tensions and evolutionary changes. Along this line of reasoning, Akamatsu explained specifically how the evolutionary process of industrial development transpires in terms of interactions – and gaps – between 'economic activity/reality [A]' and 'economic policy/order [P]', which create 'demand and supply linkages':

> ... it is a situation in which the increase of population and traffic (A) exceeds the capacity of the roads furnished by the nation's policy (P). As the growth of A becomes larger, the discrepancy between A and P – I call this 'the restraining discrepancy' – becomes more intense, and, although the growth of A is restrained,

the pressure of the discrepancy increases. This discrepancy gives rise to a new economic policy, and a policy of road construction is effected . . . The construction of roads will take place on a larger scale than needed to exactly match the existing traffic volume, and an inequality occurs again. This is what is called the 'stimulating discrepancy.' This discrepancy in turn stimulates the increase of traffic volume A, and A and P at length may become equal. Nevertheless, a restraining discrepancy is formed again in the process of a further development. The situation in which economic policy is activated through the initiative of economic activity corresponds to *demand linkage*, and the situation in which economic policy stimulates economic activity corresponds to *supply linkage*. (1961, p. 214)

What Akamatsu means is that a process of economic development is in essence a continuation of *disequilibrium* conditions constantly created – and only momentarily adjusted – during the course of its unfolding events. His perspective is equivalent to what Harvey Leibenstein (1957) called a 'quasi-equilibrium system', where 'the equilibrium state is only quasi-stable as it is from time to time subject to stimulants and shocks, and as a consequence, if ever, gets a chance to pursue undisturbed the path toward equilibrium' (p. 34). Akamatsu's concept of 'homogenization' or 'uniformization' is basically an equilibrating process, in the sense that it is a gap-closing process. And 'heterogenization' or 'differentiation' is a disequilibrating process as it creates and expands gaps. The economy as a whole – if not a particular activity or industry – can *never* become homogenized as heterogenization starts somewhere else.

In this connection, it should be noted that in a famous article, 'The Irrelevance of Equilibrium Economics', Kaldor (1972) stresses 'the theorem of endogenous and cumulative change' in reference to Young's (1928) contributions: 'It means that the counter forces which are continually defeating the forces which make for economic equilibrium are more pervasive and more deeply rooted than we commonly realize. Myrdal (1957), writing twenty-five years later, called this the principle of circular and cumulative causation'. (p. 1245).

Given the pervasive trend of dialectic evolutionary unraveling, any first goose country may not remain a leader for long in the global economy. The internal logic of a FG formation of interactive growth is such that the lead goose ineluctably loses competitiveness, if not in all areas of industrial activity, in an increasing number of areas, as knowledge creation/infusion at home is gradually overwhelmed by knowledge dissemination/diffusion from home. The only way to put off the day of reckoning is to make sure that the rate of knowledge infusion is greater than that of knowledge diffusion – say, by way of promoting scientific endeavors such as R&D. Yet this is easier said than done. Globalization facilitates knowledge dissemination across borders and often leads to even knowledge creation being offshored.

In short, what Akamatsu wanted to emphasize is that economic structures go through evolutionary transformation, experiencing contradictory outcomes and continuous disequilibria and adaptations, which is the very dynamics of growth – and that these features can be elucidated by way of dialectic reasoning.

2.6.1. Hegelian Lineage in Marx, Engels, and Schumpeter

Akamatsu was not the only one influenced by Hegelian dialectic. This section briefly reviews how others have been equally inspired. This in turn helps us better understand Akamatsu's analysis from the perspective of evolutionary economics, which adopts a dialectic way of thinking. In the first place, it is well known that much earlier dialectics had greatly affected Karl Marx (1818–83) and Friedrich Engels (1825–95). They applied dialectic reasoning to the analysis of civilization and socio-political change, an analysis that came to be known as 'dialectical materialism'.[5] Their approach is based on three basic laws: (i) the law of the interpenetration of opposites, (ii) the law of the transformation of quantity into quality and vice versa, and (iii) the law of negation of the negation (Engels, 1872–82/1940, as cited in Peng and Ames, 2001). According to Marx and Engels, for example, 'revolutionary change comes as a result of contradictions in the concretely existing modes of production rather than as a result of supernatural or mystical phenomena', and 'each economic system may have tendencies that can be seen, but they should not be taken to be inevitable' (Young and Arrigo, 1999). The dialectical triad of thesis-antithesis-synthesis is also clearly observable in Marx's transformational sequence of the 'commodity (C) vs. money (M)' cycle: $C \rightarrow M \rightarrow C$ or $M \rightarrow C \rightarrow M$.

In modern times, Joseph Schumpeter, too, was very much inspired by Marx and Engels' dialectical materialism. In his book, *Capitalism, Socialism and Democracy* (originally published in 1942 and revised in 1950), Schumpeter initially predicted that 'a socialist form of society will *inevitably* emerge from an equally *inevitable* decomposition of capitalist society', but later toned down this conclusion by asserting instead that 'The capitalist order tends to destroy itself and centralist socialism is . . . a *likely* [not inevitable] heir apparent' (cited in Bottomore, 1976, emphasis added). This is because Schumpeter probably recognized that observed tendencies might have *diverse* outcomes, depending on the strength of various resistances and counter-tendencies (that is, antitheses) that would alter the course of the original tendencies in many entirely new and unpredictably stochastic directions (that is, unforeseen syntheses) – hence, *no* inevitability or determinism is implied or admitted.

In his 1934 classic, *The Theory of Economic Development*, Schumpeter examined how an initial stationary state of 'a circular flow' at a given level of national income (that is, a thesis) would be disturbed by an entrepreneur with a new combination or innovation (that is, an antithesis), who was then followed by a swarm of other emulating entrepreneurs or imitators, and in the end, another circular flow (the *synthesis*) would be attained at a newly notched-up higher level of national income. Here, the principle of what he called 'creative destruction' (which is an oxymoron phrase) characterizes and permeates the dynamic dialectical process of structural change under capitalism.

We can also discern the now often-used and familiar concept of 'path-dependence' or the 'lock-in' effect in Schumpeter's evolutionary analysis. This concept, however, needs to be recognized as an *ex post* concept describing only one outcome from many stochastic possibilities that have previously existed, hence it does not mean determinism. Schumpeter observed that 'Every concrete process of development . . . rests upon preceding development . . . Every process of development creates the *prerequisites* for the following. Thereby the form of the latter is altered, and things will turn out differently from what they would have been if every concrete phase of development had been compelled first to create its own conditions' (Schumpeter, 1934, p. 64). This matches what Richard Nelson and Sidney Winter, in their book, *An Evolutionary Theory of Economic Change* (1982, p. 19), reiterated: the economic condition in each time period 'bears the seeds of its condition in the following period'. This is the essence of evolutionary analysis reflective of Hegelian dialectic.

Interestingly enough, the recently emerged 'chaos theory' is said to be a natural outcome of the human quest for knowledge along the lines of dialectical thinking. In fact, Schumpeter's vision of economic development punctuated by 'creative destruction' in the aftermath of revolutionary 'new combinations' – instead of incremental improvements – and the subsequent 'swarm-like appearance' of follower entrepreneurs foreshadowed chaos theory (Rostow, 1990). The logic and power of dialectic are thus clearly observable in Schumpeter's analysis of the dynamics of economic development and change.

There are, indeed, many similarities between Akamatsu's and Schumpeter's thinking, though the latter is much more clearly formulated and articulated as a theory. Yet both are concerned with the dynamics of change in economic structures under the forces of capitalism, and are strongly influenced by Hegelian dialectic.

2.7.　SUMMING UP

What Akamatsu identified as the 'fundamental' pattern of flying-geese formation, namely the MPX sequence of introducing and building up a new modern industry under an infant-industry protection policy, was based on Japan's bygone-era experiences of industrial development. Such a protectionist approach was accepted before and immediately after World War II – but no longer at present. Trade and investment liberalization is becoming the zeitgeist of the present global economy. After all, MNCs can almost instantly set up new ventures or industries in developing host countries and bring about local production, import substitution, and export simultaneously in one fell swoop – without any prolonged sequencing of MPX. Therefore, what he called 'secondary or auxiliary patterns' (reflecting structural upgrading and a hierarchy of countries) are, in fact, turning out to be decisively more relevant than the MPX sequence in interactive growth under today's global capitalism.

In many respects, Akamatsu preceded and complemented Western scholars in conceptualizing about the fundamentals of economic development. His dialectical perception and approach resonate with major Western thinkers who looked at the process of structural transformation and growth as an evolutionary one. Dialectical thinking is called for in understanding the fast-changing global landscapes that bring forth contradictory events and unintended consequences. Seemingly paradoxical outcomes may not be so paradoxical after all (as seen, for example, in the sequence of 'import restriction as import promotion'). There is always a dynamic evolutionary chain of causalities running through future events. We ought to think in flying-geese terms – that is, to think in dialectic, evolutionary, and interactive terms.

As explained in his historical model sketched out above, Akamatsu's theory of economic development treats trade and cross-border migration of production as the integrative compositional phenomenon of growth in the developing world – in the best tradition of classical 'grand' theories of trade and growth (especially, Adam Smith's, Ricardo's, and John Stuart Mills'). It is a dynamic theory of *trade-driven* industrialization and structural change. In particular, Akamatsu stressed the role of economic nationalism in reaction to the forces of imperialism. This largely reflected the international situations of his day, facing Japan in the pre-World War II period when the FG theory was originally expounded.

Given the rapid changes in the global economy and polity, many of his specific analyses (such as the sequence of MPX and protectionism to foster national industries) may no longer be relevant. Nonetheless, the key fact that capitalism spreads growth and prosperity, if unevenly, across the globe, though creating disruptions, contradictions, and tensions in the process, remains true and particularly policy-relevant. Hence, his analytical framework is still useful so long as it is appropriately reinterpreted and reformulated, as this study intends to demonstrate.

Obviously Akamatsu depicted his flying-geese theory with very broad strokes of the brush and left many aspects of his model unelaborated – hence, the title of this chapter bears the phrase 'in the rough'. His model is subject to many different interpretations and further theoretical elaborations. Thus, his followers have their work cut out to expand on his ideas. We will present reformulations and adaptations of Akamatsu's original theory in what follows.

NOTES

1. Also, it was early on called '*henkei* [variant pattern]'. But *fukujikei* (auxiliary pattern) is more appropriate, since the three patterns (one fundamental plus two auxiliary patterns) reveal the three structural features of the same process of catch-up industry development. All three are functionally connected.
2. Akamatsu (1962) spells English words, 'homogeneization' and 'heterogeization'. Throughout this book, however, the alternate spellings, 'homogenization' and 'heterogenization', are used instead. Also, Akamatsu (1961) uses 'differentiation' and 'uniformization'.
3. The stages model described here is based on Akamatsu's two articles (1961 and 1962). The 1961 article briefly touches on a four-stage model that describes how Europe (initially homogeneous) was transformed by the Industrial Revolution into a heterogenized region, which in turn was first homogenized but later differentiated again. In contrast, the 1962 article focuses on how Asia's economic structure has evolved in response to initial contact with the advanced West in terms of seven stages of interactions.
4. Ginzburg and Simonazzi (2005), for example, observe that, 'In the West, Akamatsu's ideas are interpreted simply as a version, or a completion of Vernon's product cycle theory' (p. 1052).
5. 'Marxist dialectical thought recognizes the permanence of opposition and contradiction in *the real material world*, and therefore in thought about reality. According to Marx and Engels, the process of historical development is endless because the synthesis itself becomes a new thesis and is in turn negated by a new antithesis producing a new synthesis and so on *ad infinitum*' (Peng and Ames, 2001, pp. 3634–5, original emphasis).

3. A dynamic stages model of structural upgrading, industrial transplantation, and knowledge diffusion

3.1. THE LADDER OF ECONOMIC DEVELOPMENT DEFINED

3.1.1. Trail-blazers' Legacy

What are the causes of structural upgrading from one stage to another – that is, Akamatsu's progression 'from crude and simple goods to complex and refined goods' and 'capital goods following consumer goods'? In other words, what factors propel a catching-up economy to scale the ladder of economic development – and in what manner? To answer this question, we must first define the ladder of economic development itself. This notion has long been popularly cited in the economics of industrialization, but surprisingly without any clear definition other than casually referring to a gradual process of upgrading from low-productivity to higher-productivity industrial activity. Yet, what exactly are the *rungs* of such a ladder?

In neoclassical economics, economic development is conceived as a process of *capital accumulation*, that is to say, a country's *capital-to-labor* endowment ratio increases. This merely means, however, that any growing country becomes increasingly more capital-abundant as national income rises, resulting in greater savings. Yet, capital accumulation is an effect or a result and not the cause of growth per se. What really brings about a spurt of growth and structural change under capitalism is *innovation*, both technological and organizational, or breakthrough technological progress that creates brand-new industries, as stressed by Joseph Schumpeter (1934). Capital investment only follows innovations.

Therefore, the ladder of economic development can be defined by tracing out the actual historical path of industrial (hence technological) development driven by innovations. The model to be presented here may be called a 'leading-sector stages model' à la Schumpeter, in which a sequence of growth is punctuated by stages (five stages so far, as will be seen below), and in each stage a certain industrial sector can be identified as the main engine of structural transformation (Ozawa, 1992, 2005). In other words, long-term growth is not input-driven incrementally and marginally – it is not 'due to a quasi-automatic increase in population [labor] and capital' (Schumpeter, 1942, p. 82) – but is set in motion by innovation, which then eventually leads to rapid capital formation in innovation-initiated new industries that serve as leading sectors. A given set of innovations (a breakthrough technological progress and its accompanying organizational and technical improvements) creates a new *rung* on the ladder of economic development.

In sum, the capitalist process of growth can be neither incrementally additive nor smoothly cumulative in capital formation as posited by neo-classical economics, but is driven by the logic of 'the perennial gale of creative destruction' (Schumpeter, 1934). This perspective is also in line with what Rostow (1960) emphasized: 'it is useful to characterize an economy in terms of its leading sectors; and a part of the technical basis for the stages of growth lies in the changing sequence of leading sectors' and in terms of 'economic history as a sequence of stages rather than merely as a continuum, within which nature never makes a jump' (p. 16). The notion of 'a ladder' metaphorically means 'a series of ranked stages or levels' (as defined in *The American Heritage Dictionary*). Therefore, the stages model is most appropriate for defining the rungs of the development ladder.

3.1.2. A Structural Stages Model of Growth

More specifically, this leading-sector stages model is built on the historical evidence that the world economy has so far witnessed five tiers of leading growth industry emerge in a wave-like progression ever since the Industrial Revolution in England. The five tiers are schematically illustrated in Figure 3.1. These tiers give some defining characteristics to the erstwhile nebulous notion of 'the ladder of economic development'. Following close on the heels of Great Britain, other Western countries emulated and replicated the pattern of industrialization in England, each furthering the growth of each tier in terms of follow-up technological contributions. Non-Western countries, notably Japan – and more recently, the Asian NIEs, and now China and India, likewise have been retracing the paths of industrial upgrading pioneered by earlier industrializers. The ladder of development defined and presented in Figure 3.1 can also be regarded as a 'flight map', so to speak, for 'follower geese' to be guided in their drive to catch up on growth.

The first dominant industry that appeared was what may be called the 'Heckscher-Ohlin' endowments-driven (natural resources- or 'raw'

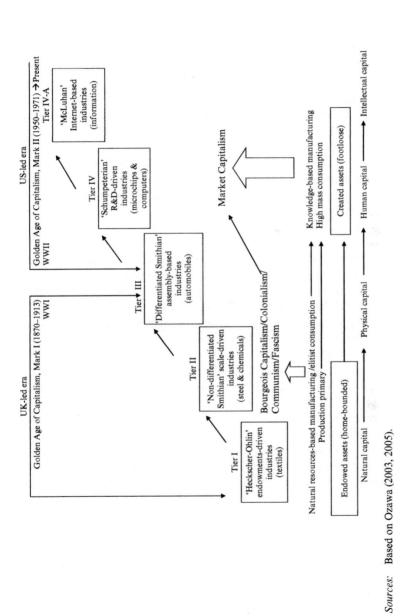

Sources: Based on Ozawa (2003, 2005).

Figure 3.1   The ladder of economic development: industrial upgrading under UK- and US-led global capitalism

labor-intensive light) industries – best represented by textiles in labor-abundant countries and by raw industrial materials, energy, and agricultural goods in resource-rich countries. (The first stage is named after the Heckscher-Ohlin trade theory that explains the doctrine of comparative advantage in terms of different factor proportions between countries and different factor intensities between goods.) The factors most intensively used in this Stage-I growth are largely 'natural assets' that are endowed by nature (hence, alternately often called 'endowed assets'). Any developing country has an opportunity to kick-start industrialization by first exploiting readily available 'natural assets'. And trade is characterized by the *inter*-industry pattern and based on the doctrine of comparative advantage.

The first stage was historically almost immediately entailed by the 'non-differentiated Smithian' scale-driven (physical capital-intensive, natural resource-processing) heavy and chemical industries, such as steel and basic chemicals (mostly homogeneous/non-differentiated goods). Steam power replaced animal and water power, revolutionizing transportation. The factory system that had taken over the putting-out system in manufacturing came to be run by steam engines. Mechanized textile production, shipbuilding, and mining lay the ground for modern machine and engineering industries. Iron and steel and basic chemicals met the needs of heavy industry. Meanwhile, steam power was in turn substituted for by internal combustion and electricity. This all led to the rise of heavy and chemical industries as the lead sector in the second stage. (Stage-II growth is named after Adam Smith who stressed gains from dynamic increasing returns to scale.)

Indeed, the Golden Age of Capitalism, Mark I (1870–1913) stemmed from the rapid growth of these first two phases of technological/industrial development under Britain's hegemony. That Golden Age's need – and its fervent search – for natural resources (for example, iron ore and non-ferrous metals) and overseas markets for textiles and capital goods fostered colonialism. And scale-driven heavy and chemical industrialization was pursued relentlessly under imperialism as part and parcel of an arms race among the imperial powers that had to expand, protect, and control their colonies.

The rise of the US as the industrial hegemon after World War II originated from American ingenuity in the innovation of interchangeable parts and assembly-line operations, which eventually culminated in the American manufacturing system of mass production on the supply side and the America-initiated pattern of mass consumption on the demand side, both of which would set the tone for the rest of the world. The 'differentiated Smithian' assembly-based industries (notably automobiles) emerged as the leading growth sector in the US, following the introduction of Ford's assembly lines and Frederick Taylor's scientific management ('time and motion study'). Fordism-cum-Taylorism thus became the dominant manufacturing paradigm, which was aimed at exploiting increasing returns to scale through the *standardization* of products (as initially exemplified by the Model T), work processes, and parts and components. With the entry of many competing producers in both the US and Europe, however, automobiles became increasingly differentiated in engineering, design, function, optional features, and add-on accessories to satisfy consumers' diversified preferences. (Hence Stage-III growth is identified as 'differentiated Smithian'.)

The stage of assembly-based industries, which also include electric machinery and appliances, is by nature far more consumer-oriented and far more responsive to diversified consumer tastes than its previous counterpart of heavy and chemical industrialization. The growth of these consumer-focused industries necessitated – and is compatible with – strong market democracy where people are able to vote with their dollars to determine desirable types of consumer goods. Individual freedom of choice became the *sine qua non* of the age of high mass consumption. Consumerism is the market ideology of US-led global capitalism – and the hallmark of the Golden Age of Capitalism, Mark II (1950–71). And diversified tastes gave birth to intra-industry trade among those advanced countries that had reached Stage-III growth.

Rising consumerism in turn spurred R&D activities in corporate America in search of new products. As a consequence, especially in the post-World War II period, the Schumpeterian R&D-driven industries came to represent the next stage of economic growth. The outcome was innovations of mostly knowledge-based consumer goods, such as TV sets, computers, semiconductors, washers and dryers, dishwashers, microwave ovens, tape-recorders, and antibiotics. In the 1950s and 1960s, many large corporations in science-based industries began to set up R&D centers. Notable were IBM's Watson Labs and AT&T's Bell Labs. The 'age of corporate laboratories' (Best, 2000) was thus ushered into the US economy, leading to America's technological leadership in many emerging high-tech sectors. 'Created assets' began increasingly to substitute for and replace 'endowed natural assets'. Indeed, this structural transformation of the US economy was captured in the product-cycle (PC) theory of trade and investment (as distinguished from the FG theory in Chapter 2).

The latest stage of economic growth is driven by information technology (IT). It has emanated from the configuration of Schumpeterian industries. The new stage is built on the Internet and other forms of IT, which have revolutionized the way we communicate with each other. The IT-based stage can be most appropriately called the 'McLuhan' Internet-enabled phase of growth, in which we now live – named after Marshall McLuhan, the guru of mass communications. Indeed, the phenomena of 'The Medium is the Message' (McLuhan and Fiore, 1967) and 'The Global Village' (now web-enabled) (McLuhan and Powers, 1989) are the hallmarks of our present age of information. This new growth sector was pioneered in the US, particularly during the first tech boom of the latter half of the 1990s. The New Economy has thus come into existence. Moreover, the newest two sub-phases of R&D-driven growth are already in the making as additional spin-offs from the Schumpeterian industries and as subsystems of the New Economy. One is based on the biotechnology (BT) revolution, and the second is the nanotechnology (NT) revolution. In fact, these three revolutions of IT, BT, and NT are fast converging.

3.1.3.   First under British Hegemony – and then under American Hegemony

We can recapitulate the sequential path and nature of modern industries introduced under Anglo-American global capitalism as follows: What British hegemony introduced were initially labor-intensive light industries (of the 'Heckscher-Ohlin' type) as typified by textiles and then resource-intensive, scale-driven heavy and chemical industries (of the 'non-differentiated Smithian' type) as epitomized by steel, basic chemicals, and heavy machinery. These stages represent the Old Economy. They were once developed and thrived as the leading growth sectors in the advanced countries in the pre-World War II period – under a variety of economic systems; unfettered bourgeois capitalism and colonialism (early on in Great Britain and other capitalist powers), communism (in the Soviet Union and China), fascism (in Germany, Italy, and Japan), and welfare/socialist capitalism (in Scandinavia).

In contrast, in the post-World War II period American hegemony created the highly components-intensive, assembly-based, genuinely consumer-oriented, and R&D-intensive industries (the 'differentiated Smithian' and 'Schumpeterian' stages) as best represented by mass-produced (more recently 'lean-produced') automobiles and electronics. And the most recent phase is Internet-enabled information-intensive industries (the 'McLuhan' stage). In particular, IT-driven industries are built on 'intellectual and entrepreneurial capital' and strongly geared to, and closely tied with, the needs of final consumers in product development, distribution, and consumption. The New Economy is the latest creation of US-led capitalism. As Baumol (2002) argues, free market capitalism is the most efficient 'innovation machine', producing a stream of innovations, satisfying consumer needs and demands because of its 'survival of the fittest' effect of fierce competition. The rise of consumerism explains at least in part why Soviet communism tumbled down in the late 1980s and why China began to switch to a market economy by opening its doors at about the same time.

Market capitalism is therefore the necessary institution for Pax-Americana-nurtured industries, especially for the New Economy, where individuals are increasingly empowered more fully to exercise the freedom of choice and communicate with each other at the grass roots more freely than ever before in real-time exchange of information at the click of a mouse, thanks to the IT revolution. (No wonder, then, that authoritarian governments are trying to control the public in the use of the Internet so as to suppress any expression of democratic values and criticism of such regimes.)

3.1.4. From Coal to Oil – and to Alternative Energies?

There has been a drastic shift in the main source of energy from coal under Pax Britannica to oil under Pax Americana. And the rise of assembly-based industries, especially automobiles for mass consumption, inevitably increased demand for oil as both fuel and raw materials. The US and all other advanced countries are now entrapped in – and 'addicted to' – oil.[1] America's military engagement in the Middle East for the stability of the region reflects the high intensity of oil use in both consumption (as fuel) and production (as raw materials for synthetics) in the present world. The collapse of the Soviet Union has meant a focal shift of geopolitics from ideology (capitalism vs. communism) to oil security, which involves rising cultural conflicts between the West and the Islamic World. No doubt, oil has become 'the ultimate geopolitical commodity'.[2]

And the recently surging demand for oil in China and India, as they enter the oil-dependent stage, is further contributing to soaring oil prices. Both are currently in the midst of heavy and chemical industrialization (Stage-II growth) and exhibit voracious appetites for industrial commodities, especially oil (more on this in Chapter 5). Asia has become the world's biggest source of new oil demand. China alone accounts for half the recent global increase in demand. This heavy oil dependence may prove to be the Achilles' heel of US-led capitalism unless new sources of energy (such as wind power, solar energy, hydrogen, nuclear, and biofuels) are harnessed to replace oil. In this regard, the next possible technological progress may be an 'energy revolution' that produces a new stage of economic growth in the near future, if properly guided and supported by government policies.

In the meantime, the energy-rich countries are basking in Stage-I (resource-based) growth, thanks mainly to the economic growth of China and India and the inability of the advanced world to wean itself off oil consumption. Furthermore, the oil-exporting countries themselves are sparking their own demand for oil and other commodities, as they emulate the capitalist mode of production and consumption. In 2008, the soaring price of oil made it possible for OPEC's (Organization of Petroleum Exporting Countries) annual revenue to reach the 1 trillion dollar level. As will be pointed out in Chapter 8, what made the matter worse is that oil has become a commodity ('black gold') just like other commodities on which investors place their bids speculatively in the futures market, driving up oil prices. Speculation has been abetted because of expansionary monetary policy in the US, as excess liquidity finds its way into commodities. Be that as it may, soaring commodity prices are to be predicted by the FG paradigm of structural upgrading when such huge economies as China and India happen to be simultaneously in the midst of Stage-II growth.

3.1.5. Vertical Segmentation in Each Tier

In addition to the basic five stages of structural upgrading described above, each advanced stage has produced a widening range of *vertically* concatenated (hence, fragmentable) multi-segments, the upper end of which is technologically sophisticated and highly capital-intensive, while the lower end is technologically standardized and labor-intensive – hence, the latter is more readily transferable to low-wage developing countries (see Figure 3.2). As a consequence, even higher-stage industries, especially automobiles, electronics, and telecommunications equipment, are transplanting their *low-end* production (mostly of standardized parts/components/accessories, as well as the low value-added, low-profit lines of finished goods) to low-wage locations in the developing world. The same can be said about services such as back-office jobs, as seen in the growth of call centers and data processing in developing countries, most notably India. In short, both industrial upgrading (of the inter-industry/stage type) and refined vertical chains of value-added (of the intra-industry/stage type) have created structural opportunities for firms in both advanced and the developing countries to pursue a new division of labor in production across borders.

This vertical division of labor is related to what is known as 'production fragmentation' and has been theorized by Arndt and Kierzkowski (2001) and Cheng and Kierzkowski (2001). Here trade occurs within a given firm (between the home-based office and overseas suppliers), hence an intra-firm transaction. And the doctrine of comparative advantage (both neofactor and neotechnology types) still applies – in addition to the competitive

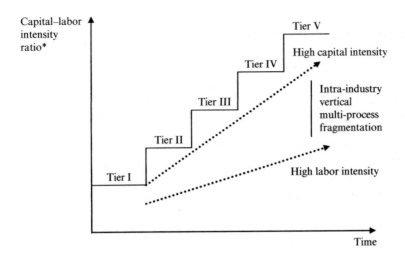

Note: *Capital includes human/intellectual capital.

Figure 3.2   Production fragmentation along capital–labor intensity ratios

advantage emanating from the increasing returns (scale economies) that necessarily occur, since trade promotes specialization and agglomeration.

3.1.6.   Latecomers' Paths to Catch-up Growth: Stages Co-mingling, Reconstructing and Skipping

What has been described above is the evolutionary unfolding of industrial structure as a series of innovations introduced into one leading sector after another in a wave-like fashion over the past two centuries in the presently advanced world. The stages progression toward higher value-added industries (measured on the vertical axis in Figures 3.2 and 3.3) and the time involved (measured on the horizontal axis) necessarily indicate a monotonic one-way relationship from a historical (longitudinal) perspective. Yet, for present-day catching-up countries, the progression can be modified, its order sidetracked, and its pattern made non-monotonic and non-linear. After all, the historical path described above presents only a broad flight map which follower-geese countries can consult in planning their own catch-up strategies. In other words, they are in a position to design their own paths by taking shortcuts whenever and wherever possible. The consequence is no longer an exact duplication of moving up the ladder of development, but stages (rungs) co-mingling and even stages skipping occur.

These possibilities are made all the more available, since in addition to the inter-industry progression toward higher value-added industries, there has occurred intra-industry vertical deepening and fragmentation in each industry, with high-skill, capital-intensive production at the top and low-skill, labor-intensive production at the bottom (Figure 3.2). This development is creating trade opportunities for a new division of labor in which advanced and developing countries can further participate according to the logic of the Heckscher-Ohlin theory – that is, with advanced countries specializing in the higher-end markets, and developing countries specializing in lower-end markets (at least initially, as the first step in joining the global economy).

This increased opportunity for a vertical division of labor is made possible in part because of the rise (Stage-III growth) of components/parts-intensive industries (such as automobiles and electronics) and in part because of the IT revolution (Stage-V growth) which has considerably reduced transactions costs. Some developing countries are now able to initiate their catch-up growth from the IT-based services sector and then try to move toward Stage-I labor-intensive manufacturing, as is the case with the recent strategy adopted by India. And this widened window of business opportunity is being actively used by MNCs – not only from the advanced world but also from fast-emerging countries – to craft cross-border networks of production and other business operations.

The new paths followed by Asia's catching-up countries are illustrated in Figure 3.3. It should be noted that Japan moved, on the whole, directly (almost monotonically or linearly) up the inter-industry sequence pioneered by the West, ratcheting up the industrial structure, stage by stage – each stage being compatible with prevailing factor endowments and overall technological sophistication at home. In scaling the available ladder of economic (and technological) development, Japan was scarcely dependent on direct help from foreign MNCs. This is because postwar Japan, though war-devastated at the start of reconstruction, was already a fairly industrialized economy equipped with institutions and a large stock of basic industrial knowledge. In sharp contrast, China has been far more open to, and more dependent on, inward FDI in practically all stage-specific industries simultaneously in a co-mingled fashion (that is, stages co-mingling). It has been first starting at the low-end of each industry – and then 'racing to the middle' (that is, to strive for higher-end goods). South Korea's and Taiwan's experiences have been closer to Japan's, though they have entered each tier from much lower-end segments. Hong Kong and Singapore skipped heavy industry and large-scale assembly manufacturing and moved into the services sector (finance, research and engineering, healthcare and the like) (that is, stages skipping). On the other hand, the ASEAN-4 countries

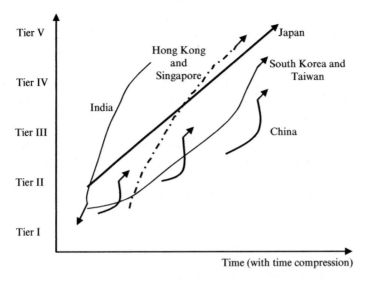

Figure 3.3   Followers' paths of catch-up industrial upgrading: stages co-mingling, reconstructing, and skipping

have been similarly moving into each tier from the bottom – but they have not been able to move up by exploiting intra-industry opportunities. And as mentioned above, India began seriously to capitalize on the forces of US-led global capitalism by first opening up its information industry and presently striving to integrate its lower-tier industries with the outside world (that is, stages reconstructing/reversing).

Whatever strategy the catching-up countries pursue, they have grown much faster than their earlier brethren – that is, a phenomenon of *time compression*. It took the UK nearly 60 years (1780–1838) to double its per capita output; the US 50 years (1836–86); Japan 34 years (1885–1919); Turkey 20 years (1857–77); Brazil 18 years (1961–79); South Korea 11 years (1966–77); and China only ten years (1977–87) (World Bank, 1991). A similar trend is observable in the average rate of real wage increases: 'While it took English workers seventy years to raise their real earnings by roughly 150%, Korean manufacturing workers achieved a comparable gain in about 20 years (from 1955 to 1976). In just one decade, 1969–1979, real wages in Korea rose by more than 250%' (Amsden, 1989, p. 197).

The principle of time compression is at work because of the economies of concatenation in economic development. Knowledge and information are basically borderless and travel faster than ever before. Trade and other international business activities, along with international education (that is, overseas studies and research by students and scholars), not only bridge the gaps in knowledge (that is, equilibrating Wallasian-type knowledge arbitrage) but also simultaneously lead to synergistic 'new combinations' in ideas (that is, disequilibrating or gap-creating Schumpeterian-type knowledge advancement). Knowledge transfer is prevalent between advanced countries and developing ones, while knowledge creation occurs more frequently within the advanced world. This essentially means for the developing world that 'the options and prospects facing latecomers [at least, initially] are necessarily influenced by what is going on in pioneers' (Bell, 1987, p. 2), although latecomers themselves often turn into path-breakers in certain industries in the course of 'catching up and surging ahead' (Abramovitz, 1986).

In addition to time compression, FG-style economic development tends to be clustered in a particular supra-national region – that is, *space compression* – because of the economies of hierarchical concatenation, learning, and agglomeration – and the 'demonstration' effect. The logic of the Marshallian 'industrial district' basically holds at a supra-national level. Neighbors' success is contagious. Transaction costs are much lower within a region than between regions for commercial and informational exchanges. Yet, what region is amenable to growth clustering depends on a region's 'social capacity' (Ohkawa and Rosovsky, 1972; Abramovitz, 1986) to respond to, and exploit, the opportunities externally provided by global capitalism. And regions vary in social capacity. An FG formation of tandem growth thus occurs in a particular region, as it has taken place in Asia, when ideal enabling conditions happen to prevail.

3.2.   ENABLING MECHANISMS OF SEQUENTIAL UPGRADING: 'USHERS OF TRANSFORMATION'

So, what are the enabling mechanisms for industrial upgrading to reach the next stage of growth? We must search for what may be called the 'ushers of transformation'. Surprisingly, the major ushers are mostly 'insiders' in the sense that they are endogenous part of the market mechanism, though the government as an 'outsider' certainly has a key role to play in terms of policy execution and regulatory enforcement – that is, exogenous parametric factors.

3.2.1.   Wages and Flexible Labor Markets

The advanced countries no longer have comparative advantages in lower-tier (Stage-I and II) industries, especially labor-intensive light manufacturing (for example, textiles and apparel) and resource-based 'smoke-stack' low-tech heavy and chemical industries (for example, steel and basic chemicals). The US, in particular, is in the midst of losing assembly-based (Stage-III) industry, notably automobiles. Ironically, their own technological progress – hence their successful structural ratcheting-up – has made it impractical and even impossible for them to retain competitiveness in lower-tier industries – and for that matter in the low-end segments of higher-tier industries (for example, standardized final, inter-mediate, and capital goods in electronics). This loss of competitiveness is necessarily the inevitable outcome of 'creative destruction' that generates dynamic comparative advantages.

Such a structural transformation in the advanced world means that low-wage-based light industries and assembly operations of higher-tier industries (for example, assembly of electronics goods such as TV sets and cell phones) are the ideal 'entry' industries for developing countries to initiate their efforts to climb the ladder of economic development. These industries, indeed, can serve as jump-starters of development by mobiliz-ing developing countries' most abundant factor, unskilled (but readily trainable) labor, for active employment. In fact, this is the most effective *market-based* solution to reducing poverty (as will be explored in Chapter 4). Being cognizant of this fact, many developing countries are eagerly pro-ducing and exporting apparel, electronics, and other labor-intensive goods as their major manufactures. Interestingly enough, this development strat-egy usually puts female workers, especially those from poor rural areas, in great demand, since low-end manufacturing normally creates more jobs for young female workers than for their male counterparts.[3]

3.2.1.1. Flexible labor

What really matters here is not so much low wages *per se* but flexible labor markets where market principles are at work in wage determination. In this respect, the setting-up of enclaves is no doubt the *necessary* first step in developing countries if they are to capitalize on global capital-ism (as stressed by Radelet and Sachs (1997) in Chapter 1). East Asia as a whole – but especially China despite (or rather on account of) its communist rule (centralized economy) – has ironically but fortuitously benefited from its 'flexible' labor markets largely because of the establish-ment and spread of capitalist enclaves. In China, indeed, practically its entire manufacturing sector has already morphed into a capitalist system from the special economic zones. And it is only in recent years that labor has been gradually unionized and higher (more decent) labor standards adopted. By comparison, India is still experiencing some difficulty in fos-tering labor-intensive manufacturing because of its strong labor unions and socialist labor laws despite the fact that it has already set up more than a dozen special economic zones modeled after China's.[4] Hence, enclaves alone are *not* a sufficient condition unless they are freed from labor market rigidities.

Critics of labor-driven industrialization charge that it is a dead end or 'race to the bottom', entrapping a developing country in perpetual labor exploitation by foreign interests.[5] The reality is, however, quite contrary. It opens up a way to higher wages and higher value-added activities. On the theoretical front, the Heckscher-Ohlin trade theory provides two major reasons: (i) when a developing country concentrates on labor-intensive production, demand for the country's most abundant factor, namely labor, rises more than for its scarce factor, capital; and (ii) a factor-price (wage) magnification effect occurs, in which the wage increases more than proportionately than the price of the exports the labor produces. More importantly, furthermore, on an empirical/factual front, wages have increased rapidly as Asian countries have gone through the labor-driven stage of catch-up growth. China and India are experiencing labor shortages in some skill areas and suffering soaring labor costs. In fact, this development is desirable from a social point of view as it leads to the rise of the middle class, which in turn expands domestic markets, soon supplementing export markets – all this creating a virtuous circle (an upward spiral) of economic expansion.

3.2.1.2. Outward FDI as a substitute for immigration
Flexibility in the labor market also means that once low-wage industries become comparatively disadvantaged, they are readily contracted and shifted to still lower-wage countries abroad. This type of wage-driven industrial transmigration occurred first from Japan to the NIEs, then from the NIEs to the ASEAN-4, and more recently to China – and to Vietnam at the present. Furthermore, this relatively swift transplantation across the region has been made possible because the comparatively disadvantaged (hence, contracting) industries are on the whole (i) free from labor market rigidities (for example, layoff restrictions) and are (ii) not rescued and sustained by inflows of low-skill labor from abroad, and therefore can no longer be retained at home. No significant labor immigration has so far occurred in Asia's manufacturing sector (except in construction and services). It should be kept in mind that transferring labor-intensive manufacturing activities abroad can substitute for inflows of relatively unskilled labor at home. The upshot is that resources tend to be quickly reallocated to higher value-added (hence higher wage) manufacturing at home, and productivity-raising and labor-saving innovations are induced. The economic consequence of this structural change is perhaps

most succinctly summarized in a once oft-quoted observation: 'While Japan is getting robots, Germany is getting Turks.'[6] It should be noted, however, that Japan's automobile industry is now becoming dependent on migrant workers from Latin America, especially those who are Japanese descendants.

Special economic zones like EPZs are an effective way of introducing a flexible labor market (unregulated enclave) to attract foreign multinationals' investment and offshore production in the labor-driven phase of catch-up growth. They are, however, no longer useful in the subsequent stages of growth that require far larger amounts of capital investment both in infrastructure and in production facilities, and more intensive uses of human skills and cutting-edge technologies. After all, what matters at higher levels of growth is created assets, and no longer so much endowed assets at home. In addition, modern industries (for example, steel, heavy machinery, chemicals, and automobiles) are characterized by (i) large-scale operations (large minimum efficient scales) that can reap the benefits of increasing returns, (ii) vertical (intra-process) and horizontal (multi-variety goods) specializations, and (iii) the need for a higher degree of coordination in matching input supplies and in creating and meeting the demand conditions (Balassa, 1980).

In sum, a rapid rate of structural upgrading in more advanced countries, combined with flexible labor markets on the part of catching-up countries, facilitates a transmigration of labor-intensive manufacturing, FG-style, from higher developing to lower developing countries across Asia. This provides one major explanation of why so-called Third-World multinationals come into existence in the relatively early phase of their home countries' industrialization. It also explains the oft-observed phenomenon of relocating back of FDI (or reverse FDI) in which MNCs from the advanced world which once eagerly set up factories in low-wage countries such as China and other transition economies (Central and Eastern Europe) are now relocating back closer to home due to rising labor costs abroad – and more recently, to rising energy and shipping costs.

3.2.2. Currency Valuation

It is said that developing countries' currencies tend to remain undervalued relative to advanced countries' (Bhagwati, 1984; Kravis and Lipsey, 1983). In fact, most developing countries want to keep their currencies undervalued, if possible, to gain export competitiveness and protect domestic industries from imports. An undervalued home currency is thus normally a plus factor in export-led and import-substituting growth. Yet, the very success of such a currency strategy ironically and inevitably leads to home currency appreciation as the trade balance improves. If the exchange rate is nominally fixed, the currency becomes even *more* undervalued – that is, the real exchange rate depreciates. This may strain trade relationships with other countries and eventually cause increasingly high domestic prices of imported capital goods and industrial materials. In other words, the benefits of an undervalued currency begin to be outweighed by the costs in the course of rapid catch-up growth.

Some argue that the Bretton Woods system of fixed exchange rates has been revived in Asia, where exchange rate fluctuations against the dollar are contained by Asian governments' foreign exchange market interventions (Dooley et al., 2003) – and that such stabilized exchange rates may be even a desideratum for catch-up growth and should not be disturbed by rate adjustment (McKinnon, 2005a, 2005b – observed in defense of China's present currency policy). Currency undervaluation is thus regarded as one key variable that can explain Asia's phenomenal catch-up growth. It has even come to be described as a new paradigm for economic development in Asia.

Paradoxically, however, any undervalued currency eventually meets the fate of sharp appreciation in the course of export-driven industrialization. For example, in the wake of Japan's swift catch-up growth accompanying the rising current-account surplus, the yen became grossly undervalued. Consequently, soon after fixed exchange rates were abandoned in 1973, the yen began to soar in market value and even became overvalued. It gained more than fourfold in value against the dollar in 1995. As a result, many Japanese firms were compelled to shift their manufacturing activities out of Japan into neighboring countries – not so much because they had lost real comparative advantages, but rather because the abnormally high yen made it disproportionately more costly to produce at home than abroad (Ozawa, 2005).

Although less dramatic, a similar exchange-rate effect has been observed in the NIEs' overseas investments in the ASEAN-4 and China. In 1985, the NIEs' currencies likewise began to exhibit a secular trend of appreciation. Meanwhile, the ASEAN-4's currencies and China's yuan in particular became undervalued. Indeed, because of China's export-driven growth, the yuan has become grossly undervalued as the Chinese government kept it tied to the US dollar, and has only gradually been allowed to appreciate. These trends in currency appreciation have no doubt played a key role in the rapid *transmigration* of labor-intensive production, first from Japan to the NIEs and then from the NIEs to the ASEAN-4 and China.[7] The potential and inevitable appreciation of the yuan has already been compelling multinational, as well as Chinese, firms to move production out of China to Vietnam, Cambodia, and other still low-cost nearby locations. Indeed, this exchange rate factor gives another explanation for the emergence of Third

World multinationals from rapidly catching-up countries. In fact, China in particular encourages its firms to make overseas investments, including acquisitions (such as the buyout of IBM's personal computer division by Legend), so as to secure technology sources and established brands – in addition to relieving upward pressure on the yuan (as Japan once did).

All these changes in currency valuation that occur *pari passu* with structural upgrading and economic growth will be discussed further in terms of a stages model of development finance (Chapter 7). The value of a home currency on the foreign exchange markets is a macroeconomic variable that alters along the path of structural upgrading, as well as a strategic variable often manipulated by governments for trade policy purposes.

3.2.3. Ricardo–Hicksian Limits of Industrialism

Industrialization at each stage is not an endless process. It cannot go on forever. Building, say, steel mills and chemical factories and all the necessary physical infrastructure take up space, putting strains on the environment, especially in any space-constrained, small countries. A rise in consumption *pari passu* with economic growth, too, leads to a host of ecological problems such as air pollution, water contamination, mal-sanitation, traffic congestion, and shrinkages of the natural surroundings. The early stages of economic development, notably Stage-II growth of heavy and chemical industrialization, are plagued by the environmental problems. London was once notorious for heavy smog and poor public health, especially in the latter half of the 20th century. At the height of Japan's Stage-II growth in the late 1960s, Tokyo, too, experienced serious air pollution that made birds practically disappear, children faint in school backyards, traffic policemen seek fresh air supplies from oxygen tanks every hour or so, and Mt Fuji invisible from the city center. Now, Beijing, Shanghai, and other cities in China are going through similar experiences. Bangkok, Jakarta, Kuala Lumpur, Bangalore, and other Asian cities all suffer from the ecological costs of rapid economic development.

One theoretical perspective was put forth by John Hicks in his Nobel memorial lecture (1973). He stressed that growth under the 'impulse of an invention' would come up against the ecological limits and slow down:

> Obviously, in a limited world, the expansion that is due to a single improvement [a major innovation] cannot go on forever. If railway-building, for example, went on forever, the world would in the end become cluttered up with railways. The profitability, or productivity, of a railway depends on its locations; the time must come when a new railway project which will yield any surplus over cost, must be hard to find. For unlimited expansion of a particular kind, such as that induced by a particular invention, there is not enough space . . .

> The first economist to see this at all was [David] Ricardo . . . He supposed that the supply of labour was indefinitely extensible; it would increase without limit, so long as subsistence for the increased labour force would be provided; so his operative scarcity was scarcity of agricultural land. This was responsible for his 'declining rate of profits.'

> . . . it would still be true, even in the socialist economy, that *irremovable scarcity would cause the rate of return on the spreading of the original improvement to diminish*. In either case the *impulse* of the original improvement would in time peter out. (Hicks, 1973, pp. 128–219, original emphasis)

The idea that any economic growth triggered by a lead sector (that is, a major innovation that spawns a brand-new industry – hence a new growth stage) is, sooner or later, bound to hit the limit can thus be called the 'Ricardo–Hicksian bottlenecks theory of industrialization' (Ozawa, 1979). The natural environment is fast becoming an irremovable scarcity in any growing economy, especially in a land-scarce small economy. This is one reason why a successful company at a particular stage of growth is compelled to expand its production in overseas locations in the developing world. This also provides an additional reason for the emergence of multinational firms from the rapidly catching-up countries that quickly run into environmental constraints.

It should be noted that while ecological problems are rather the inevitable companions of industrialization, once an economy reaches a certain level of development (that is, a critical average income), those problems begin to subside because people come to value the environment more than many more factories and because proper environmental regulations are to be adopted. Thus, there is an inverted-U relationship between economic development and environmental indicators (for example, water and air pollution), the relationship known as the 'environmental Kuznets curve' (resembling the Kuznets curve which exhibits a similar U-shaped trend between economic development and income inequity) – so named by Grossman and Krueger (1993).

This may give solace to those developing countries over the environmental costs of economic catch-up and encourage them to adopt a policy prescription: Grow first, then clean up. Such policy, however, may make the developing countries 'pollution havens' that attract environmentally unscrupulous MNCs. The relationship between economic development and ecological issues is complex and controversial, dividing scholars, researchers, and policymakers largely into two groups, optimists and pessimists about the impact of growth on the environment (Dasgupta et al., 2002). It all seems to depend on an individual host country's institutional and regulatory capacity and technical ability to deal with the environmental costs of economic growth. Be that as it may, economic growth raises the costs of doing business as regulations are increasingly enacted and enforced (as has recently been evidenced in China).

In sum, the FG-stages model of structural transformation introduced above can shed light on the environmental Kuznets curve – that is, how environmental problems begin to turn serious but soon moderate during the course of climbing the ladder of economic development.

3.2.4. Outflows and Reverse Flows of Industrial Knowledge and Skills (Brains)

The production of created assets necessitates government involvement as the auxiliary investor in education and healthcare, since created assets (knowledge) engender social benefits that are far larger than the benefits reaped by private investors because of positive externalities for society. This is commonly understood and accepted as the legitimate justification for government investment in knowledge formation, especially in the realm of science and engineering that is directly supportive of high-tech stages of growth.

3.2.4.1. Hume's knowledge retrogradation
It is a received theory that the *rate* of knowledge and skill formation instrumental for industrial activity rises *pari passu* with economic growth up to a certain level and then tends to decline (again an inverted U-shaped trend curve). In fact, this tendency was pointed out by David Hume as far back as the mid-18th century. He argued: 'When the arts and sciences come to perfection in any state, from that moment they naturally, or rather necessarily, decline, and seldom or never revive in that nation, where they formerly flourished' (Hume, 1754/1985, p. 135). This climax in industrial sciences may then be identified as 'Hume's theory of endogenous retrogradation' (Elmslie, 1995).

Unfortunately, young people in the advanced world tend to shy away from science and engineering and show interest mostly in less academically rigorous fields such as liberal arts (languages, history, visual arts, and music) and finance. Affluence diminishes the 'hungriness' of the young to better their lives by achieving degrees in science and engineering. With their higher standards of living in advanced countries, people place a premium on leisure, liberal arts, and humanities. They shy away from demanding hard studies and 'boring' technical training. Science, math, and engineering are inferior goods, in the sense that a rise in income leads to a decline in the public's interest in learning hard sciences. In successfully developing countries, on the other hand, engineering skills are in great demand, and science and engineering diplomas serve as tickets to better-paid employment. Hence, this brings about a virtuous circle of learning in critical areas and successful economic growth.

One clear advantage enjoyed by catching-up Asian economies is, therefore, young people's interest in, and pursuit of, science and engineering (S&E) – for example, compared to the US:

> With regard to education, the number of Americans obtaining science and engineering degrees is small and declining. In 1999, for example, the United States graduated 220,000 students with B.S. degrees, about the same as in 1985 and down 5 percent from ten years ago. China graduated 322,000 and India 251,000. Both countries have much larger populations, but their economies are only a fraction the size of the U.S. economy. And the Indian and Chinese numbers are set to double in the near future. Japan, with half the U.S. population, graduated 235,000 with B.S. degrees, and the EU-15, with a population about one-third larger than the United States, graduated 555,000 with B.S. degrees. Except in the life sciences, the U.S. number is lower now than it was in 1985. (Prestowitz, 2005, pp. 132–3)

Over all, the US is still the dominant leader in high-technology manufacturing. It has 'the single largest value-added world share (35 per cent in 2005) of any country in high-technology manufacturing industries', ranking 'first in three of the five-technology industries (scientific instruments, aerospace, and pharmaceuticals)' and 'second in the other two (communications equipment and office machinery and computers)' (NSF, 2008). But, America's high-technology activities are becoming increasingly dependent on immigrant scientists and engineers and foreign students who come to the US for graduate studies and remain for employment.

> Over the past decade, both the U.S. college-educated workforce and the science and engineering (S&E) workforce have grown dramatically. *An important factor in that growth has been immigration . . . Three-fourths of all immigrant scientists and engineers [in the US] were born in Asia or Europe (56% and 19%, respectively).* (NSF, 2007b, emphasis added)

Thus, the Asian group *dominates* (56 percent). And Indians and Chinese are predominant (27.5 and 17.4 percent, respectively, of that Asian contingent) – followed by Filipino (16.3 percent), Korean (6.4 percent), Taiwanese (6.4 percent), Vietnamese (5.2 percent), Pakistani (2.7 percent), and Japanese (2.5 percent)[8] (NSF, 2007b).

3.2.4.2.   Brain drain and brain return
The US obviously benefits from the much-needed inflow of brains. The Asian countries that send human capital may suffer a 'brain drain' in

the short run. Yet they can also enjoy a 'brain gain' (or a 'brain return') in the long run, as those who studied and stayed on in the US for work eventually return home with practical training and experience. In fact, *the high-tech industries across Asia have been spawned and fostered largely by those returnees from the US.*

The same thing can be said about Europe, though to a lesser extent. 'The US share of foreign students declined in recent years, although the US remains the predominant destination for foreign students (accounting for 22% of internationally mobile students in 2004), followed by UK (11%), Germany (10%), and France (9%)' (NSF, 2008). In short, a global trade in knowledge capital (intellectual talent) has rapidly developed with a host of important policy ramifications for both sending and receiving countries – and for international and regional organizations as coordinators (Kapur and McHale, 2005).

More recently, Japan too has emerged as a key host for foreign students, if not yet for immigrant scientists and engineers. Japanese companies are increasingly hiring those foreign students who study at Japanese universities and want work experience in Japan. At the moment, however, the impact of this trend on the economic development of students' home countries seems to be relatively small.

Actually, Japan has developed a powerful technological capacity since World War II. Japan is the world's key location for important technological competencies – measured in terms of what the National Science Foundation (NSF) calls 'high value patents':

> In 2003, inventors residing in Japan produced approximately 72% and 82% of the number of triadic [the US, EU, and Japan] patents produced by US and EU-based inventors, respectively. *Given Japan's much smaller population, its inventive productivity on a per capita basis is well in excess of the per capita productivity of the United States or the EU.* (NSF, May 2007a, p. 32, emphasis added)

Japan's emergence as Asia's first advanced economy in the post-World War II period is owing to its capacity to innovate and scale the ladder of economic development. This contributed to rapid structural transformation, enabling Japan to graduate quickly from low-wage-based light industry and move up to higher-tier industries. Many significant innovations have been made by Japanese firms as they climbed the ladder: processing technologies in heavy industry (notably steel), 'lean production' in assembly-based industry (automobiles and electronics), micro-chip technology in electronics, and new Net access technology in the information industry. All this has helped Japan leave behind low-tier (low-tech) industries for other catching-up Asian neighbors to move into and make additional innovations of their own.

In this process, the rest of Asia has become the most important importer of technology from Japan. Especially in the early postwar period (1950s and 1960s), about half of Japan's technology exports headed for its neighboring Asian countries, involving mostly light industry that had already been developed in the prewar period and revitalized during Japan's Stage-I growth in the immediately postwar years (Science and Technology Agency, Japan, 1969). With Stage-II growth in full swing during the latter half of the 1960s, Japan's technology exports began to be increasingly made by heavy and chemical industries, replacing those by light industry almost completely in the early 1970s – a clear indication of Japan's swift industrial upgrading.

In short, the rest of Asia has thus been benefiting from inflows of industrial knowledge not only from the advanced West (notably the US) but also from Japan. Japan has been shedding comparatively disadvantaged industries by way of overseas investments and has also started to export state-of-the art technologies from its newly developed (comparatively advantaged) industries since the mid-1960s. Similar progress has no doubt been duplicated in the NIEs. As a consequence, catching-up Asian countries (late latecomers) now have many more sources of knowledge to draw on, which helps them accelerate their growth in a time-compressed fashion.

3.2.5.   Institutional and Market Organizational Factors

3.2.5.1.   Coordination failure
So-called coordination failures, especially in investment activities, are expected to occur as a developing country strives to move up the ladder of development (Rodrik, 1995 for South Korea and Taiwan; Okazaki, 1997, for Japan). And this calls for government involvement as a legitimate coordinator. This is actually nothing new; Alexander Gerschenkron (1962) earlier observed that developing countries as latecomers to industrialization tend to rely on institutional arrangements (notably direct state involvement) rather than on the market – for the very simple reason that the market mechanism has yet to develop.

In climbing up the higher rungs of the development ladder, individual firms or entrepreneurs themselves may be neither willing nor capable of taking investment risks in new technologies and modern industries unless they are encouraged and assisted financially by their government. In other words, what may be called a 'socially justifiable moral hazard' needs to be created (Ozawa, 2005). Therefore, industrial or structural policy, along with special public funding for infrastructure in particular, is required, and government involvement thus entailed. This is especially the case when a developing country strives to industrialize as a matter of national endeavor.

It is for these reasons that the 'big push' doctrine of catch-up development was once advocated in order to take care of the *simultaneous* coordination of supply and demand requirements – that is, to solve the coordination failure issues associated with the early stages of development. Here, some Japanese experiences can illustrate the point in terms of institutional setups. The *keiretsu* industrial groups (instrumental in solving coordination failures), the main-bank system (crafted to inject ample credit for capital-intensive industries in lieu of equity finance), and the state-run long-term banks (devoted to investment in infrastructure) were once all arranged to cope with coordination failure and facilitate the reconstruction and modernization of Japan's scale-driven heavy and chemical industries in the early postwar period (Ozawa, 2005).

3.2.5.2. Trade as a market coordinator

In addition, developing countries face a supply gap in vital industrial inputs when manufacturing activities begin to take root, requiring new intermediate goods which are not yet readily available at home. In this regard, trade and multinational corporations' investment activities serve the role of market coordinators in filling the gaps in supply and demand conditions for intermediate goods. Neoclassical trade theory predicts two gains: 'exchange gains' and 'specialization gains'. However, 'coordination gains' need to be added in the dynamic context of structural upgrading in an outward-focused developing country that can rely on trade and MNCs to fill the supply gap. In fact, export-led growth in all the East Asian follower geese has become equally dependent on imported parts, components, and accessories from the advanced countries, especially from Japan. 'In 1987, [the NIEs] obtained from Japan almost 50% of their total imports of technology-intensive manufactures (up from about 41% in 1980 as compared to 26% from the United States)' (Park and Park, 1991). Shinohara (1987) noted that Japan interacts with the rest of Asia more strongly from the supply side (that is, as a supplier of inputs) than from the demand side (that is, as a buyer of finished manufactures).

It is therefore correct to argue that Asian countries are not simply export-driven but also *strategically import-driven* at the same time. Imports of industrial knowledge, capital goods, and intermediate supplies, notably through multinationals' operations, are critical to the success of export-led growth. Indeed, an 'import- and export-led growth' paradigm (Klein, 2000; Dutta, 1999) is appropriate – with the exception of Japan that developed a rather self-sufficient industrial structure under infant-industry protection and without much reliance on imported capital goods.

3.2.5.3. Getting fundamentals right

According to the World Bank (1993), the high-performing Asian Economies (HPAEs) got the fundamentals right by way of (i) carefully limited and 'market-friendly' government activism, (ii) strong export orientation, (iii) high levels of domestic savings, (iv) accumulation of human and physical capital, (v) good macroeconomic management, (vi) acquisition of advanced foreign technology, (vii) flexible labor markets, and (viii) 'shared growth' (in which the benefits of growth spread to all groups). All these features are pro-business in nature. Indeed, policy matters – in building market-compatible (if not totally market-dictated) economies. There is an abundance of literature on the key role of government as a market-facilitating or market-enhancing agent in East Asian growth (*inter alia*, Amsden, 1989, 2001; Aoki et al., 1997; Wade, 1990), hence no need to detail it here. Here it suffices to say that East Asia's 'social capacity' – a term coined by Ohkawa and Rosovsky (1972) and popularized by Abramovitz (1986) – is neither innate nor manna from Heaven but has been created and governed by government. This pro-activist approach is in sharp contrast to the neoclassical stance of placing full trust in the market mechanism, which was at one time reflected in the so-called 'Washington Consensus'.

In this respect, Stiglitz (2003) advocates a 'new (i.e., post-Washington Consensus) paradigm of development'. This consists of a 'more holistic approach to development', whose features 'were in fact, incorporated in the development strategies of the fastest [Asian] developers' (Stiglitz, 2003, p. 92). In other words, the new paradigm is built on, and modeled after, the successful growth of Asia.

3.3. SUMMING UP

We have defined the hitherto casually used concept of 'the ladder of economic development' in terms of the actual legacies of structural upgrading pioneered by the advanced world and further refined by close followers, first under the hegemony of the UK (with coal as the main energy) and then under the hegemony of the US (with oil as the main energy). The rungs so far built are the five tiers of leading growth industry. The current dependence on oil is unraveling as the Achilles heel of global capitalism.

No doubt, industrial evolution continues to unfold as further scientific discoveries are made, technologies are spawned, and innovations are sparked under the Schumpeterian 'creative distruction' machine of capitalism. And new alternate sources of energy are bound to be discovered or invented in market economies where human creativity is unhampered. The next new stage that is to be shaped by an 'energy revolution' may be in the offing around 2015 when the energy crisis is expected to reach a climax, forcing the world to radically reorganize the mode of production and consumption.

Any stages theory of growth needs enabling mechanisms for moving up the development ladder from one rung to the next. Rises in wages, currency appreciation, flows of cross-border knowledge and human capital, and institutional factors are examined as the key forces that facilitate and propel the sequence of industrial upgrading in catching-up countries. And technological and institutional innovations continue to be the driver of structural upgrading in the lead-goose countries to stay ahead of their emulators. All these determinants are endogenous to economic development in the sense that they are the variables *inherent* in the development process itself. In other words, they constitute an 'endogenous growth' model.

It is worth re-emphasizing that catching up is not likely to be a 'monotonic' linear progression up the existing ladder of economic development. It involves stages-jumbling, as well as time and space compression. This is more so with late latecomers such as China and India (and with those in Latin America and the Middle East) – and even much more so with late-late latecomers in Africa.

NOTES

1. The Pax Americana is characterized by the car culture. One billion cars are expected to be on the road worldwide by 2020. 'Automotive: The Journal Report', *Wall Street Journal*, April 17, 2006, p. R1.
2. Lohr, Steve, 'Who's Afraid of China Inc.?' *New York Times* (on the Web), July 24, 2005.
3. It is an important – often politically and emotionally charged – issue whether female workers are made better off or simply exploited, as many feminists contend. It is, however, beyond the scope of this study, since it requires careful analysis and justifies no generalization, as all depends on specific situations and circumstances. For a balanced analysis, see Bhagwati (2004).
4. At least another 75 new zones are said to be in the pipeline. 'India, Known for Outsourcing, Expands in Industry', *New York Times* (on the Web), May 19, 2006.
5. Many incidences of labor abuse no doubt occur unless the minimum work and safety standards are effectively enforced by the host governments. Here, NGOs and the codes of conduct observed by multinationals are helpful in reducing the abuse of workers.
6. This saying was reportedly popular when Germany's postwar economic miracle introduced the *Gastarbeiter* program ('Economic Focus: Be my Guest', *Economist*, October 8, 2005, p. 86).
7. Although the undervaluation is not emphasized, Kwan (1994) observes how changes over time in the exchange rates of East Asian currencies contributed to transmigration of production in an FG fashion across the region.
8. It is said that 'In 2003, of the 21.6 million scientists and engineers in the United States, 16% (3,352,000) were immigrants' (NSF, 2007).

4. Comparative advantage recycling in labor-driven growth: an unprecedented opportunity for the poor to rise?

4.1. REPLICATION OF LABOR-DRIVEN GROWTH

Looking at the experience of Asia, one can easily notice that a newly attained comparative advantage, especially in labor-intensive (Stage-I) industries (such as toys, garments, and sundries), has not lasted long in any rapidly catching-up country. Paradoxically, *the relatively more labor-abundant a developing country happens to be, the faster the occurrence of labor shortage and rising wages when it exploits its endowed comparative advantage in labor-intensive goods.* The rise in wages is the ineluctable outcome of labor-driven growth. It compels local firms to search for lower-wage labor via FDI or subcontracting in other developing countries where labor is still abundant. True, adopting labor-saving technology is an alternative to going overseas. But this approach takes time and often proves expensive. The most likely way out of rising labor costs at home is, therefore, overseas investment in still lower-wage countries.

This process of industrial transmigration in labor-intensive goods has been repeated in a staggered fashion across the region. Low-wage light industry manufacturing shifted first from Japan to the NIEs (initially in the 1950s and 1960s), then to the ASEAN-4 (in the 1970s), more recently to China (after its open-door policy of 1978), and most recently to Vietnam and Cambodia. In other words, Stage-I growth (of the labor-driven type) has been replicated, in one country after another, as labor-intensive manufacturing was transplanted down the East Asian hierarchy of economies, boosting wages in each country. Such an occurrence may be called 'comparative-advantage recycling', since the trade advantage has been recycled or relayed from more successful catching-up countries to still less developed ones. Here, FDI and other international operations (such as licensing, subcontracting, outsourcing, and production sharing) of MNCs are the major enablers of comparative-advantage recycling.

The themes of this chapter are (i) that intra-Asian comparative-advantage recycling in labor-intensive Stage-I industry and the lower-end segments in each higher-tier industry is the primary cause of creating demand for unskilled workers, thereby contributing most effectively to poverty alleviation across the region, and (ii) that outward FDI is bound to emerge from the catching-up countries *even* in their early stages of growth during the very course of comparative-advantage recycling (contributing to the rise of Third World multinationals,[1] as touched upon in Chapter 3).

4.2. POVERTY ALLEVIATION

Asia's economic development, especially in its early phases, has been accompanied by impressive poverty reduction as a consequence of sharp rises in demand – hence, incomes – for unskilled labor. In fact, this 'unique' feature (a double play of growth and poverty alleviation) was already recognized as 'shared growth' by the World Bank's 1993 study of the development experiences of the 'high performing Asian economies', the phenomenon which exhibited 'unusually low and declining levels of inequality, contrary to historical experience and contemporary evidence in other regions' (1993, p. 29).

Indeed, the incidence of extreme poverty practically disappeared first in post-World War II Japan and then in the NIEs. And there has also been a considerable reduction of abject poverty in the ASEAN-4 – and more recently, and most dramatically, in China. It is estimated by the Asian Development Bank (2004), for example, that the headcount ratio for those living on $1 a day in China decreased from 53.1 percent in 1984 (more than half the entire population of 1.3 billion) to 26.5 percent in 2001, that in Indonesia from 37.8 percent in 1984 to 7.5 percent in 2002, and that in Thailand from 17.8 percent in 1988 to 1.9 percent in 2000. These are remarkable accomplishments. India, too, has been experiencing noticeable alleviation in poverty, especially in urban areas, as a consequence of its recent stepped-up pace of economic development; the headcount ratio declined from 46.3 percent in 1987 to 36.0 percent in 2000 – though, admittedly, the absolute number of the poor is still large.[2] Interestingly enough, therefore, poverty reduction has been occurring, again flying-geese style (that is, in tandem) among these rapidly catching-up Asian economies. Given such a track record of poverty alleviation, most Asian countries are expected to meet without much difficulty the goal of the UN Millennium Project to halve the proportion of the population in extreme poverty ($1-a-day baseline) by 2015.[3]

Therefore, the major question we must ask is: Why has Asia as a whole – but especially East Asia, relative to other developing regions – been so successful in managing its economic growth so as to reduce poverty? Why hasn't the same phenomenon occurred evenly across the world? Is there any particular reason specifically endemic to that region? So far, the usual answer is that the East Asian countries have adopted both pro-growth and pro-poor policies and established the appropriate institutional arrangements to achieve equality, as epitomized in the practice of 'shared growth' – and also benefited from the region's egalitarian tradition based on communitarianism, stemming largely from the influence of Confucianism (or a 'strong culture' adaptable to the forces of globalization).

This chapter, however, argues that although such practices and tradition are no doubt instrumental and necessary for a desirable outcome, what matters most is the distinct way in which East Asia has initiated, and continues, its catch-up growth, first by capitalizing on its most abundant asset, unskilled labor, for labor-intensive manufacturing for export at the start of its economic development. Therefore, the notion of 'comparative-advantage recycling in labor-intensive goods' can provide a useful framework within which Asia's effective poverty alleviation is comprehensively explicable. Indeed, those Asian countries that have actively participated in the flying-geese formation of labor-driven growth are the ones that have experienced significant poverty reductions.

4.3.   GLOBALIZATION, GROWTH, AND POVERTY REDUCTION

To explore the 'globalization→growth→poverty' nexus, one can adopt a reduced form of analysis and/or a structural form of analysis. It is generally accepted that there are three key events and two causal linkages: globalization affects growth, and such globalization-driven growth then impacts on poverty (that is, in two logical steps), as illustrated in Figure 4.1. And two opposing views, positive and negative, prevail about the impact of globalization on poverty via growth. The positive view argues (i) that globalization (via international businesses) favorably affects (fosters) developing countries' growth and wages for workers, thereby contributing to poverty alleviation, whereas the negative view holds (ii) that globalization aggravates poverty – whether or not it stimulates or stunts developing countries' growth because globalization entails inequality in favor of the rich and against the poor.

The negative view stresses the belief that the market-driven (capitalistic) process of economic development causes an adverse income distribution

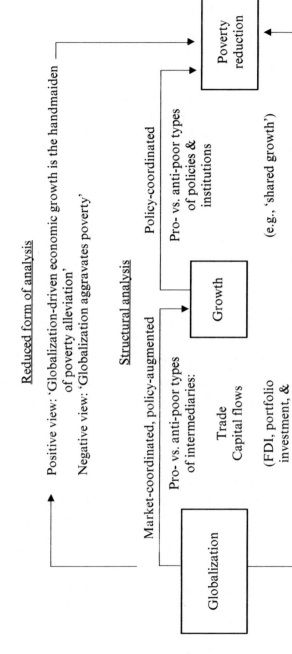

Figure 4.1 Globalization, economic growth, and poverty reduction

against the poor. On the other hand, the positive view argues that *even* with such an adverse income distribution effect, the growth effect of globalization (via freer trade and inward FDI) can more than compensate for any income inequality – so long as developing countries implement appropriate policy and set up necessary institutional arrangements. Each side has legitimate grounds to support their positions. For reasons to be discussed below, however, the general consensus among economists is that both 'shrewd [on-the-field] observation and scientific evidence' are in strong support of the positive view. As summed up by Bhagwati (2004), 'The scientific analysis of the effect of trade on poverty is even more compelling' (pp. 52–3). After all, the Asian experience arguably attests to the positive outcome.

4.3.1.   Scientific Evidence for Growth-led Poverty Reduction

Scientific (empirical) evidence is strong, indeed. Dollar and Kraay (2001, 2002) found a close correlation between growth and poverty reduction by observing 92 developed and developing countries. A similar study was made – and a similar result obtained – by the Asian Development Bank (2004) that is concerned with developing countries alone: 'In particular, growth of 1% is associated with a 1.5% decline in the incidence of $1-a-day poverty on average' (ADB, 2004, p. 32). Focusing on Asia alone (27 countries in East Asia, Southeast Asia, and South Asia), however, we can observe an even *stronger* relationship between growth and poverty alleviation. 'Each 1% of growth is associated with an almost 2% decline in poverty incidence on average' (ADB, 2004, p. 33). In other words, the efficacy of growth in lessening poverty is as much as one-third higher for Asia.

4.3.2.   Policy and Institutions Matter

By nature, market-driven growth, at least initially, tends to cause an unfavorable distribution (in relative terms) in relation to the poor. But if an economy grows vigorously enough (which is the case with capitalism, since it is the most powerful engine of development), there is a positive spillover from growth that can more than offset the adverse distribution effect. And this is exactly what has happened in Asia:

> [The] driver of rapid poverty reduction in Asia has been growth and not distribution change. Indeed, the largest reductions in poverty in Asia have all taken place in the context of distribution changes that went *against* the poor. There were nine spells in which poverty declines on average by 1.5 percentage points or more a year. In each of these nine spells, distribution changes were such that

poverty would have increased in the absence of growth. In the case of rural PRC, for example, . . . distribution changes alone (i.e., in the absence of any growth), would have increased poverty 1.2 percentage points a year on average during the 1993–1996 spell. Nevertheless, poverty reduction was rapid over this period (4.8 percentage points a year on average) *because the positive growth effect more than matched the adverse effects of purely distribution change on the poor.* [These] episodes . . . have been experienced widely across the region, encompassing countries not only from East Asia and Southeast Asia but even two South Asian economies (namely, Bangladesh and Pakistan in the late 1980s and early 1990s). (ADB, 2004, p. 35, emphasis added)

It should be noted, however, that the Asian governments *proactively* intervened to lessen the adverse distribution effect on the poor rather than focusing only on their pro-growth strategy. It cannot be overemphasized, therefore, that *both* policy and institutional arrangements need to be specifically crafted to enhance the positive growth effect and concurrently abate the negative distribution effect. Asia's practice of 'shared growth' epitomizes such policy-cum-institutional matrices.

As early as the start of the 1990s, the World Bank (1993) took notice of the fact that HPAEs achieved *both* high growth and income equality simultaneously, and reduced poverty to a much greater extent than economies in other regions:

> . . . For the eight HPAEs, rapid growth and declining inequality have been shared virtues, as comparisons over time of equality and growth using Gini coefficients illustrate . . . The developing HPAEs clearly outperform other middle-income economies in that they have *both* lower levels of inequality and higher levels of growth. Moreover . . . improvements in income distribution generally coincided with periods of rapid growth . . . Given rapid growth and declining inequality, these economies have of course been *unusually successful* in reducing poverty . . . Increases in life expectancy have also been larger than in any other region . . . (World Bank, 1993, pp. 31–2, emphasis added)

One legitimate question, then, arises: 'Why has growth served the poor in East Asia better than the rest of the developing world on average?' (p. 33). Put differently, why has the region been so 'unusually successful in reducing poverty?' (p. 32).

Although separately listed, we must keep in mind that all these features are often mutually augmenting and cumulatively causational. For example, a rapid rise in income with declining income inequality leads to higher primary and secondary school enrollments (human capital formation), which in turn further fosters catch-up growth and poverty alleviation. And these desirable linkages are advanced and reinforced by appropriate government policies. Indeed, policy and institutional arrangements matter – in creating market-compatible pro-poor growth.

The Asian approach to growth and poverty alleviation is in sharp contrast to the neoclassical stance that places full trust in the market mechanism, an approach best exemplified by the 'Washington Consensus'. In the East Asian experience, rapid growth is consciously governed in such a way as to moderate adverse distributional change. As Bhagwati (2004, p. 52) put it, 'It's policy, stupid'. In reference to India's experience,

> . . .growth was not a passive, trickle-down strategy for helping the poor. It was *an active, pull-up strategy* instead. It required a government [of India] that would energetically take steps to accelerate growth, through a variety of policies, including building infrastructure such as roads and ports and attracting foreign funds. (p. 54, emphasis added)

Here, Bhagwati's growth model chimes with Stiglitz's (2003) formulation of what he calls 'a new paradigm of development', a paradigm that is an amended version of the Washington Consensus:

> . . . the rapid growth of most of the East Asian economies showed that development was possible, and that successful development could be accompanied by *a reduction of poverty, widespread improvements in living standards, and even a process of democratization.* . . . these countries did not follow the standard prescriptions. In most cases, national governments played a large role. (p. 81)

Stiglitz's 'new (i.e. post Washington Consensus) paradigm of development' constitutes a 'more holistic approach to development' (2003, p. 92). It boils down to the notion of 'social capacity' to learn from and catch up with the advanced world. Such capacity depends on government policies and institutional arrangements to create a market-compatible, if not totally market-dictated, economy. Social capability requires more than mere (unconditional) acceptance of the so-called Washington Consensus (a set of 'neoliberal' economic policy prescriptions).[4]

In this connection, we may argue that growth under globalization (that is, the globalization–growth link) can be best coordinated by market forces – that is, should be left fundamentally to the market by adopting market-enhancing policy if growth is to be most effectively maximized. On the other hand, however, growth-led poverty reduction (that is, the growth–poverty link) ought to be coordinated proactively by policy and relevant institutional arrangements. In other words, we can have the best of both worlds; growth (an increase in the size of the pie) is market-driven, whereas poverty eradication (an equitable division of the pie) is assigned to both the state (that is, appropriate public policies) and the private sector (inclusive of enterprises) that can create job opportunities for the poor/ unskilled.

This is because poverty eradication is basically a public good (a social desideratum) which the market itself is poorly qualified for, and incapable of resolving. As Dunning (2003) observes, the market is 'less well designed for the production and exchange of *public* or social goods and services than *private* goods and services' (p. 32). It is, indeed, often said that 'Like fire, the market is a good servant, but a poor master' (Eatwell, 1982).[5] Put differently, the market is basically neither goal-setting nor goal-pursuing; it is goal-neutral at best and sometimes even goal-hindering. In essence, the market is merely a resource-allocative mechanism, not a goal-oriented and fulfilling entity (Ozawa, 1996). Poverty amelioration is essentially a *social* goal of human endeavor.

In short, the growth–poverty reduction nexus has been both conceptually explored and empirically verified throughout Asia where trade and investment have been considerably liberalized and pro-poor policies and institutional arrangements are actively organized. Yet, as seen below, by contrast the nexus between globalization and growth seems still to be lacking in a comprehensive framework that can capture the more fundamental, underlying forces of global capitalism.

4.3.3. Globalization–growth Nexus

What is the causality from globalization to growth – and vice versa? How do economists conceptualize this linkage? In economics, trade and capital flows (especially FDI) are naturally considered the major conduits of globalization impacting on the growth of the developing host world.

The nexus between trade liberalization and growth has already been well established as positive in trade theory (that is, trade is a national income-raising activity via gains from exchange and specialization – plus coordination, as seen in Chapter 3) and empirically verified in most cases (for a survey on this topic, see Winter, 2004). The impact of trade on growth is, furthermore, examined with respect to two opposing trade policies: outward-focused, export-led policy versus inward-oriented, import-substituting policy. The former has proven growth-conducive, whereas the latter is not so much growth-stimulating – or is even growth-stunting. East Asia, in particular, has succeeded in outward-focused, export-driven growth. And it is often compared with Latin America, which once experimented with, but suffered from, inward-oriented import-substituting strategies and had to switch to the East Asian model.[6] (More on this in Chapter 6.) Strong export promotion is thus now regarded as preferable – as a desideratum – for successful catch-up growth than import substitution. Yet what kind of goods a country specializes in and exports influences how trade impacts on demands for labor, hence poverty. For instance, the promotion of primary exports has long been recognized as a less desirable strategy of economic development than that of manufactured exports.

As to the impact of inward FDI by MNCs on the growth of host countries, there are both boon and bane stories. Graham (2000) distinguishes inward FDI in internationally competitive activities (competitive FDI) from FDI in internationally non-competitive activities (non-competitive FDI). He relates the former to a situation in which the host country pursues export-oriented development policy, and the latter to a host country's import-substituting protection policy. This distinction actually clearly matches a differentiation made much earlier by Kojima (1973) between 'pro-trade' (export-creating) and 'anti-trade' (import-substituting) FDI.

No doubt, FDI can thus be 'designed' to become a positive link between globalization and growth. It should be noted that another form of capital flows, portfolio investment ('hot money'), is by comparison less desirable – and often disruptive for developing countries where financial markets are underdeveloped, because of its speculative and quickly reversible flow. International bank loans, which are mostly inter-bank loans, are considered not as desirable as FDI because of their relatively short-term commitments and volatility in loan renewals (though less volatile than hot money).

In sum, two forms of globalization linkage – trade and capital flows – have been extensively studied – but only separately, without unifying framework. That is to say, the existing studies cannot really explain why trade and FDI in East Asia have been so strongly and so distinctly pro-growth and pro-poor simultaneously in outcome. There are actually more fundamental forces at work in producing rapid growth – hence more substantial poverty reduction – throughout East Asia than individual country-specific pro-growth and pro-poor policies and institutions themselves can explain. As will be seen below, the FG model of comparative-advantage recycling in labor-driven goods, which most cogently fits the East Asian experience, can provide a holistic, comprehensive, and integrative explanation in terms of a structural form of analysis by linking the process of globalization more directly with the successful decline in poverty.

4.4. COMPARATIVE-ADVANTAGE RECYCLING IN LABOR-INTENSIVE GOODS – WITHIN A HIERARCHY OF COUNTRIES

The model of 'comparative-advantage (or market) recycling in labor-intensive goods' is built on Akamatsu's two derived patterns of FG formation in combination (that is, a pattern of industrial upgrading and an alignment of countries), the two patterns that are crucial in sparking catch-up growth in the present global economy, as discussed in Chapter 2 . Our model is a comprehensive framework within which we can explain how Asian economies – first, Japan and then, the NIEs, the ASEAN-4, China, and Vietnam in tandem – have successfully initiated a succession of labor-driven growth (by developing and exporting labor-intensive goods mostly to the relatively open markets of the United States and the EU), the event that has proved to be most effective in poverty reduction.

The model of comparative-advantage recycling is built on: (i) the stages of industrial upgrading pioneered and trail-blazed by two hegemons of global capitalism (first under British hegemony and later under American hegemony), which can serve as the ladder of economic development for followers to scale (Chapter 3); (ii) the catch-up growth of each Asian economy starting from the bottom rung of the development ladder, that is, labor-intensive manufacturing and exports (notably textiles and garments); (iii) the role of US markets as the major demand provider; (iv) the sequential recycling/relaying of US markets for labor-intensive goods from one Asian country to another; (v) the role of Japan – and more recently, the NIEs – as the capacity (comparative-advantage) augmenter for the lower-ranking follower-goose countries by way of FDI and technology transfer; and (vi) the resultant opportunity given to each follower goose to create strong demand for unskilled labor (so long as the labor market is kept flexible and appropriate government policies are adopted), thereby contributing to poverty reduction. In short, the model serves as a comprehensive framework to capture not only the static gains (allocative efficiency) of trade and FDI but also – and more importantly, the dynamic gains (adaptive efficiency) and poverty alleviation of economic integration.

4.4.1. The US as the First Lead Goose: the Originator of Concatenation Economies

What has happened in East Asia is the result of the convergence of three earlier structural dynamisms: (i) the US pioneered the development of new R&D-driven industries such as computers and microchips, (ii) Japan moved up the ladder of development from the lower tiers by first modernizing its war-torn heavy and chemical industries (that had already been established before World War II) and then by entering into higher-value-added industries, as its wages rose and its capital accumulation proceeded, and (iii) other Asian countries at lower stages of economic development soon initiated their catch-up growth by developing labor-intensive manufacturing for export, one group of economies at a time in a staggered sequence.

In the postwar period the US, the hegemon of postwar capitalism, adopted a liberal trade policy toward Asia, especially during the Cold War. It has provided the major market for Asia's exports of labor-intensive goods. And the US market for such goods, the market captured early on but soon discarded by Japan, was quickly handed over to the NIEs, which in turn soon relayed it to the ASEAN-4 – and more recently to China and Vietnam. The successful growth of export-oriented labor-intensive manufacturing in Asia has been facilitated by FDI not only from the US and Europe, but also – and more significantly – from Japan, the NIEs, and even the ASEAN-4, that is, from within East Asia itself. FDI normally transplants to the developing host countries modern management, technology, and access to export markets so as to activate or reinforce developing countries' comparative advantage in labor-intensive goods and services (that is, comparative advantage augmentation). Those developments have combined to produce the phenomenon of intra-regional recycling of comparative advantage in low-end manufacturing via FDI, as illustrated schematically in Figure 4.2.

4.4.2.   The Role of a Second Goose: Japan – and then the NIEs

In this connection Japan has been playing a critical role as the principal second goose. It first captured the US market for labor-intensive exports and then handed it over to other Asian countries by way of transplanting Japan's comparatively disadvantaged industrial activities through Japanese multinational firms' operations. Simultaneously Japan has been successful in scaling the ladder of development. As a consequence, Japan's rapid industrial upgrading has contributed to the spread of its low-end production of both the inter-industry and the intra-industry types to the rest of Asia.

Interestingly, Japan's evolutionary sequence of industrial upgrading (that is, the ladder of economic development) after World War II has been accompanied by a corresponding sequence of outward FDI and other business operations: (i) the elementary stage of offshore production (or low-wage-seeking investment centered on labor-intensive light industries, such as toys and apparel), (ii) resource-seeking and house-cleaning types of investment by heavy and chemical industries, (iii) assembly-transplanting investment (inclusive of low-cost-labor-seeking investment in parts, components, accessories, and low-end lines of products) by manufacturers of electronics and automobiles, and (iv) alliance-seeking (strategically networking) business operations in production, marketing, and R&D (often and increasingly via M&As).

The faster the pace of Japan's catch-up growth by climbing the ladder of industrial upgrading, the greater the pressure on – and the easier it has been

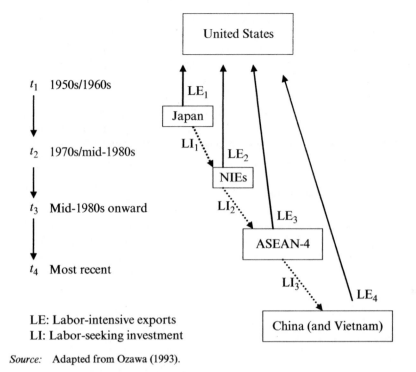

Source: Adapted from Ozawa (1993).

Figure 4.2   Comparative-advantage recycling in labor-intensive manufacturing via FDI and outsourcing

for – Japanese producers to transplant disadvantaged (low value-added) industrial activities in all tiers to low-cost locations in Japan's neighboring countries so that they would be able to maintain and, in fact, enhance competitiveness in the world market (Ozawa, 2005). Structural upgrading is no doubt one of the major sources of productivity growth, since it involves both technological progress and a reallocation of resources from low value-added to higher value-added activities. And the subsequent rises in productivity lead to higher wages overall, but especially to higher wages for skilled workers (thereby giving incentives for workers to upgrade their skills). Japan's high societal propensity to seek higher education and for firms to give on-the-job training under job security prepared for, and facilitated, labor's adaptability to higher-productivity activities. The supply of low-skilled labor quickly declined, and such labor became a scarce factor. Japan's small archipelago and its nationwide network of compulsory universal education and public health did not allow the existence of a rural hinterland where an oversupply of uneducated and unskilled labor might have been marooned.[7]

The Japanese experience was soon to be replicated by the NIEs that followed in Japan's footsteps. The NIEs have all in turn quickly graduated from the labor-driven phase of catch-up growth and transferred (recycled) their labor-intensive manufacturing (hence their shares of the US markets) first to the ASEAN-4 and more recently to China and Vietnam. This 'orderly' recycling/relaying of labor-intensive manufacturing is rather endemic to East Asia, the phenomenon that no other region has so far been unable to replicate.

4.4.3.   Empirical Evidence

The patterns of comparative-advantage recycling are mirrored in US import markets for labor-intensive goods (Figure 4.3). The vertical axis measures the shares of the US market for labor-intensive manufactures captured by Japan, the NIEs, the ASEAN-4, and China over the period of

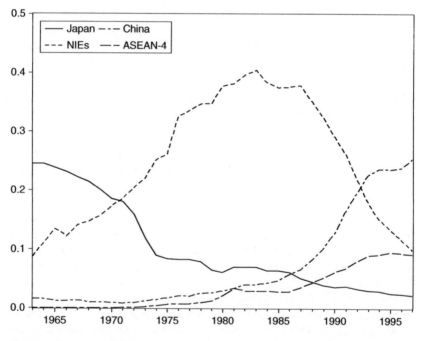

Source: Cutler et al. (2003).

Figure 4.3   US import market shares for labor-intensive goods

1963–97. It can be seen that, on average, Japan lost its lead to the NIEs as the start of the 1970s. The NIEs, in turn, were able to attain a rising market share until the early 1980s and then began to experience a rapidly declining share; in 1992 they were finally taken over by China. By 1997, the shares of both the NIEs and Japan had dwindled and fallen behind both China and the ASEAN-4, whose exports of labor-intensive goods to the US had started soaring in the mid-1980s onward. It is also interesting to note that the US market shares of the ASEAN-4 and China reversed in 1981 and that since then China's share has risen much faster than the ASEAN-4's, more than doubling in the late 1990s. Such soaring Chinese exports to the US have been made possible by foreign multinationals' export-oriented investments and outsourcing operations attracted to, and induced by, China's low wages after the adoption of its open-door policy in 1978. In 1995, for example, FDI inflows into China registered $35.8 billion, while those in the ASEAN-4 were $12.0 billion, the former nearly three times more than the latter (UNCTAD, 1997).

The above patterns have also been econometrically tested in terms of cointegration analysis (Cutler, et al., 2003), which not only affirms the pattern of comparative-advantage recycling but also points out one interesting adjustment phenomenon: the first round of recycling from Japan to the NIEs was slower than the second round of recycling from the NIEs to the ASEAN-4 (and from the NIEs to China). Why did this happen? There were several developments that were responsible for the phenomenon.

First of all, Japan began to shift away from labor-intensive exports to more capital-intensive exports (such as steel, ships, and machinery) as early as the 1950s. In other words, Japan's graduation from the labor-intensive stage was so swift that the NIEs were not yet fully prepared to take over Japan's US market share. The speed with which Japan moved up the ladder of development away from the labor-intensive tier is reflected in Figure 4.4, which shows that the ratio of labor-intensive exports to total manufactured exports from Japan declined precipitously from 40 percent in 1960 down to as low as 6 percent in 1974. At that time, indeed, the NIEs (except for Hong Kong) were still pursuing inward-looking, import-substituting strategies and were not in a position to immediately take over Japan's rapidly declining US market share. It was not until 1965, for example, that Taiwan opened its first export-processing zone in Kaohsiung – and not until 1970 that South Korea set up an export-processing zone in Masan, the first markers of their adoption of an export-oriented policy. These zones soon hosted Japanese enterprises as the major foreign investors and joint venture partners. In short, there was thus a lag between Japan's retreat from, and the NIEs' full entry into, the labor-intensive export market.

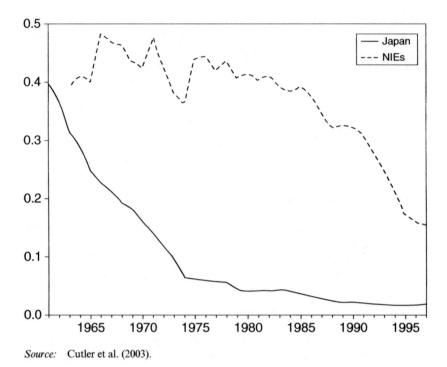

Source: Cutler et al. (2003).

*Figure 4.4   The ratio of labor-intensive exports to total manufactured
             exports: Japan and the NIEs*

In contrast, the market recycling from the NIEs to the ASEAN-4 and
China was better coordinated in timing. As the NIEs began to lose competitiveness in labor-intensive goods as a result of rapid growth in the 1970s,
the ASEAN-4 almost simultaneously, and then China in the 1980s, opened
up for inward investment in these goods. In fact, the miraculous growth
of the NIEs triggered China's decision to switch to an export-oriented
development strategy. Moreover, both the ASEAN-4 and China came to
be assisted by export-oriented investments not only from the NIEs but
also from Japan and the United States, enabling them to quickly build up
labor-intensive exports. In addition, so far as FDI in China is concerned,
the largest group of investors is neither from Japan nor from the United
States but mainly from the ethnic-Chinese NIEs (Hong Kong, Taiwan,
and Singapore) and the overseas Chinese diaspora in the ASEAN-4.
Consequently, there were much faster transplantations of labor-intensive
manufacturing through the networks of ethnic Chinese businessmen from
one place to another.[8]

Reflective of the recycling of labor-intensive manufacturing for export, it is expected that FDI in East Asia's labor-intensive manufacturing is mostly from within East Asia itself – rather than from the advanced West.[9] The MNCs from the latter are, on the whole, more likely to set up production in capital-intensive, high-tech manufacturing, though some (especially mass merchandisers such as Wal-Mart) are also active in outsourcing and procuring labor-intensive manufactures from their Asian suppliers.

This sequential process can continue down the intra-regional hierarchy of economies by repeating the same experience each time. Obviously, a multiplication of derived incomes is not as exact as is depicted above; the size of the labor-intensive, low-end markets 'captured' by followers of the leader economy certainly varies each time, and the second-rank followers – and the third-rank followers – themselves in turn add to the markets to be handed down to still lower-rank followers. These added details, however, do not negate the main point. There is a significant effect via the multiplier of tandem development on the growth of outward-oriented, labor-driven economies in Asia, as low-end markets and industries are passed around and re-exploited among themselves.

Indeed, tandem development can alleviate one problem (a 'fallacy of composition') of outward-looking, export-focused industrialization: If the developing countries adopt such an export-dependent strategy all at once, will there be still enough markets for every country? Bela Balassa gave an answer in the affirmative:

> The stages approach to comparative advantage . . . permits one to dispel certain misapprehensions as regards the foreign demand constraint for manufactured exports under which developing countries are said to operate. With countries progressing on the comparative advantage scale, their exports can supplant the exports of countries that graduate to a higher level. (1989, p. 28)

This ideal process of supplanting 'the exports of countries that graduate to a higher level' has indeed so far occurred from Japan and the NIEs to the ASEAN-4 and to China. For successful recycling of comparative advantages to occur, it is imperative that upper-echelon countries climb up the value chain quickly and willingly relay their increasingly comparatively disadvantaged production to lower-echelon countries. In other words, their capacity to metamorphose themselves structurally is one key enabling factor in comparative-advantage recycling. In this regard, Japan and the NIEs, not to speak of the US, have clearly demonstrated such a capacity in part because of institutional flexibilities in their labor markets.

The emergence of China as the world's major labor-driven manufacturer, however, is creating a problem for other developing countries that are in the same early phase of labor-driven development and are still unable to graduate to a higher level, as is largely the case with the ASEAN-4. Because of the pure size of China with its enormous labor supply, what is true for China (that is, labor-driven development pays off for China) may no longer be true for the rest of the developing world as a whole – that is, a fallacy of composition).

4.5. SUMMING UP

In what way does this FG model of comparative-advantage recycling in labor-intensive goods provide a useful framework of analysis to shed light on the unusually strong nexus of globalization, growth, and poverty alleviation in Asia, especially in East Asia? In the first place, as posited in the paradigm, the present hierarchy of industries that exists in the global economy provides a five-stage ladder of structural transformation that any aspiring catching-up country could climb, starting with the most labor-intensive segment of industrial activity. (Comparative-advantage recycling is most workable in this segment.) For example, it is clearly quixotic for any developing country (where an abundance of unskilled labor is the potential basis of its comparative advantage) to try, in its early developmental phase, to take up the task of building capital-intensive high-tech manufacturing (such as automobiles and aircraft) or R&D-driven Schumpeterian industries. Such a country obviously needs to start out with the lowest tier of industry (that is, low-tech Heckscher-Ohlin industries) which is commensurate with its labor abundance and level of technological sophistication – hence the most practical, most appropriate, and easiest to develop in terms of its natural potential for comparative advantage. At the same time, however, the higher tiers of industry, especially assembly-based manufacturing and Internet-enabled services also have created god-sent opportunities for developing countries to participate in the low-end and labor-intensive segments of advanced industries.

Indeed, all the successful Asian economies have been following such a natural sequence of orderly progression up the ladder of development, starting from labor-intensive production. The main asset of poor countries for long-term growth, whether they are endowed with natural resources or not, is no doubt their abundant labor, which needs to be mobilized and activated for gainful employment as the first requisite of industrialization. After all, employment of unskilled labor is the *sine qua non* of any poor country's development and poverty eradication. Labor-intensive manufacturing is the mandate of early-stage development.

Fortunately, the US as the hegemon of postwar global capitalism, has been willingly offering developing countries, notably in East Asia, its domestic markets for labor-intensive goods and services throughout the postwar period – during the Cold War for geopolitical reasons and more recently because of its high propensity to outsource production across borders to lowest-cost locations anywhere in the world in order to control inflation at home. Actually, this segment of the US market has also come to be used as a tool of foreign aid, as seen in the African Growth and Stabilization Act and other bilateral free trade agreements with developing countries such as Chile and Jordan.

It is against the backdrop of America's relatively liberal trade policy that the comparative advantage recycling has occurred. And in this process, the paradox of 'labor abundance as a labor shortage' has been observed repeatedly. The first lead goose, the US, has arguably been the foremost market (demand) provider.[10] Meanwhile, Japan and the NIEs as the second geese have so far been mostly the capacity augmenters, transferring and supplying all the necessary managerial, technical, and marketing skills, as well as intermediate goods – in the capacity of direct investors in, and procurers from, the lower-ranking follower geese, the ASEAN-4, China, and Vietnam. As a consequence, demand for low-skilled labor has expanded, contributing to a reduction in poverty.

In short, the evolving hierarchies of countries and industries have most cogently meshed and interacted with each other – at both market (unconscious) and policy (conscious) levels – across East Asia to produce the most dynamic pattern of mutual economic growth the world has ever seen. And this pro-growth system is providing an unprecedented opportunity for poverty reduction.

It should be noted, however, that how long this regime of comparative advantage recycling lasts all depends on the capacity of the US to absorb Asia's labor-intensive goods and services. Ironically, the US dependency on imports and foreign savings has become excessive, and its trade deficits have consequently been ballooning. Fears are expressed that the rest of the world might no longer be willing to finance the ever-rising US current account deficit, thereby leading to a crash of the dollar. (More on this in Chapters 8 and 9.)

NOTES

1. Third-World MNCs are now emerging in heavy industry as the outcome of successful Stage-II growth in some catching-up countries, especially BRICs. This chapter is concerned only with MNCs emerging out of Stage-I growth.
2. Despite the recent sharp decline in abject poverty, however, it should be noted that East, Southeast, and South Asia still had almost 690 million poor people in 2002 in terms of the $1-a-day poverty line, and as many as 1.9 billion people on the basis of the $2-a-day

poverty line (ADB, 2004). Furthermore, the Indian Ocean tsunami may add nearly 2 million more people to poverty (ADB, 2005).

3. This prediction is based on the assumptions that '(i) current rates of economic growth continue in most DMCs [developing member countries of ADB], but decline to more sustainable levels in the PRC and the Central Asian republics, and that (ii) distributions are no more unequal than those experienced in recent years, many DMCs are poised both to meet the MDG [Millennium Development Goal] target of halving the 1990 proportion of extremely poor by 2015 and to reduce the number of people living in extreme poverty' (ADB, 2004, p. 45).

4. India recently decided to keep outward-oriented development and economic changes on track when its government announced its budget and spending plans for the fiscal year 2005. Even at the cost of not trimming its fiscal deficit, New Delhi will focus on three objectives: job creation, infrastructure improvements, and social programs for the rural poor. All three will moderate the adverse distribution effect of rapid growth (which India pursues by further opening up its economy for inward investment), hence will have a favorable impact on poverty reduction.

5. This famous statement is attributed to Joan Robinson.

6. It should be noted here, however, that most recently a revisionist movement has started. Ricardo Hausmann and Dani Rodrik, both of Harvard, are said to be challenging the idea of free-market-style liberalization and advocating government subsidies on entrepreneurial projects (that is, selective industrial policy) to ignite growth, since Latin America's recent experiment with the Washington Consensus did not produce the expected results. See 'Seeking Latin America Growth: Some Economists Argue Government Policies may be the Solution', *Wall Street Journal*, February 23, 2005, A15. Their argument is similar to Stiglitz's 'new paradigm of development'.

7. How Japan used policy and institutional arrangements during its high growth period is explored in Ozawa (2005). The post-World War II land reform carried out during the occupation enabled about 4 million peasant households to acquire their own farmland and led to the eradication of rural poverty.

8. For an earlier empirical work, see also Berri and Ozawa (1997).

9. For example, more than a half of FDI in the ASEAN-4 is from Japan, the NIEs, and the ASEAN-4 themselves, and the major investors in China are from the NIEs.

10. It is said that China surpassed the US in 2004 as Japan's top trading partner. True, China replaced the US as the largest exporter to Japan ($57.6 billion from the US vs $61.7 billion from China). This reflects Japan's own procurement-aimed FDI and OEM in China, as well as transmigration of export-oriented manufacturers from the NIEs to China, especially in IT-related electronics industries. Yet, the US is still Japan's largest market ($118.6 billion to the US vs. $39.9 billion to China in 2002), though China is closing the gap at double-digit rates (for example, a 28.2 percent jump in 2002). JETRO (2003).

APPENDIX 4.1   COMPARATIVE ADVANTAGE RECYCLING IN AMERICA'S TV IMPORTS: AN EMPIRICAL EXAMINATION AND POLICY IMPLICATIONS*

A.1.   Introduction

In recent years an extensive theoretical literature has been offered examining the implications of the product cycle (PC) model of trade. Emphasizing knowledge transfers, Krugman (1979) constructed a general equilibrium model consisting of an innovating North country and an imitating South country. A key implication of the product cycle is that the North must continually innovate in the face of the South's ability to eventually imitate each new product. By contrast, the flying geese (FG) theory of trade examines conditions under which an initially imitating South country itself loses its comparative advantage in producing the mature product due to rising costs at home. The loss in comparative advantage results in the further and sequential transfer of production to other less developed South countries and the accompanying recycling of the North's import market among themselves, a phenomenon that can be called 'comparative-advantage (or market) recycling'.

This appendix specifically studies one particular mature good, TV sets, in the US market and its changing pattern of exporting economies from East Asia – first, from Japan and then from the NIEs, from the ASEAN-4, and more recently, from China. True, technological progress continues in the TV set industry (for example, digitalization, flat-panel sets, and HDTV), but set manufacturing has practically disappeared in the US (Chandler, 2001). Incremental innovations are now being introduced mostly in the South/follower countries themselves, especially in Japan, South Korea, and Taiwan. East Asia has emerged as the world's largest concentration of consumer electronics production.[1] In this sense, TV sets are certainly a 'mature' product for the US (too mature to be retained). In short, our study examines the combined phenomenon of product cycle and comparative-advantage recycling as witnessed in the US and explores policy implications for both North and South countries in the age of globalization.

There have been several tests for the existence of a product cycle.

* This appendix is based on 'The Dynamics of the "Mature" Product Cycle and Market Recycling, Flying-geese Style: An Empirical Examination and Policy Implications' (co-authored by Harvey Cutler and Terutomo Ozawa), *Contemporary Economic Policy*, **25** (1), 67–78, copyright Western Economic Association International 2006.

Tsurumi and Tsurumi (1980) found support for the product cycle by determining that the US price elasticity of demand for color TV sets increased over time as US consumers chose between domestic and Japanese-produced color TV sets. Audretsch (1987) also found support by determining that growth industries tend to be more R&D-oriented while mature industries allocate fewer resources to this activity. Cantwell (1995) concluded that over time the share of patents of MNCs located abroad increased for most countries from 1920 to 1990, which supported the internationalization of investment by technological leaders. Gagnon and Rose (1995) found that a trade surplus (deficit) of a commodity is likely to persist over a long period of time, a trend that is counter to the product cycle and more consistent with factor proportions theory (which closely parallels the FG theory).

Econometric tests of the FG theory have been limited. Dowling and Cheang (2000) found support for the FG theory by utilizing both Balassa's 'revealed' comparative advantage index and FDI ratios for East Asian countries. Using Spearman rank correlation coefficients and examining three periods (1970–95, 1970–85, and 1985–95), they found that economic development trickled down from Japan to the NIEs and then to the ASEAN-4. Cutler, Berri, and Ozawa (2003) analyzed labor-intensive trade data from Japan, the NIEs, the ASEAN-4, and China to the US and found support for the FG theory (market recycling).

In this study, we are interested in testing for the dynamics of the combined PC-FG framework. Using annual data from 1961–2002 for TV sets, we use cointegration techniques to estimate a system of multiple cointegrated vectors representing the sequential transfer of America's TV import market from Japan, to the NIEs, to the ASEAN-4, and finally to China. We develop a methodology of interpreting both the cointegrating vectors and the speeds of adjustment as a technique to test for the recycling of the US import market among the East Asian economies. We argue that our analysis has implications for the emerging HDTV and flat-panel TV sets markets as well as patterns of behavior in lower-developed South countries such as China, Vietnam, and India as these countries are actively pursuing inward FDI in higher valued-added industries.

Section A.2 presents the theoretical framework, and Section A.3 provides the data and background information about the region's TV set manufacturing. Section A.4 discusses empirical techniques and the results of the analysis. The final section touches on policy implications and offers conclusions.

A.2.   Conceptual Framework

Electronics is an R&D-based industry where new products and processes are constantly innovated, and competitiveness shifts from one product to another sequentially, an industry that is characterized by short product cycles. The Schumpeterian concept of 'creative destruction' aptly applies to innovators' home markets. A fast pace of technological standardization and maturity for a given new product leads to an equally swift outward shift of production from the innovators' (North) country to overseas, as conceptualized in the PC theory of trade and investment. In the early developmental phase of electronics, the US was the dominant source of innovations, as seen in the original PC theory, but other countries in Europe and East Asia also soon emerged as active innovators, as presented in the revised version (Vernon, 1979).[2] Nonetheless, the US still continues to play the major roles of both *technology* and *market* providers to East Asian economies. Yet, as described in the original PC theory, conventional TV sets and many other mature electronics products have followed the typical pattern of a sequence from US domestic production to exports, to overseas production, and to imports. These imports come mostly from East Asia.

What is equally interesting is that once an electronics product becomes a mature 'commodity', whose competitiveness is basically determined by labor costs, its production shifts from one South country to another in a persistent search for lower-cost locations. This development is facilitated especially when lower-echelon South countries liberalize their trade and investment regimes so as to attract production from higher-developed South countries. Such successive transmigration of production of a standardized product therefore exhibits a changing pattern of production over time within the South countries, while the US remains the major import market. This phenomenon of production transmigration down the intra-regional hierarchy of South countries differentiated in terms of the stages of economic development and levels of technological sophistication is captured in the FG model. Viewed in the above light, the PC theory and the FG model complement each other, as schematically illustrated in Figure A.1.

A *new* product is innovated first in a high-income (high-wage) country like the US and initially manufactured and exported from the innovator's home country (that is, the 'introduction' and 'growth' stages, from t_0 to t_2). However, it is doomed to be transplanted overseas as its technology matures and becomes standardized in the 'maturity' stage (a process explained by the PC theory). The production of such a quickly *matured* product moves from the US to a lead South country (Japan from t_2 to t_3), and the US starts to import from the latter, as described by the distance

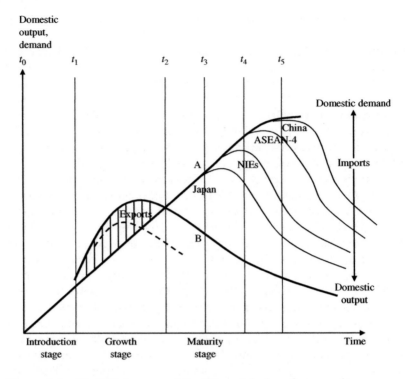

*Figure A.1   The PC theory and the FG model of market recycling
           combined*

AB. As the lead South country's production costs rise, other and lower-
developed South countries (the NIEs, the ASEAN-4, and China) begin to
produce and export to the US. In this scenario, the US thus turns from
an innovator to the major market provider. This production transmigration occurs due to the quest for lower costs (the process of industrial and
market recycling envisioned in the FG theory). A number of electronics
goods have gone through this PC-cum-FG phenomenon. Color TV sets
are a prime example and the focus of this appendix.

A.3.   Data and Background Information

A.3.1.   Data
We have collected data for SITC number 76, which represents all TV sets
that are imported by the US. Two sources of data were used to construct
the data set from 1961–2002. We obtained data from the OECD CD-ROM
for the period 1961–98. For the period 1998–2002, the US International

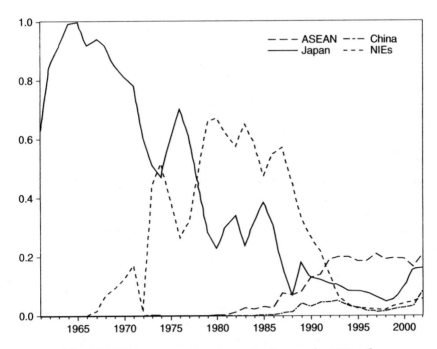

Figure A.2   *US TV import market shares for Japan, the NIEs, the ASEAN-4, and China*

Trade Commission web site was used. Merging the two sources of data was easy as they matched up very well, using 1998 as the splicing year.

To create the NIEs variable, we added the exports of TV sets to the US from Hong Kong, Taiwan, Singapore, and South Korea together and then divided this sum by total US imports of TV sets. This variable is referred to as NIEs. A similar procedure was done for the ASEAN-4 countries. For Japan and China, we simply divided their respective exports to the US by America's total TV imports to calculate their market shares. This transformation requires that all these TV set imports are in percentages. However, these percentages do not sum to unity since the US imports TV sets from other parts of the world as well. Figure A.2 displays the import shares of the US for TV sets from the East Asian group.

A.3.2. Background information about exporting countries

Japan was obviously the first Asian country to develop an electronics industry successfully. It once dominated the US market with a market share of over 80 percent for most of the 1960s. Japan's electronics industry originated with the manufacturing of radios before World War

II. But it was after the war that electronics became a major growth industry.[3]

In the early 1950s, the production of TV sets – first, monochrome and soon, color – was actively transplanted to Japan under licensing agreements by RCA (Radio Corporation of America), the dominant holder of TV-related patents. Why did the company want to produce in Japan instead of at home – at such a relatively early growth stage of the product cycle? (This actually meant a flattening of the US domestic output function as illustrated by a dotted curve in Figure A.1.) This move by RCA was reportedly in part intended as retaliation against Zenith Electronics, an initial rival and once top producer of TVs, which legally challenged RCA's 'package licensing (patent pool)' practice and won the litigation. RCA, then, decided *not* to manufacture TVs at home but to license the world so that it would be able to earn licensing fees out of its huge pool of patents. Therefore, Japan became the most promising cost-effective locus of production, and RCA began to import made-in-Japan TVs in competition with Zenith (Curtis, 1994).[4]

In 1962, Sony innovated a 'micro-TV set', which immediately caught the fancy of American consumers. In 1965, Japan also began to export color TV sets, and it surpassed the US in color TV production in 1970 (Kagami and Fukunishi, 1981). And before long, 'made-in-Japan' color TV sets dominated the US market. (This corresponds to the maturity stage $t_2 - t_3$ in Figure A.1, where TV imports from Japan begin to replace US domestic output.) In fact, Japan was the only country that exported TV sets to the US in 1965, capturing a 100 percent import market share (Figure A.2). Japan's initial dominance as a TV-set exporter explains why TV production and exports to the US have been so concentrated in, and retained by, East Asia, as such activities have been passed around the region. Although Japan's industrial policy did not focus specifically on TVs alone, the Japanese government was bent on promoting the growth of the electronics industry as a whole under a series of targeted laws.[5] The TV set industry as part and parcel of electronics thus benefited from a variety of protective and promotional measures.

As Japan's labor costs rose in the wake of its rapid catch-up growth, however, Japanese producers of TV sets started to innovate higher value-added TV models and other electronics goods (such as VCRs) and transferred low-end TV sets to other Asian countries, first to the NIEs and then to the ASEAN-4. Consequently, the latter's TV exports to the US quickly overtook Japan's market share in the US (Figure A.2). The rush to overseas investments not only in TVs but also in other electronics goods and their components was further intensified by the 1985 Plaza Accord, which made the yen appreciate against the dollar dramatically.

In 1993, electric and electronics goods soon became the largest part (approximately 50 percent) of Japanese foreign direct investments in Asia (Ernst, 1996).

A similar development occurred also in the NIEs. With the exception of Hong Kong, the other three economies' governments were all equally involved in electronics-targeted industrial policies. In the late 1960s, Korea's electronics industry started out as assemblers of consumer electronics (first, for radios, then tape recorders, and TVs) using imported components, mostly from Japan. *Chaebols* (large industrial corporations, mostly family-owned), such as LG Group, Samsung, Hyundai and Daewoo, initially followed this sequence of consumer electronics manufacturing. But they soon advanced into industrial electronics, producing their own parts and components, with the strong support of the Korean government (Pecht et al., 1997). Taiwan and Singapore too trod a similar path of developing their own electronics industries (Beane, 1997). All this development culminated in an export drive by the NIEs to the US market. Their market share expansion from 1966 to 1980 closely followed Japan's market share contraction in the US market (Figure A.2). And a similar policy experience was largely replicated in the ASEAN-4, soon followed by China (Pecht et al., 1999).

China's open-door policy in 1978 provided an impetus for manufacturers in Japan and the NIEs to shift production of TV sets to the vast and fast-growing mainland Chinese market. (This situation matches the market recycling illustrated at t_4 in Figure A.1.) In China, color TV production started at the then state-owned Tianjin Radio Factory in 1971 (followed by color VCRs in 1981). 'By the end of 1985, more than a thousand contracts [involving licensing, joint ventures, and subcontracting] had been signed with foreign companies, [resulting in the establishment of] 113 color TV assembly lines with a manufacturing capacity of 15 million sets per year' (Pecht et al., 1999, p. 84). China soon began to export TV sets to the US under original equipment manufacturing (OEM).

A.4.   Empirical Analysis

Given the fact TV sets are already a mature product for the US, we are not concerned with the early stages of the PC phenomenon *per se* where new technology is initially transferred from the US to East Asia but with the role of the US as the key provider of a market, thanks to which the phenomenon of market recycling is observable. Here, cointegration techniques are the most appropriate way to examine the sequence of market recycling in the US imports of TV sets for several reasons. Since these data are non-stationary, cointegration is a superior econometric method of capturing both long-run and short-run movements in the variables. Perhaps more importantly, this technique allows for each of the variables to respond to disequilibrium conditions in the cointegrating vectors.

Our empirical analysis will be divided into two sections. The first part briefly describes the Johansen (1988) method of estimating cointegrated sets of variables. This will be followed by a presentation of our empirical model and results.

A.4.1.   Econometric methodology

Cointegration is a technique that estimates the relationship between non-stationary time series variables. Suppose X_t and Y_t are non-stationary; these variables are cointegrated when X_t and Y_t are multiplied by a linear vector of coefficients and their sum equals a stationary variable e_t, such that $a_1 X_t + a_2 Y_t = e_t$. Assuming that both a_1 and a_2 are positive requires that X_t and Y_t move in an inverse manner. The variable e_t represents the departure of X_t and Y_t from its equilibrium relationship. When $e_t > 0$, the equilibrium relationship implies that either X_t or Y_t has to fall, or some combination of both has to occur to achieve long-run equilibrium.

A generalized cointegration system can be summarized by the following equation:

$$\Delta X_t = \Gamma_1 \Delta X_{t-1} + \Gamma_2 \Delta X_{t-2} + \ldots + \Gamma_{k+1} \Delta X_{t-k+1} + \Pi X_{t-k} + e_t \qquad (1)$$

The variable ΔX_t represents a p-element vector of observations on all variables in the system at time t, the $\Gamma_i \Delta X_{t-i}$ terms account for stationary variation related to the past history of system variables, and the Π matrix contains the cointegrating relationships. All variables must be non-stationary in levels. It is hypothesized that $\Pi = \alpha\beta'$, where the cointegrating vectors are in the β matrix and the α matrix describes the speed at which each variable changes to return the markets to their long-run equilibrium.

A.4.2.   Econometric results

Testing whether the series are non-stationary.   The first step in the process of applying cointegration is to establish whether the series are non-stationary. A popular technique used to distinguish these types of series is the Augmented Dickey-Fuller (ADF) approach. Table A.1 presents the ADF results for each of the market shares. It is clearly the case that since the test statistics exceed the critical values, all of the market shares are non-stationary. When we difference the variables, all the series are stationary.

We used the Akaike Information Criteria test and the Schwarz Bayesian Criterion and determined that the optimal lag length was five. We

Table A.1   Unit root tests for the system variables

Variable	ADF Statistic No Trend	ADF Statistic with Trend
Japan	−1.86	−1.17
NIEs	−1.26	−1.37
ASEAN-4	−0.02	−1.83
China	−0.27	−2.10

Notes:
(1) The critical value for the ADF statistic with no trend is −2.94 and −3.53 with trend. The values refer to statistically significant ADF values, which indicate these variables are stationary.
(2) The above results used two lags in the ADF tests but alternative lag structures did not seem to influence the results.

experimented with a variety of shorter lag lengths and the results did not vary in any meaningful way. We used four lags in our analysis.

Using cointegration implies that there are several levels of hypothesis testing that have to be successful. First, the number of cointegrating vectors has to be consistent with predictions from theory. Second, the coefficients in the cointegrating vectors have to be of the predicted sign and significant. The third level of hypothesis testing occurs with respect to the estimates of the speeds of adjustment or which variables are responsible for re-equilibrating each vector. We maintain that the PC-cum-FG theory makes specific predictions for each level of testing.

As noted, the structure of this system has been implied by the FG theory: as Japan lost its comparative advantage in the production of TVs in the 1960s, this production was transferred to the NIEs. In this case, Japan was the North, and the NIEs were the South. However, in the late 1980s and early 1990s, the NIEs also lost their comparative advantage in this sector. Consequently the ability to produce TV sets began to be transferred to the ASEAN-4 and China. Hence, in the 1980s, the NIEs had become the North and the ASEAN-4 and China had become the South. Therefore, these three relationships are consistent with three cointegrating vectors. They are the Japan/NIEs vector, an ASEAN-4/NIEs vector and a China/NIEs vector. For identification reasons, there has to be a unique variable in each vector and in our four-variable case, one of the variables has to be common to each of the vectors. Understanding the chronology of the technological transfer implies that NIEs should be the common variable and there should be unique vectors for Japan, the ASEAN-4, and China.

We used the trace and maximum eigenvalue tests to determine the number of significant eigenvalues and the associated number of cointegrating

Table A.2   Maximum eigenvalue and trace tests

		Maximum Eigenvalue Test		
Null Hypothesis	Alternative Hypothesis	Test Statistic	95% Critical Value	90% Critical Value
$r <= 0$	$r = 1$	36.63	31.79	29.13
$r <= 1$	$r = 2$	30.78	25.42	23.1
$r <= 2$	$r = 3$	17.80	19.22	17.18
$r <= 3$	$r = 4$	7.33	12.39	10.55
		Trace Test		
Null Hypothesis	Alternative Hypothesis	Test Statistic	95% Critical Value	90% Critical Value
$r <= 0$	$r >= 1$	92.55	63	59.16
$r <= 1$	$r >= 2$	55.92	42.34	39.34
$r <= 2$	$r >= 3$	25.14	25.77	23.08
$r <= 3$	$r >= 4$	7.33	12.39	10.55

Note: (a) The letter r represents the number of cointegrating vectors.

vectors to determine if the data support the predicted number of cointe-grating vectors. These results appear in Table A.2. Both tests indicated at the 10 percent level that there are three cointegrating vectors, which supports our theoretical priors. It is interesting that Johansen has pointed out many times that even if the eigenvalue tests do not support the theory, it is not unreasonable to just impose the theoretical number of vectors and proceed to the next stage of the analysis. We are fortunate that these tests support our implied structure but Johansen maintains that this is not a critical stage in the testing methodology.

Estimation of the television sector revealed the following structure:

$$1.0 \text{Japan} + 0.26 \text{ NIEs} = \varepsilon_{jnt} \quad (2)$$
$$(0.04)$$

$$1.0 \text{China} + 0.17 \text{NIEs} = \varepsilon_{cnt} \quad (3)$$
$$(0.01)$$

$$1.0 \text{ASEAN} + 0.04 \text{NIEs} = \varepsilon_{ant} \quad (4)$$
$$(0.01)$$

The numbers in parentheses are standard errors.

The three cointegrating vectors are consistent with the economic development of this region. Equation (2) reflects the Japan/NIEs relationship, equation (3) reflects the China/NIEs relationship while equation (4) represents the ASEAN-4/NIEs link as the FG theory predicts. Considering equation (2), the NIEs variable comes in with a positive sign in this vector, which reflects the inverse relationship between the market shares for the NIEs and the market shares for Japan. As discussed above, of all the East Asian economies Japan was able to adopt the technology earliest. But by the early 1960s, the NIEs were in a position to adopt the standardized technology and start producing and exporting TVs. Japan started to shift out of low-end TV manufacturing and into the production and export of higher-level goods such as VCRs and personal computers. This explains the inverse relationship between Japan and the NIEs as estimated in equation (2). In other words, as Japan fell, then ε_{jnt} would start to fall. But the rising value for NIEs exports to the US would offset this fall in ε_{jnt}. These offsetting impacts result in ε_{jnt} being stationary.

The further evolution of the production shift can be seen in the estimates for equations (3) and (4). It wasn't until later in our sample period that both China and the ASEAN-4 were developed enough to take the standardized technology and start producing and exporting TVs. As the NIEs began to consider production of other goods such as microchips, there was an opening for both China and the ASEAN-4 to obtain a portion of the export market to the US Equations (3) and (4) represent respectively the inverse relationship between China and the NIEs, and the ASEAN-4 and the NIEs. As the NIEs grew rapidly, they started acting like a North country, transferring production to the ASEAN-4 and China.

Our next area of analysis is how the transfer of markets described by the PC-FG model occurs. The vector error correction model (VECM) represented in equation (1) relates each variable's growth rate to previous departures from equilibrium in the three cointegrating relationships. This adjustment process is referred to as the speeds of adjustment and is represented by the reduced rank regression estimates of $\forall$, where $A = \forall \exists'$. Considering the Japan/NIEs market (equation (2)), suppose the market share for Japan fell, thus causing a negative value for ε_{jnt}. The adjustment back to equilibrium requires either Japan or NIEs to rise; however, the PC-cum-FG theory predicts that the NIEs' market share should rise as it takes over part of the export market for TVs from Japan.

There are two aspects to this adjustment process that can provide an in-depth look at the PC-cum-FG theory. When $\varepsilon_{jnt} < 0$, the speeds of adjustment estimates indicate how Japan and the NIEs respond to disequilibrium. We describe this adjustment process as a 'pull' if the NIEs respond by increasing exports of TVs to the US, this causes ε_{jnt} to move back to zero

Table A.3   Speed of adjustment estimates

Variable	ε_{jnt-1}	ε_{cnt-1}	ε_{ant-1}
ΔJapan	−0.72*	−6.5**	5.1*
	(0.41)	(2.6)	(2.9)
ΔChina	−0.01	−0.85**	0.25
	(0.04)	(0.40)	(0.35)
ΔASEAN-4	−0.04	1.36**	−0.60**
	(0.10)	(0.65)	(0.27)
ΔNIEs	−1.70**	8.9**	−14.8***
	(0.64)	(4.0)	(4.5)

Notes:
(1) The numbers in parentheses are standard errors.
(2) The symbol * refers to a 10 percent significance level, ** refers to a 5 percent significance level, and *** refers to a 1 percent significance level.
(3) The term EC_{jnt-1} refers to the disequilibrium residual in the Japan/NIEs relationship.

or long-run equilibrium. If at the same time, Japan responds to the negative value of ε_{jnt} by further reducing their exports of TVs to the US, this causes further disequilibrium in the market and a greater response by the NIEs. We would describe this situation as a 'push' by the North (Japan) as it recognizes the advantages that NIEs have in producing TVs and it continues to cut its production. As our results below indicate, it is the pull by the South that dominates the adjustment process.

Table A.3 reports the relationship between the four variables in the system and the disequilibrium response to the three markets. The results depict a highly integrated relationship between the four groups in East Asia. The NIEs clear the Japan/NIEs vector, where Japan is a newly emerged North (higher-developed South) and the NIEs an imitating South. The speed of adjustment estimate is −1.70 and significant at the 5 percent level. As Japan declined with respect to exporting to the US, it was the NIEs that increased their market share of exports to the US to offset the impact from Japan. In other words, the 'pull' effect appears to dominate. However, as the NIEs declined in the 1980s with respect to equations (3) and (4), it was China and the ASEAN-4 that together rose to begin to take over TV exports to the US. The estimated speeds of adjustment for China and the ASEAN-4 in their particular markets are -0.85 and -0.60, respectively. These are both significant at the 5 percent level. Here, again, the 'pull' effect stands out.

We are also able to estimate some 'push' effects with respect to the NIEs in the China vector. The speed of adjustment estimate for the NIEs is 8.9,

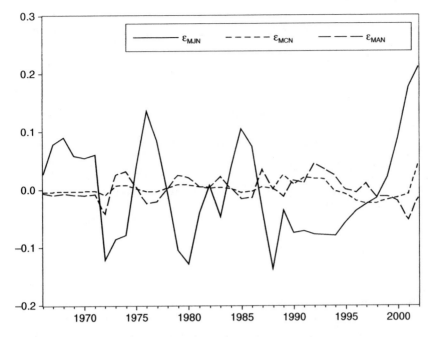

Figure A.3   Plot of disequilibrium residuals

which indicates that when the China/NIEs vector is out of equilibrium, the NIEs decreases exports to the US, which further drives the vector out of equilibrium. As an example, when $\varepsilon_{cnt} < 0$, the NIEs reduce their production, most likely in response to the realization that China is more cost effective at producing TVs. Since TV production in China moves to clear the vector, TV production in China increases even more. We do not observe any other push effects in the Japan/NIEs and the ASEAN/NIEs vectors.

Of additional interest are the characteristics of ε_{jnt}, ε_{ant}, and ε_{cnt} that reflect the similar relations noted above. Each of these variables describes the adjustment process back toward long-run equilibrium in terms of either Japan or the NIEs losing export share while the developing economies gain the export share. Figure A.3 presents the behavior of the three series. The behavior of ε_{jnt} indicates volatility in the adjustment process between Japan and the NIEs to a much greater degree than the other two relations. The variances of ε_{jnt}, ε_{ant}, and ε_{cnt} are 0.08, 0.005, and 0.002, respectively. One possible reason for the larger variance in the Japan–NIEs relations might have been that when Japan's rapid TV exports to the US caused a clamor for protection, Japanese exporters resorted to local production for a while.[6] These locally produced TV sets not only substituted for Japanese exports but also naturally competed with imports from the NIEs, thereby hindering smooth market recycling from Japan to the NIEs. The Japanese producers also began to specialize in higher-end models to retain market share – and hold on to their competitiveness in the niche market. All this must have weakened the transition to the NIEs market. The empirical evidence may reflect such strategic behavior on the part of the Japanese producers. By the 1980s, the TV exporters from the NIEs concentrated on the low-end models and did not set up assembly operations in the US. They shifted production more quickly to the ASEAN-4 and then to China as a strategy to maintain price competitiveness, thereby facilitating market recycling to the ASEAN-4, as reflected in smaller variances in the disequilibrium residuals.

A.5. Concluding Observations

This appendix has examined the PC and FG model in the context of East Asian exports of TVs to the US. The PC theory emphasizes the initial transfer of production from the US (North) to Japan (most-developed South), once the technology involved has become standardized. It also highlights the significance of the US import market as the major demand/market provider for South countries. The FG theory then examines the further transmigration patterns of TV production to lower-developed South countries in succession. We found strong empirical support for the orderly transition of the transfer of TV sets production.

In order for the lower-echelon South countries to succeed in capitalizing on the market-recycling opportunity, however, it was incumbent on their governments to liberalize trade and inward FDI so as to attract foreign multinationals' production of standardized labor-intensive goods like low-end TV sets. Besides, the technology and inputs for conventional TV sets being standardized and readily available these days, local entrepreneurs are often able to enter the industry on their own without the help of foreign multinationals, as was recently the case with China's TV sets industry. Through market reforms, a favorable business environment, including a flexible labor market, needs to be created to promote the development of local businesses, as well as to attract FDI. In this respect, policy clearly matters. For example, it is said that while India struggles to develop labor-intensive manufacturing because of its over-regulated (socialist) labor market, China has been successful in making itself the workshop of the world thanks to its deregulated labor market, especially in the so-called Special Economic Zones, initially set up in several coastal provinces, such as Guangdong and Fujian, in the 1980s. These zones are designed to absorb abundant Chinese labor by using the capital and technology of foreign multinationals as key joint inputs.

We maintain that our analysis of the PC-FG theories has strong relevance for conditions in 2006 and beyond. Consider the emerging market for HDTV and flat-panel TV sets that are currently being developed via R&D and produced in Japan and South Korea. Interestingly enough, none of these advanced latest TV sets is manufactured in the US. Therefore, these two countries are playing the role of the North as the product recycler. This represents the *evolutionary* unfolding of the PC-FG model as some higher-developing South countries join the North over time. In response, China and the ASEAN-4 are attempting to induce inward FDI by providing a slew of incentives so that they can start to produce these newer higher value-added goods. No doubt, HDTV and flat-panel TV sets are in the early stages of development with respect to the PC theory. However, time compression in the product cycles of new innovations is occurring in the sense that less expensive inputs are eagerly waiting in China and the ASEAN-4 to produce the newest TV sets. It is clear that government policies in China and the ASEAN-4 are strongly encouraging expansion in this industry in order to climb the ladder of technological development.

China, in particular, is in a promising position to attract high-end TV sets production, since it has been investing in the education of electronics engineers in large numbers. One is easily reminded of the Chinese electronics company Legend's acquisition of IBM's personal computer operations in May 2005 and its effort to build up its own computer brand, Lenovo (especially via TV commercials at the 2006 Winter Olympics), testifying to China's eagerness and technological capability to enter a high-end industry. Furthermore, China can use its huge potential domestic market as an irresistible inducement for FDI in upscale TV sets. The ASEAN-4 likewise has an advantage in compelling Japanese and Korean multinationals to use its growing regional trade bloc as a production and export base. The Philippines, for example, has already built a strong electronics industry, which now accounts for as much as two-thirds of that country's total exports. It will not be long, therefore, before HDTV and flat-panel TV sets, as they mature in technology, are eventually produced in, and exported from, these lower-echelon South countries. Therefore, we are predicting that these newer goods will transition from PC to FG goods.

We are also witnessing similar types of activity in Vietnam and India. Vietnam is also encouraging inward FDI as that country is starting to make inroads into labor-intensive goods. It is reported that because of rapid wage increases in China's coastal regions both foreign multinationals and local Chinese enterprises have begun to shift labor-intensive goods outward to Vietnam – as well as inward to China's vast interior regions

– where wages are much lower. This is in line with the FG theory. India, too, is becoming a major supplier of low- to medium-tech services such as call centers, back-office work, and tech support for computers and software. The relatively less expensive yet skilled labor in India has resulted in services offshoring from US companies. The current economic boom in India is based on skilled (mostly college-educated) low-cost labor, and not yet on an abundant supply of low-skilled labor. This is resulting in income inequality and leaving the problems of high unemployment and underemployment unresolved. Thus India needs labor-intensive manufacturing where low-skilled labor can be employed. In short, as these lower-developing countries advance in market reforms, they will be ready to more actively join the FG formation of market recycling aimed at US markets.

Rapid outflows of production from the North to the South, as evidenced in stepped-up offshoring and transplantation of even R&D activities overseas, make it imperative for the North to continue to innovate, since it becomes more and more difficult to retain R&D-sparked manufacturing at home for a prolonged period of time as envisaged in the original PC theory. In addition, we have observed the beginning of the overseas spread of R&D activities, which is diversifying the locational sources of innovations and quickening the tempo of the PC phenomenon. In response, the governments of the North (the US, Europe, and Japan) are increasingly compelled to promote science and technology at home through fiscal policies (for example, subsidies and tax incentives) – and may even resort to technological protectionism (for example, by blocking the sale of technologies via licensing and the acquisition of domestic high-tech firms by foreign interests).

In fact, the private sector in the North is becoming more cautious and less willing to transfer the latest technologies. Yet, fierce rivalry among the North countries in the face of global competition often forces innovating firms to offer technologies to the South countries – as now observed especially in China, whose government is bent on promoting absorption of cutting-edge technologies. This means that technology transfer may take place even in the introductory stage before products reach their maturity stage (that is, time compression in the PC phenomenon). Moreover, some innovating firms themselves may be quite eager to transfer the latest innovation at an early cycle stage – in part because their domestic market alone is not large enough to recoup the ever-rising R&D investments in high-tech industries, notably electronics. After all, when truly multinational firms initiate R&D projects these days, they look at a global market, not a domestic market, as their potential target.

The criticality of the US markets for Asian exports as the major demand provider means that further growth in FG goods like conventional TV sets

– as well as new PC goods like HDTV and flat-panel TVs – all depends on the economic prosperity of the US. America's current boom is, however, built on heavy borrowing from the rest of the world and relatively cheap imports from Asia that help reduce inflationary pressures. Fears are increasingly expressed that foreign investors might stop financing the ever-widening deficit on the US current account, thereby causing a crash of the dollar and a global economic crisis. If this hard-landing scenario plays out, US market recycling in labor-intensive goods including TV sets will be seriously disrupted. Yet a gradual dissolution of the US trade imbalance (that is, a soft-landing scenario) is also possible, and the US will then continue to lead the world in the foreseeable future. So long as the US maintains its position as the economic and technological leader in the world economy, the PC and FG model itself – if in its evolving form – is likely to remain relevant as a predictor of the long-term trend of US-targeted exports from Asia.

NOTES

1. At present, electronics is indeed the top number-one manufactured export of the East Asian developing economies (except Indonesia and China where electronics nevertheless ranks among their top ten exports).
2. Vernon introduced an updated version of the PC theory in which R&D activities are dispersed by MNCs throughout the advanced world and the US industry often plays merely the role of an importer and no longer the role of an innovator in some product lines.
3. In the 1920s, Japan was producing simple home electric appliances such as space heaters, electric irons, fans, and switches. In 1925, radio broadcasting began in Japan, and made-in-Japan radios were produced for the first time by Hayakawa Electric (the present Sharp Corporation) under licensing agreements with the RCA. And Japan's radio output reached the level of 876,000 units in 1941 (on the eve of World War II) (Kanasaki, 1982; Koizumi, 1990).
4. In 1955, Japan's TV production stood at 240,000 units, but soon soared to 2,850,000 units only four years later, in 1959, a nearly 12-fold increase. It continued to rise by about 1 million units each year thereafter, turning Japan into the world's largest producer of black-and-white TV sets. By 1957, as many as 57 Japanese companies had been licensed to manufacture TV components by RCA, Western Electric, EMI, and Philips (Namayama et al., 1999). The result was the extremely competitive conditions where the principle of survival of the fittest was at work.
5. More specifically, the Law on Temporary Measures for the Promotion of Electronics Industry of 1957, the Law on Temporary Measures for the Promotion of Specified Electronics Industries and Specified Machinery Industries of 1971, and the Law on Temporary Measures for the Promotion of Specified Machinery and Information Industries of 1978.
6. For example, Japan's major color-TV exporters set up plants in the US to avoid trade frictions. Sony opened a TV assembly plant in San Diego, CA, in 1972; Sanyo Electric in Forrest City, AR, in 1977; Mitsubishi Electric in Santa Ana, CA, in 1980; and Matsushita Electric in Franklin Park, IL, in 1989. But all these operations have been closed down or shifted to Mexico, especially after Mexico's accession to the North American Free Trade Agreement.

5. Structural upgrading, infrastructure development, and the insatiable quest for natural resources

5.1. INTRODUCTION

Infrastructure is the backbone of economic development and growth. The faster the rate of growth, the greater the need for infrastructure in support of both productive and consumptive activities. Infrastructure is basically a non-tradable good, since it is location-bound. As in any other sectors of an economy, furthermore, infrastructure facilities have evolved in types and services, especially in the way they are operated – *pari passu* with economic growth, technological progress, and changes in the modalities of production and consumption. They were traditionally provided as public goods by local and state governments in individual countries.

Many state-run infrastructure facilities, however, have turned out to be inefficient and costly. This is not so much because of the poor quality of the physical facilities *per se* but because of how they are operated and maintained in providing services. In this respect, infrastructure-specific software (institutional arrangements including policies, regulatory framework, and oversight) is the decisive factor. Moreover, modern infrastructure requires sophisticated management and operational skills. Without such requisite software provision, no physical infrastructure is itself capable of functioning effectively and efficiently.

In the recent past, consequently, some types of infrastructure have been privatized, and MNCs have begun increasingly to engage in the construction and management of infrastructure facilities in host countries. After all, MNCs from advanced countries possess valuable firm-specific knowledge, skills, and experiences to run the physical facilities efficiently and productively. And in doing so, they are making the non-tradable sector *indirectly* 'tradable' through direct local operations.[1]

As a matter of fact, MNCs' involvement in overseas infrastructure is nothing new. It originated during the 18th to early 20th centuries when Western powers pursued colonialism in the hunt for natural resources and markets subsequent to the Industrial Revolution.[2] Some even argue that the early chartered trading and colonizing companies (such as the Russia Company, the East India Company, and the Virginia and Plymouth Companies) of earlier centuries (the 15th through 19th centuries) were the predecessors of modern MNCs (McNulty, 1972). They established their 'trading posts' abroad (the *first* trade-supporting infrastructure overseas).

Most recently, however, China's diplomacy to obtain resources, notably in politically sensitive regions of the world such as Africa (notably Sudan), has become controversial and is causing frictions with the advanced countries that also import resources but use trade sanctions against the rogue states. In its efforts, furthermore, China is building high-profile infrastructure facilities like dams, power stations, railways, and ports in resource-rich developing countries – in collaboration with existing political regimes under its 'no-strings-attached' policy (whether or not they are oppressive and undemocratic). Also, India has begun to make deals with dictatorial states in Africa as it seeks energy resources abroad. Interestingly enough, Japan too was once most actively engaged in its own resource diplomacy during the high-growth period of heavy and chemical industrialization (in the 1970s), causing frictions with the West. Its scramble for resources, however, has since considerably subsided and stabilized as Japan's GDP became proportionately less resource-dependent.

The leitmotifs of this chapter are (i) that any fast-growing country that has reached Stage II of resource-intensive heavy industrialization searches aggressively for resources overseas by making whatever investments in project-specific infrastructure are necessary (and even providing general-purpose infrastructure to secure local goodwill) in resource-rich countries, and (ii) that a structural stages model of infrastructure development can shed light on such economic behavior.

5.2. ECONOMIC GROWTH AND INFRASTRUCTURE

As might well be expected, aggregate spending on (or stocks of) a variety of infrastructure facilities and services is significantly correlated with growth. This relationship is, for example, empirically found in a World Bank study (1994) that used the variables of telephone main lines (per thousand persons), of paved roads (kilometers per million persons), household electricity (percentage availability), and of access to safe water (percentage of the population) – all these infrastructure variables closely correlated with GDP per capita (in PPP dollars) in developing countries. Obviously the income elasticity of infrastructure provision differs across types (as shown by the different slopes of regression lines). The Bank's study also notes the changing shares (relative importance) of different types of infrastructure, depending on income levels. The share of power, telecoms, and roads (including highways) as a group becomes even greater in higher-income countries than that of sanitation, water, irrigation, and railways. Why, however, does this trend occur?

Although no explicit explanation was given, it is intuitively understandable that the latter group of infrastructure is largely of the more basic and elementary kind, while the former includes more technologically advanced forms of infrastructure, embodying recent innovations. For instance, telecoms have lately (since the early 1990s) undergone the so-called 'information technology (IT)' revolution, morphing from fixed-line to wireless transmission and from analogue to digital technology. And the Internet and the World Wide Web (www) have drastically altered the telecoms industry. At the start of the 1990s when the Bank's study was made, however, these new developments were still inchoate and not yet quite noticeable – hence could not be considered. Telecoms' share must have risen most noticeably since then with a steady and more recent trend of incessant technological innovation. Power generation has likewise experienced drastic, though perhaps less glamorous, changes towards the nuclear, solar, wind, ocean/river-current, and geothermal systems. Modern transport (especially air), though not included in the Bank's comparison, surely belongs to the high-income-elastic group.

So, the questions to be asked are how the new forms of infrastructure have come into existence, in what way their shares have changed over time, and why MNCs have begun to be involved in certain (modern) types of infrastructure development and operations overseas. And perhaps more importantly, why has China suddenly emerged as the major financier of infrastructure development in Africa? To explore these and other related questions, a 'flying-geese' stages model of infrastructure development can be introduced to provide an analytical framework for the issues of infrastructure provision and MNCs' involvement.

5.3. A STRUCTURAL STAGES MODEL OF INFRASTRUCTURE DEVELOPMENT

Given the fact that developing countries emulate the experiences of more advanced countries in catch-up growth, infrastructure development and MNCs' involvement can be similarly examined in terms of a reformulated flying-geese model – that is to say, changes in infrastructure development are evolutionary and stages-delineated, and MNCs play the role of knowledge transplanters to facilitate the structural transformation of developing countries. Infrastructure development necessarily accompanies the

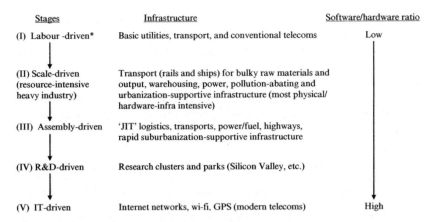

Stages	Infrastructure	Software/hardware ratio
(I) Labour -driven*	Basic utilities, transport, and conventional telecoms	Low
(II) Scale-driven (resource-intensive heavy industry)	Transport (rails and ships) for bulky raw materials and output, warehousing, power, pollution-abating and urbanization-supportive infrastructure (most physical/ hardware-infra intensive)	
(III) Assembly-driven	'JIT' logistics, transports, power/fuel, highways, rapid suburbanization-supportive infrastructure	
(IV) R&D-driven	Research clusters and parks (Silicon Valley, etc.)	
(V) IT-driven	Internet networks, wi-fi, GPS (modern telecoms)	High

Note: *At Stage-I, resource-rich developing countries normally pursue 'resource-driven' (in lieu of labor-driven) growth, exporting primary goods such as petroleum, natural gas, minerals, timber, and agricultural goods. Stage-II countries (as is currently the case with China and India) eagerly seek resources overseas, thereby creating strong demand and driving up the price of resources. This promotes growth in resource-rich countries. The infrastructure required are basic utilities (including desalination in the Middle East), transport, pipelines, ports, and LNG stations.

Figure 5.1   Stages of growth and infrastructure development

progression of industrial upgrading as technological innovations spawn new leading sectors. This is summarized in Figure 5.1.

Historically speaking, the labor-driven stage (initiated by the Industrial Revolution in England) *once* required only basic infrastructure provision such as water, sanitation, basic transport (roads and canals), and power (at first only animal power and wind/water mills but steam engines soon afterwards). Farm labor was mobilized as industrial labor in the factory system such as textile factories and foundries (as a result of the 'foreclosure' movement that turned peasants into low-wage laborers). In those days any economy was largely production-oriented with an extremely skewed income distribution (without a dominant middle class). The labor-driven stage was thus the very first stage of industrialization, as discussed in Chapter 3. The infrastructure associated with this stage was largely designed to support production and meant only tangentially for consumptive purposes. And in modern times this stage has come to be replicated repeatedly in labor-abundant developing countries, particularly after World War II – albeit with newer types of infrastructure.

It was at the next stage of heavy and chemical industrialization that more modern physical infrastructures, notably power (coal-powered and hydro-electric), transportation (rails and sea), and conventional telecoms, came to play a pivotal role in supporting the resource-processing operations of heavy industry and the shipping of raw materials and bulky outputs. Paradoxically, resource-poor countries (notably England) were among the very first to undergo this second stage (Stage II) of growth, importing raw materials and exporting heavy industry goods – and to actively make investments in resources-extractive and market-exploiting infrastructure in their colonies (for example, power, rails, shipping, and dock facilities). Soon afterwards, other newly emerged imperial powers followed suit:

> For both economic and political reasons, British, French, Belgian and Dutch manufacturers preferred to source their raw materials from their colonial territories. American firms favoured Canada, Mexico and Chile for minerals and agricultural products (Lewis, 1938), while Japanese firms owned valuable iron ore deposits and coal mines in China. On several occasions, particularly in colonial territories, [MNCs] themselves built roads, railroads, docks and warehouses facilities, and supplied the necessary housing and educational facilities for their workers. (Dunning, 1993, p. 110)

As noted earlier, this intensively resource-based stage has recently been repeated in successfully catching-up countries (such as postwar Japan, the NIEs, and now China and India) with high growth rates (8 to 12 percent per year). High growth is the hallmark of Stage II, leading to rapid *urbanization*, thereby requiring more *urban infrastructure* (such as urban transport, electricity, and sewerage). Present-day Stage-II countries, like their European counterparts in the past, act strategically in order to secure resources overseas by investing in project-specific infrastructure (and also in 'goodwill-diplomacy' projects) in resource-rich developing regions. Therefore, they are the eager developers of infrastructure in resource-exporting regions like the Middle East, Latin America, and Africa, as the latter themselves in turn enjoy an opportunity for resource-driven growth. (This stage-specific development will be investigated in detail below in terms of a comparative analysis of Japan's and China's resource-seeking efforts.) Heavy and chemical industrialization also causes environmental and ecological problems (pollution in air, water, and soil) that require infrastructure for environmental clean-up and betterment. Environmental consciousness, which was practically non-existent in the early days of industrialization during the 19th century and the early 20th century, has lately been elevated to the global level. The Kyoto Protocol is one indication of the new consciousness.

The arrival of the stage of assembly-based manufacturing (as best exemplified by automobiles) revolutionalized land transportation. Highways, along with bridges and tunnels, began to be used not only for commerce (material transport and goods distribution) but also for more consumption

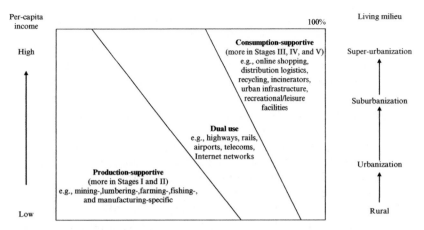

Figure 5.2   Infrastructure for production vs. consumption purposes (shares, %)

(personal use). It was at this juncture on the path to growth that production (supply) became *consumer-focused more strongly than ever before*, since the growth of an economy had reached the stage of 'high mass-consumption' (Rostow, 1960). Model-T cars and Fordism-cum-Taylorism symbolized the beginning of this new era. Motorization led to a brand-new culture of car-based lifestyle and consumption, as seen in the births of gas/service stations, motels, drive-in theaters, drive-in fast-food restaurants, shopping malls with huge parking lots, and drive-in banks – first in the United States but soon spreading to other countries. And all these infrastructure facilities for consumers were normally provided as *private goods.* The phenomenon that more infrastructure for consumptive purposes comes into existence *pari passu* with economic growth is schematically illustrated in Figure 5.2. Some types of infrastructure are obviously of *dual* use, namely for both production and consumption. Rising per-capita incomes require more and more consumption-supportive infrastructures.

Just as America's mass production replaced Europe-originated craft production, the post-World War II innovation of 'lean or flexible production' (originating as the Toyota production system) drastically altered auto-assembly operations and other assembly-based manufacturing activities, especially through the adoption of the 'just-in-time' delivery method for parts, components, and accessories on the factory floor. What matters most in lean production is the *logistics* of procuring these upstream inputs from the suppliers. And 'just-in-time' logistics became a critical form of soft infrastructure for transport and distribution (as opposed to hard infrastructure such as rail, highways, and warehouses).[3]

Meanwhile, ever-rising consumerism spurred R&D activities, first in the United States and then in other advanced countries, in an intensive search for new products for consumers. This was an early post-World War II peacetime phenomenon, since pent-up consumer demand existed. As a consequence, R&D-driven, high-tech 'Schumpeterian' industries came to represent Stage-IV growth, innovating in rapid succession a myriad of knowledge-based consumer goods, as discussed in Chapter 3. It became imperative for science-based industries to set up corporate R&D centers. Consequently, the importance of 'high-tech industrial districts, à la Marshall', as typified by the success of Silicon Valley, was recognized as a new type of industrial infrastructure, and many local governments began to promote the development of high-tech parks.

This stage of knowledge-based economic growth in the advanced world once coincided with the development of air transport infrastructure (commercial airlines and consumer-oriented airports) and the containerization of cargo shipping with all its accompanying infrastructure provision (for example, ports with container loading and unloading facilities). What is more, since R&D-based knowledge creation is the linchpin of this growth phase, protection of intellectual property rights is all the more required, and the institution of a legal system serves as intangible (soft) infrastructure.

The latest stage of growth was ushered in by the IT revolution with the introduction of the Internet, the World Wide Web (www), and multi-functional cellular phones. Accordingly, new types of infrastructure came into existence. At the basic level, cellular phones require transmission towers (the backbone of every cellular network) and their accompanying power source. For high-speed Internet services a WiMax network that uses wireless broadband technology is the latest rage. Its most advanced use has been reportedly in Japan (by KDDI) and Korea (by Korea Telecom). But India's Tata Communications is about to set up the world's largest commercial network for services in 115 cities nationwide, and America's Sprint is scheduled to offer a WiMax network in Washington in 2008, and in other cities the following year.[4] It is now clearly recognized that in order for any modern economy to compete in this information-intensive century it needs to adapt to the growing needs of the digital age by investing in IT infrastructure. In this regard, the Geneva-based World Economic Forum (WEF) keeps track of the 'e-readiness' of countries around the world in its annual publication of the *Global Information Technology Report*. E-readiness means how well a country is equipped with IT infrastructure, which also includes IT-related higher education.

In the wake of continuous and fast technological advances that enable the use of the Internet for phone calls and online videos, interestingly enough, it is said that its infrastructure may already be fast obsolescing. Internet pioneers, such as Larry Roberts and Len Bosack, themselves are reportedly striving to redo the same technology, as they believe it is far behind the times – and are striving to innovate *new routers* to carry the ever-heavier traffic.[5] The infrastructure for the Internet age involves high technology, which is private industrial property. Google's competitive advantage lies in how computers are arranged to form a unique network, that is, Google's own firm-specific infrastructure – rather than the algorithms behind its search tools.[6] Understandably, therefore, Google keeps secret the number of computers deployed in its vast clusters.

Because of the technology-intensive nature of the Internet-driven phase of growth, its infrastructure is provided by technology-owning corporations – usually, if not totally, then at least jointly in developing countries that often treat telecoms as a strategic industry. The transfer of knowledge, especially when it comes to private property, involves high market transaction costs. Hence it is normally implemented internally (via intra-firm transactions) instead of externally (via market transactions).

In sum, different new types of infrastructure have emerged *pari passu* with economic growth and structural transformation, each type compatible and consistent with the needs of each growth stage. These stage-specific infrastructure facilities and services have increasingly become more sophisticated in technological and organizational characteristics and proportionately more software-intensive and more firm-specific in management and operation (that is to say, economic growth has became increasingly dependent on 'soft infrastructure', as reflected in the rising ratio of software to hardware infrastructure in Figure 5.2). At the same time, as might easily be expected, the infrastructure that supports consumption has gained in importance relative to that devoted solely to production. The sequential phenomenon of urbanization→suburbanization→ super-urbanization (inclusive of re-urbanization in the core cities) has also been concurrent with economic growth (Figure 5.2).

5.3.1. Recapitulation

As seen above, the structural stages model of infrastructure development is useful in understanding the stages-specific needs of infrastructure and how fast-growing Stage-II countries are engaged in infrastructure building, both at home and abroad. More specifically, it helps us understand

(i)   why the shares of different types of infrastructure change *pari passu* with economic growth;

(ii)   that when the advanced West early on underwent Stage-II growth, it pursued colonialism in search of resources and markets, resulting in the first wave of infrastructure development abroad;

(iii)   ● that prewar Japan (which succeeded in heavy and chemical industrialization with an eye to bolstering its military strength) followed suit in Manchuria, Korea, and Taiwan;

        ● that when Japan repeated Stage-II growth by rebuilding and modernizing heavy and chemical industries in the 1960s and the 1970s, Japan's MNCs again had to strenuously seek overseas resources (such as oil in the Middle East, copper in Latin America, and iron ore and coal in Australia by offering resource-extractive infrastructure);

(iv)   why China, which is in the midst of Stage-II growth – and India, too, though in a somewhat delayed fashion – is currently active in the quest for oil, natural gas, and minerals abroad by similarly developing infrastructure in the host countries; and

(v)   that resource-exporting (Stage-I) countries in the Middle East, Africa, and elsewhere are, in turn, presently benefiting from the rise of Stage-II countries, especially China and India, attracting MNCs' involvement in infrastructure projects, notably in telecoms, transport (sea, land, and air), and urban infrastructure.

5.4.   STAGE-II QUEST FOR OVERSEAS RESOURCES: JAPAN VS. CHINA

As seen above, Stage-II growth is most intensive in the use of raw materials and energy and strategically engages in the development of overseas resources and related infrastructure. As emphasized above, any economy, but especially those that are resource-indigent, which goes through this stage struggles to secure stable supplies of resources abroad.

At present, China is most conspicuously active in its efforts to obtain overseas resources and its voracious appetite is driving up the price of commodities in world markets – from copper and steel to petroleum to natural gas. The recent swift rise of China's middle class is also contributing to global price hikes in corn and other kinds of grain as its consumption of meat and other high-income-elastic foods increases. China's resource-seeking efforts in Africa, Latin America, and the Middle East are now often the target of criticism from advanced countries, notably the United States and the EU. Though perhaps not widely known, China closely studied the postwar Japanese experience of Stage-II resource procurement during the 1960s and the 1970s.

In fact, Japan's search for raw materials and energy abroad once caused political tensions with the West (though the world seems either to have a very short memory about this or is too overwhelmed by China's voracious appetite for natural resources to recall it at the moment). In those days Japan was compared to the United States as a resource-hungry giant in a well-known study, *Two Hungry Giants: The United States and Japan in the Quest for Oil and Ores* (Vernon, 1983). Japan was then an unwelcome upstart that had suddenly emerged as a rival to the West in the global commodities markets, just as China has only recently entered this phase. Japan once actively offered aid to resource-rich developing countries to build infrastructure facilities such as multipurpose dams, irrigation and flood controls, power plants, railways, roads, airports, sea ports, telecommunications, and the like – exactly what China is currently doing.

5.4.1.   Japan's Resource Diplomacy during its High-growth Period

Stage-II growth made the Japanese economy become very much dependent on overseas resources. In the late 1960s Japan ranked second only behind the United States in the consumption of such basic industrial resources as petroleum, copper, zinc, aluminum, nickel, and crude steel. From 1964 to 1968, for example, Japan's demand for petroleum expanded at an average annual rate of 17.6 percent, more than twice the growth rate of the non-communist countries taken as a whole; for copper at 11.7 percent, more than seven times as much, and for zinc at 8.0 percent, four times as much – and for aluminum, 21.0 percent; for nickel 25.2 percent, and for crude steel, 20.0 percent, each far exceeding the average rate of the Free World countries at that time.[7]

Interestingly enough, furthermore, most of these growth rates were overall much greater than that of Japan's GNP (10.6 percent per annum over the same period). This circumstance reflected a rapid shift in Japan's industrial structure away from light manufacturing (Stage I) to heavy and chemical industries, sectors that are both more resource-intensive and more energy-consuming (Stage II). The upshot was again reflected in the fact that among OECD member countries Japan's share of trade in iron ore climbed from 23.7 percent in 1964 to 39.3 percent in 1969; in coking coal from 15.8 percent to 41.6 percent; in timber from 15.4 percent to 29.9 percent; in copper from 9.5 percent to 19.1 percent; and in crude oil from 12.6 percent to 15.6 percent.[8] (Ozawa, 1979).

Conversely, Japan's increased reliance on overseas supplies had resulted in an equal or even greater dependence upon the Japanese market by some of the major resource-exporting countries, making economic dependence a two-way problem of interdependence. In 1971, for example, practically all of Malaysia's and 96.3 percent of Indonesia's exports of bauxite went to Japan. In the same year, Australia sent 84.6 percent of its iron ore exports to Japan and India 96.3 percent. Canada sold 93.5 percent of its exports of copper ore to Japan, the Philippines 92.7 percent.[9]

The sharp increases in crude oil prices announced by OPEC in 1974 and 1979 heightened Japan's sense of insecurity and vulnerability to any disruption in resource inflows to its industry. Japan's search for stable supplies of resources was, of course, nothing new: Japan, being indigent of natural resources, had been striving to secure them from abroad ever since the start of the modernization of its economy in 1868. Japan's imperial aggression into Manchuria, for instance, mirrored its dire need for raw materials in the prewar period. Yet, Japan's successful Stage-II development of heavy and chemical industries in the 1960s and the 1970s exhibited a renewed national sense of urgency, calling for new resource diplomacy.

And there clearly developed a strengthened triumvirate connection between Japan's economic aid to industrialization in resource-exporting developing countries, the assured supplies of resources to itself secured in exchange for such aid, and the simultaneous use of assistance as an internal aid to the overseas investment activities of Japanese industry in large-scale resource development ventures abroad. These activities were usually carried out through the formation of consortia or group investments involving a large number of Japanese firms as joint ventures. Once an overseas venture had been designated as a 'national project', government aid took the form of participation by the Overseas Economic Cooperation Fund (OECF), Japan's official aid agency, as the major stockholder of a semi-public investment company set up by the consortium involved in such a project.

The Japanese government also provided low-interest concessionary loans both to the Japanese partner and to the host government from the Export-Import (Ex-Im) Bank of Japan, loans often used as equity capital by both parties. In addition, another aid agency, the Japanese International Cooperation Agency (JICA) gave support to infrastructure development, in the form of both hardware (such as port facilities) and software (via technical and managerial training).

This new form of economic assistance – simultaneous aid to both the host country and corporate Japan – evolved into, and came to be established as, 'the Asahan formula', a formula originally worked out in connection with a regional development project in Indonesia. It took the characteristic of being a national project entailing a political commitment by the Japanese government, and set a precedent for Japan's resource-related ventures in other developing countries (Ozawa, 1979, 1980).

5.4.1.1. The Asahan formula

The Asahan project involved the construction of a large dam, a hydroelectric power station on the Asahan River and an aluminum refinery that would use the power generated and related infrastructural facilities in Sumatra, Indonesia. The Indonesian government first brought the idea to the attention of Sumitomo Chemical, which organized a feasibility study team in August 1970 – in collaboration with two other Japanese smelters, Nippon Light Metal and Showa Denko. Soon afterwards, the group was expanded to include Mitsubishi Chemical Industries and Mitsui Aluminum, thus becoming a collaborative venture among Japan's top industrial groups.[10]

The Asahan project was the first and most significant 'show case' venture of Japan's postwar resource diplomacy undertaken by its government and industry in close collaboration with the host government. Even before the final agreement was signed between the two countries in July 1975, the project had long been publicized in Indonesia as 'the TVA [Tennessee Valley Authority] of the Suharto Government'. Several big Western aluminum companies that had initially participated in international bidding withdrew when they learned of the desire of the Indonesian government to seek a comprehensive project that included a power station, an aluminum refinery, and all the related infrastructure facilities (seaport and land transportation) in a regional development plan. For a while, the project seemed likely to become a joint venture with the Aluminum Company of America (Alcoa) and Kaiser Aluminum & Chemical, as they both expressed interest in joining the project. However, those American companies, too, decided in the end to withdraw as the estimated project costs doubled quickly from the initial $400 million to $800 million (and later even more), and as world demand for aluminum precipitously declined in 1974. From then onwards it became a mammoth project that Japanese industry was left to undertake alone.

The five Japanese companies comprising the initial consortium subsequently enlisted the participation of their respective *keiretsu*-affiliated trading companies as co-investors, joint-project coordinators, and trade intermediaries: Sumitomo Corporation joined with Sumitomo Chemical; Marubeni Corporation with Showa Denko; Mitsubishi Corporation with Mitsubishi Chemical; Mitsui & Co. with Mitsui Aluminum; and three other trading companies, C. Itoh & Co., Nichimen Co., and Nissho Iwai Co., with Nippon Light Metal. And this new 12-company consortium sought long-term, low-interest funds from the government-affiliated financial institutions.

The refinery was initially 90 percent-owned by Japanese interests, but in 1980, 25 percent of ownership was transferred to the Indonesian government. The hydroelectric power station, with a capacity of 510,000 kilowatts, was to be turned over to the Indonesian government after 30 years of operation. The latter was thus a long-term version of BOT.

Capital investment on the Japanese side was fully backed with credit from both official and private sources. Official sources covered approximately 70 percent of the total cost of the project – funding for the power station came from the OECF; for the aluminum refinery from the Ex-Im Bank of Japan; and for port facilities, service roads, and other infrastructure from the JICA. The balance consisted of loans from Japanese commercial banks. The 12 participating Japanese enterprises formed an investment company, Nippon Asahan Aluminum Co., in which the Japanese government became the major shareholder (50 percent), through stock ownership by its agency, OECF. A comprehensive training program for the Indonesians to operate the power plant and smelter was also arranged at both the project site and Japanese aluminum plants. In the end, rising labor and material costs turned the venture into a more than $2 billion investment.

In the 1970s, Indonesia was the second largest supplier of petroleum to Japan; the first having been Saudi Arabia. Japan's economic cooperation in the Asahan project was clearly based on the significance of the host country in that capacity. The project also created a favorable environment in which all other Japanese investments in practically all areas were welcomed by Indonesia. No wonder, then, that Japan's FDI, which had lagged behind that of the United States in both Indonesia's manufacturing and extractive industries until 1973, expanded with astonishing swiftness and captured the lion's share of FDI in the host country.

5.4.1.2.   Other Asahan-formula ventures

The Amazon project in Brazil, another large Japanese investment in aluminum, was actually modeled on the Asahan project. It was also a regional economic development project pursued between Brazil and Japan, involving an aluminum project in the Amazon basin.[11] It called for the construction of a dam, a hydropower plant, and a smeltery with an annual production capacity ultimately reaching 340,000 tons. Forty-nine percent of the ownership was taken up by the Japanese side and the rest by Brazil's state-owned mining company, Companhia Vale do Rio Doce (CVRD) (Ozawa et al., 1976). The Japanese group, consisting initially of five major smelters, expanded into another semi-governmental investing company, Nippon Amazon Aluminum Co., with as many as 32 private enterprises as co-investors and capital participation by the OECD as the major stock-holder. Although the Japanese corporations were the actual participants who implemented the plan, negotiations basically were carried out between the two governments.

When the recession that followed the first oil crisis of 1973 delayed Japan in making a firm commitment, Brazil approached European nations and succeeded in securing a promise from France for an extension of a loan to be used for the hydropower plant. Fearful of losing out to its European competitors, Japan's government and industry conferred together to make all the necessary arrangements for a final commitment. Japan's Minister of International Trade and Industry, Komoto, was dispatched to Brazil in July 1976 to work out details with the Brazilian government. And corporate Japan as represented by *Keidanren* (the Federation of Economic Organizations) announced its all-out support for the project (then estimated to cost at least $1 billion), urging the Japanese government to provide ample financial assistance. The final contract was then signed by the two countries on the occasion of Brazilian President Geisel's visit to Tokyo in September 1976. The Japanese government gave the project a $490 million loan from the OECF and a $140 million from the Ex-Im Bank of Japan.[12]

Subsequent to the Amazon project, the Asahan formula was again applied to a petrochemical venture in Singapore in the late 1970s. The project, initially conceived by Sumitomo Chemical, involved an $800 million petrochemical complex on a small island off Singapore. The core plant was to use locally refined oil to initially produce 300,000 metric tons per year of ethylene, which were expected to spawn downstream production of plastics and other chemical-based products.

Keen on the petrochemical project as it symbolized a more advanced stage of economic development, the Singapore government, working closely with Sumitomo Chemical, maneuvered to secure funds from the Japanese government. From the start, Sumitomo's plan needed cooperation from other Japanese firms as well as from the Japanese government. Both Sumitomo and the host government publicized it as the most significant development project for Singapore. The host country, though a resource-poor city-state, is situated on the Malacca Strait, the critical sea-lane through which pass the tankers transporting the vital supply of oil needed to keep Japan's industrial wheels rolling. A stable and friendly Singapore was a logistic necessity for Japan's resource diplomacy.

Whenever Prime Minister Lee had an opportunity to talk with Japanese political leaders either in Singapore or in Tokyo, he never failed to seek a commitment from the Japanese government to the project. In the meantime, Sumitomo Chemical recruited other large Japanese companies, including Mitsubishi Petrochemical, Showa Denko, Idemitsu Petrochemical, Mitsui Toatsu Chemicals, Mitsui Petrochemicals, and Asahi Chemical Industry. Thus, again, all major industrial groups came to be represented in the consortium. Because of concerted pressure exerted by these powerful industrial groups and the Singapore government, the Japanese government finally moved in May 1977 to support the project with funds from the OECF and the Ex-Im Bank of Japan. Later on, the Japanese consortium further expanded to become a group of 23 companies, forming the Japan-Singapore Petrochemicals Company. Again, the OECF became its major shareholder, acquiring 30 percent of the initial capital investment.[13] Basic civil engineering work to make the island suitable for a petrochemical complex was first carried out and then completion of the petrochemical plant followed in 1982.

About the same time as the Singapore project was given financial support by the Japanese government, another huge petrochemical project planned by the Mitsubishi group in Saudi Arabia similarly secured Japan's official commitment. The plan called for the construction of a petrochemical complex, including an ethylene plant with an annual capacity of 341,000 tons, at Al Jubaylah in northern Saudi Arabia. In 1976 the Mitsubishi group decided to suspend its plan for three years because of the poor prospects for marketing ethylene. However, for fear of losing Saudi Arabia's confidence in Japan's economic and technical cooperation, the Japanese government stepped in and made a commitment in 1977 to help the Mitsubishi group finance the project with funds from the OECF and the Ex-Im Bank of Japan. The project, thus adopting the Asahan formula, was considered to be a key element in Japan's extension of economic cooperation to Saudi Arabia. As many as 54 Japanese companies joined together to form an investment company, Saudi Petrochemicals Development Co. This Japanese company – again, with the OECF as its major shareholder – and the host country's Saudi Arabian Basic Industries Corporation agreed to share equally the project's total cost of about $1.25 billion.[14]

Similarly, with an eye to securing Mexico's oil, Japanese industry proposed to construct harbor facilities and an oil pipeline in Salina Cruz on the Pacific coast, a project reportedly welcomed by Pemex, Mexico's state-owned oil corporation. The plan was formally made official on the occasion of a visit to Mexico by the president of the Industrial Bank of Japan in October, 1978. It was developed into a more specific form of economic cooperation with the visit to Mexico of an economic mission headed by Toshio Doko, president of *Keidanren*, as well as with the visit to Japan of Mexico's President Jose Lopez Portillo soon afterwards. The Industrial Bank of Japan was soon joined by two big trading companies, Mitsubishi Corporation and Mitsui & Co. in 'laying down the foundation for concrete talks with Mexican authorities'.[15] The rest followed along the familiar lines of Japan's other resource projects.

5.4.1.3. Local development of 'infrastructure inputs'
Japan's economic cooperation was also extended to help the host countries develop what may be called 'infrastructure-inputs' industries such as cement, steel, trucks, and the like, which would be used to produce the necessary

Table 5.1   Japan's projects in return for oil and natural gas in the Middle East shortly after the first oil crisis of 1973

Host countries	Projects
Abu Dhabi	An LNG station and a cement plant
Algeria	2 cement plants, an oil refinery, an ethylene plant, and telecoms
Iran	3 cement plants and a steel-sheet plant
Iraq	3 fertilizer plants, an LNG plant, and an oil refinery
Kuwait	2 desalination plants and a power plant
Saudi Arabia	2 oil refineries, 2 cement plants, and a steel-pipe plant
Syria	An oil refinery
Qatar	A steel plant
Egypt	A steel plant

Note: In addition, economic development advice was offered to Algeria, and agricultural development planning to Saudi Arabia. Projects were mostly joint ventures but infrastructures (e.g., power plants and desalination plants) were BOTs.

Sources: Ozawa (1974b); information gathered from newspaper articles and government reports.

inputs/materials in the construction of infrastructure facilities including highways and bridges, pipelines, ports (sea and air), and warehouses.

As summarized in Table 5.1, Japan's MNCs were once actively engaged in building cement plants, steel mills, and steel-pipe plants in the Middle East – in addition to local infrastructures such as LNG (liquid natural gas) stations, telecoms, and desalination plants.

As vital partners for Japan's resource diplomacy, Japanese MNCs also turned their attention to resource-rich Latin America, notably Brazil, and invested in infrastructure-inputs industries for iron and steel, hydraulic turbines, electric generators, telecoms equipment, trucks, earthmoving equipment, and ships (Ozawa et al., 1976). Infrastructure development thus not only backs up industrial expansion and economic growth but also can provide backward linkages to stimulate upstream heavy industry in terms of input–output relations.

This approach has most recently been redeployed in 2007 when Japan offered economic cooperation to India to assist the latter's five-year plan to modernize power and transport infrastructure, especially the Delhi-Mumbai rail system. India's Stage-II rapid growth (around 9–10 percent) is outpacing infrastructure development, which is said to be set for up to 5–6 percent growth (Kumra, 2007). Kawasaki Heavy Industries will set up a joint venture with Indian Railways to produce 1,900 freight cars over the next 15 years. Mitsubishi Heavy Industries will invest in local production of boilers, while Toshiba Corporation will make generators and turbines in India. Komatsu is already locally producing hydraulic excavators and dump trucks to be used at coal mines, and also plans to produce construction equipment for infrastructure development.[16] All these outputs will be used as inputs for the construction and development of India's power supply and transport service.

5.4.1.4. Summary of the Japanese experience: problems of Stage-II growth
The above analysis of the Asahan formula as it emerged as a recognizable pattern of Japan's resource diplomacy during the 1970s is meant only to illustrate how resource-indigent Japan once endeavored to secure natural resources at the height of its Stage-II growth, at which time heavy and chemical industries became the leading sector of the Japanese economy, thereby intensifying the use of minerals, petroleum, and natural gas. In 1970, for example, the resource requirements of Japan's industrial structure were once the world's highest, despite the fact that Japan is one of the most resource-poor countries. Yet compared with the United States and Germany (West), Japan, exhibited the *highest* concentration of industry in the sectors consuming the most resources and the lowest concentration in the sectors consuming the least resources (Ozawa, 1979), a clear sign of its Stage-II growth. Small wonder, then, that Japan was compelled so aggressively to secure resources overseas.

Although Japan's economic cooperation was welcomed by resource-rich developing countries, its resources requirements also had to be additionally satisfied by stepped-up resources imports from advanced countries with rich natural endowments such as Canada and Australia. These advanced countries, however, felt uncomfortable watching their trade relations with Japan evolve into the old colonial pattern – exporting natural resources and importing manufactures. This feeling was clearly expressed by a high-ranking Canadian official during the Trudeau administration:

> It is not much of an exaggeration to say that Japanese governments have looked upon Canada in recent years as a large open-pit mine; as an endless and reliable source of raw materials to satisfy the Japanese industrial appetite . . . it will be necessary for Japan to recognize the quality and the competence of Canada in a variety of economic and non-economic fields; to do more than, as is now the case, regard Canada primarily as an object of its 'Resource Diplomacy'.[17]

A similar resentment was also felt in Australia and the United States, which developed a trade pattern of importing manufactured goods such as automobiles and electronics, while selling primary goods for a large part of their exports.

In the meantime, however, Japan, as the world's resource-processing workshop importing raw materials and then exporting finished products – and as a geographically small archipelago country – was quickly coming up against the environmental limits of concentrating on pollution-prone heavy and chemical industries at home. Indeed, the environmental decays in Japan had already reached intolerable levels by the early 1970s, and its quest for overseas resources brought about tensions with the advanced West, whose oil majors and other resource-extractive companies were then controlling and governing the world markets for those commodities.

With the above developments as a backdrop, the Japanese government adopted an epoch-making policy to restructure Japan's industry, a proposal made by the Industrial Structure Council, the MITI's consultative organ. The policy emphasized a shift from 'pollution-prone' and 'resource-consuming' heavy and chemical industries towards 'clean', 'knowledge-intensive', and 'consumer-oriented' industries, and assigned overseas investment a new role – that of catalyst to 'house-clean' the economy by way of transplanting resource-processing activities where resources are located (as exemplified by FDI in aluminum smelting). The Japanese popularly described this shift as a move away from '*ju-ko-cho-dai* [heavy-thick-long-big]' goods such as steel, ships, and heavy machinery (Stage-II goods) and a push for '*kei-haku-tan-sho* [light-thin-short-small]' goods, as best represented by Japan's fuel-efficient subcompact cars (Stage-III goods) and miniaturized consumer electronics such as transistor radios, portable TV sets, and transistorized CVRs (Stage-IV goods).

As Japan's industrial structure was successfully upgraded to climb the ladder of economic development, as predicted by the FG paradigm, its resource requirements began to mitigate relative to its ever-rising GDP levels, if not in absolute terms. In fact, Japan soon transformed itself into one of the most efficient users of energy. Its energy and resource-saving innovations, too, helped accelerate this development. Japan's dependence on overseas resources, therefore, accordingly declined relative to its GNP. As illustrated in Figure 5.3, when viewed from a resource-exporting country's standpoint (such as Australia), Japan's share as a resource export market began to decline considerably (as its per-capita GDP rose), while other catching-up countries quickly replaced Japan as they entered Stage-II growth. This vicissitudinous pattern is appropriately called the 'boomerang' effect. But it also represents a flying-geese pattern of tandem growth among the Asian countries: Japan was followed closely by Taiwan and Korea (NIEs, while Hong Kong and Singapore mostly skipped Stage II), and then by the ASEAN-4. China and India are now about to tread the same path. All this is just meant to illustrate that a country's excessive resource dependency (relative to GDP) is a *transitory* stage-specific

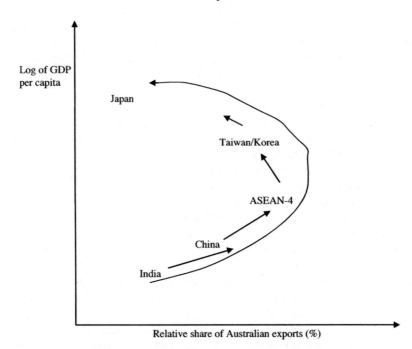

Source: Adapted as stylized flows from Chart 5 (a data-based figure) in 'A Survey of
Australia', *Economist*, May 7, 2005, p. 10.

Figure 5.3   'Boomerang' – demand for Australian resource exports

phenomenon, which eventually moderates at higher mature stages of
growth.

In short, the resource diplomacy pursued by Japan during the height of
Stage-II growth can be summarized as follows:

(i)   Close collaborative efforts between industry and the home govern-
       ment, though usually initiated by the private sector, in search of stable
       supplies of overseas resources.
(ii)   Such joint efforts were crafted as goodwill diplomacy in the form of
       economic cooperation to assist *regional* economic development in
       partnership with the host government, and its implicit selling point was
       that Japan was in an ideal position to offer advice on industrialization
       since it had only lately succeeded in miraculous catch-up growth (that
       is, the 'Japanese model'). And Japan's assistance in infrastructure
       development ranged from dams, power plants, railways, highways,
       and roads to airports, seaports, telecommunications, and others.[18]

(iii) The Ex-Im Bank of Japan played the role of major financier, along with other foreign aid agencies, OECF and JICA. The Ex-Im Bank provided finance for the machinery exports that were needed for a project and extended long-term concessionary loans to the host government, while OECF became the major shareholder of a Japanese investment company (consisting of a consortium of Japanese firms) specifically set up for the overseas project involved. JICA gave technical and managerial training to the local partners and provided assistance and funding for the development of project-specific infrastructures. The participating Japanese corporations were able to secure funding from their *keiretsu*-affiliated banks, whose liquidity was in turn augmented by the Bank of Japan, which was under the purview of the Finance Ministry in those days.

(iv) Japan's economic cooperation focused not only on infrastructure per se but also on developing 'infrastructure inputs' industries such as cement, steel, rolling stocks, machinery, and others that could contribute directly to the construction of infrastructural facilities and that would also serve as the providers of capital goods for the host economies.

(v) Japan's resource diplomacy was also supported by its effort to reduce excess foreign exchange reserves (that is, to recycle trade surpluses by investing overseas) so as to ease upward pressure on the yen – that is, exchange rate management. When Japan was in the midst of Stage-II growth during the 1970s, it was enjoying ever-growing trade surpluses and hence rising foreign exchange (mostly US dollar) reserves. Japan tried to avoid any abrupt rise in the value of the yen after the collapse of the IMF system in the early 1970s, and encouraged overseas investment as part of the 'yen defense' program.

5.4.2.   China's Quest for Overseas Resources

Now that China is in the midst of Stage-II expansion, its growth is registering inflection-point rates hovering around 10 to 12 percent a year, and its efforts to acquire resources overseas are exhibiting many similar characteristics to Japan's. At this point in time, China still has one leg in (though it is about to graduate from) Stage-I labor-driven manufacturing, but also has the other leg in Stage-II industries – and simultaneously its toes in all higher-stages industries with the assistance of foreign multinationals in its all-out efforts to catch up. Being highly export-oriented, China has been accumulating a huge amount of foreign-exchange reserves (about \$1.3 trillion by the end of 2007). Being desperately in need of raw materials and energy, therefore, China is thus in a fortunate position to exercise its enormous purchasing clout in procuring resources overseas.

Realizing that even resource-scarce Japan successfully rebuilt and modernized heavy and chemical industries in the postwar period, Chinese officials visited and studied Japan's approach to resources acquisition abroad. Hence, there are, as might be well expected, some *near-identical* parallels between the two countries' approaches; these include the offer of advice and aid for economic development in the host countries, with each using its own successful catch-up model as a key selling point, the role of each country's Ex-Im Bank as the major financier of resource-extractive projects, a collaborative endeavor between the state and the private sector, and the use of abundant foreign-exchange reserves as the source of funding overseas investments (and as a way of moderating upward pressures on their currencies) – and all this against the backdrop of some serious growth-induced environmental problems at home. As detailed below, nevertheless, China's approach is very different in its political aspects and impact from Japan's.

Over a short span of time China has already emerged, at amazing speed, as the world's largest producer of steel, cement, flat glass, and aluminum. In addition to a rapid buildup of heavy industry, the recent rise in China's standard of living means more Western lifestyles geared to high energy consumption. For example, the Chinese quickly abandoned bicycles and are eagerly buying automobiles. China is now the world's second largest producer of cars and trucks after the United States, surpassing Japan. Furthermore, all this is accompanied by headlong infrastructure development, whose facilities are highly intensive in the use of steel, cement, chemicals, and energy. These changes in industrial structure and lifestyle quickly translate to an explosive rise in demand for more raw materials and energy. What makes China's need for resources even more urgent, moreover, is that its heavy industry plants, shopping malls, and residential houses do not operate as efficiently, or control pollution as effectively, as their counterparts in the advanced world. The *New York Times* (Kahn and Yardley, 2007), for example, reports, citing the World Bank as a source of statistics:

> Chinese steel makers, on average, use one-fifth more energy per ton than the international average. Cement manufacturers need 45 percent more power, and ethylene producers need 70 percent more than producers elsewhere . . . Each year for the past few years, [moreover,] China has built about 7.5 million square feet of commercial and residential space, more than the combined floor space of all the malls and strip malls in the United States . . . Chinese buildings rarely have thermal insulation. They require, on average, twice as much energy to heat and cool as *those in similar climates in the United States and Europe* . . . A vast majority of new buildings – 95 percent, the bank says – do not meet China's own codes for energy efficiency. (p. 8, original emphasis)

These inefficient uses of energy surely leave a lot of scope for conservation that allows for reducing energy requirements – and simultaneously alleviating the environmental problems.

Be that as it may, it should be kept in mind that China's current aggressive search for minerals, petroleum, natural gas, and other commodities is *nothing but a replay* of what the advanced West was once engaged in and what Japan likewise more recently exhibited in its resource diplomacy, though their modus operandi are expectedly quite different. Interestingly enough, as Japan risked criticism of its neocolonial trade pattern, China is now similarly criticized for reviving a colonial relationship in Africa, as seen below.

5.4.2.1. No-strings-attached

The most controversial feature of China's scramble for resources abroad is that it eagerly extends favor-currying goodwill diplomacy in the form of economic cooperation to local regimes whether or not they are dictatorial, authoritarian, and/or corrupt. This 'no-strings-attached' approach is understandably welcomed by the local regimes in Africa, Latin America, and elsewhere in the Third World. In contrast, the United States and Europe – and the international organizations such as the World Bank – tie loans and aid to the sensitive issues of human rights, democracy, and governance. However, China separates business from politics abroad, as it does at home. After all, capitalism, pragmatically permitted and tolerated at home since the 1978 open-door policy, merely serves as a means of bolstering national wealth and power under communism. This unique 'Chinese model' of catch-up is marketed in combination with commerce and aid – all in return for resources. The model shows that *market capitalism can be made compatible with any non-democratic political regimes (including authoritarianism) in the developing world*. This is the *core* of China's pragmatic state (communism)-led capitalism or hybrid economy.

In addition, China has remarkably succeeded in reducing poverty to a significant extent (more than 100 million people lifted out of absolute poverty), a valuable experience that led China in 2005 to set up a development center, the International Poverty Reduction Center, in China with the support of the United Nations and World Bank. The Center trains about 300 anti-poverty officials, mostly from Africa.[19]

In comparison, Western aid to developing countries is centered on *intangible* general public areas such as education and health (notably combating malaria and AIDS). China's aid, on the other hand, is focused on *tangible* bricks-and-mortar infrastructure such as dams, power plants, railroads, highways, port facilities, succor stadiums, technical institutes, farming parks – and even presidential palaces and satellite launching.

At present China's no-strings-attached partnership is most extensively and intensively offered to Africa where China early on established ideological solidarity against Western colonialism during the Cold War, carving out its sphere of influence. Maoists used to give hospitals, football stadiums, and railways to win Africa's hearts. Now China just likes to win African resources by building on its past partnership. China's recent stepped-up involvement in Sudan, a civil war-torn country with the humanitarian catastrophe in Darfur, is a prime example:

> China is Sudan's biggest investor and buys two-thirds of its oil. During his visit there [in early 2007], Hu [Jintao] offered a $12.9 million interest-free loan to build a presidential palace for Sudan, wrote off $70 million in debts to China, reduced import tariffs on Sudanese goods, and offered a $77.4 million loan for infrastructure and a grant of $40 million.[20]

Similarly, other telling examples are China's cooperation programs with Angola and Nigeria:

> Across Angola, Chinese workers are busy rebuilding roads, railways and technical institutes. The work is financed by a US$2 billion low-interest loan from China Ex-Im Bank. One of the key Chinese-funded projects is the reconstruction of the 1,300-kilometre railway from the west coast city of Benguela to Angola's eastern border with the Democratic Republic of Congo.[21]

> [China is] helping Nigeria to launch a second satellite into space. Some officials, *disillusioned with the Western development model*, say that *China gives them hope that poor countries can find their own path to development*. (emphasis added)[22]

And in addition to China's big state-owned oil and mining companies, whose investments in Africa, the Middle East, Central Asia, and the Americas are sparking off political frictions with the US and Europe, its private businessmen are also joining the hunt for resources abroad by adopting a consortium approach:

> Private Chinese companies are looking to places such as Indonesia and Ecuador. In April [2007], 40 such companies traveled to Pakistan and signed deals to develop oil fields, refineries, pipelines and coal mines worth a total of more than 10 billion yuan ($1.28 billion) . . . The highest-profile member of that delegation was Gong Jialong, chairman of Great United Holding Co., a consortium of several dozen private Chinese companies involved in small-scale oil production and refining.[23]

In short, China's search for resources is focused on the developing world at the moment, often involving those countries that are shunned by or even sanctioned by the West for political reasons. To cite major examples, China is scrambling for oil in Africa (Angola, Somalia, Sudan, Zimbabwe, Ethiopia, Libya, Nigeria, and Gabon), the Middle East (Saudi Arabia and Iran), and Latin America (Venezuela); for copper and cobalt in the

Democratic Republic of Congo and Zambia; for uranium in Namibia; for bauxite in Guinea; for iron ore in South Africa and Brazil; for timber in Gabon, Cameroon, and Congo-Brazzaville.

5.4.2.2.   New colonialism?

China's enormous appetite for resources has significantly contributed to high commodity prices, which are no doubt benefiting resource-exporting Stage-I countries. This has been a boon to most of Africa in particular. Yet China's charm offensive is not always welcomed by ordinary African people, though it is surely appreciated by incumbent politicians and government officials. There is reportedly a spreading grass-roots backlash against Chinese investments, goods, and the settlers who create a Chinese diaspora. Sudan alone hosts more than 30,000 Chinese businessmen and construction workers who are catered for by their restaurants, supermarkets, and recreational facilities.[24] Chinese workers, rather than local workers, are mostly employed to construct infrastructure facilities. These situations often cause local frictions and backlash, and more are expected as China steps up its effort to lock in resources even in the remotest corners of Africa. 'A Chinese diaspora in Africa now numbers perhaps 80,000, including labourers and businessmen, who bring entrepreneurial wit and wisdom to places usually visited only by Land Cruisers from international aid agencies'.[25]

Resentment among the local populace is said to be the strongest in Zambia – mainly because of the tragic explosion of a Chinese-owned factory that produced explosives for the region's mining industry, killing 46 Zambian employees in April 2005, and the way the factory handled the post-accident situation.[26] And even when South African President Thabo Mbeki signed up to and launched the China–South Africa economic trade and cooperation, he warned that China might be risking 'to replicate in Africa a "colonial relationship" of the kind that existed under white rule'.[27]

A colonial pattern of trade is rather a natural outcome of China's resource offensive. Besides, China may be entrapping Africa in the familiar 'resource curse', including what may be called 'Chinese disease' to paraphrase the term 'Dutch disease', in which the bid-up price of commodities and the cheap price of manufactured imports from China crowd out investment for the local manufacturing sector and discourage labor-driven economic development. Resource extraction may also be carried out in environmentally incorrect ways. *The Economist* editorializes on these issues:

> China is doing its bit to improve infrastructure, building roads and railways. But it could do more to open up its own markets. China is quite open to yarn, but not jerseys; diamonds, but not jewellery. If it has as much 'solidarity' with

Africa as it claims, it could offer to lower tariffs on processed goods. Chinese firms have also ignored international initiatives to make project finance greener (the 'Equator Principles') and to make mining industries cleaner (the 'Extractive Industries Transparency Initiative'). Even with China's backing, these outside efforts might not succeed: honesty and greenery come from within. Without it, they will certainly fail.[28]

It is in the same vein that China's infrastructure projects overseas, notably in Africa, are criticized as gaps are revealed 'between China's commitment to international standards regarding good governance and environmental protection and actual practice on Chinese projects' (Bosshard, 2007, p. 1).

Interestingly enough, most African countries being former colonies of Europe, the EU has recently taken the initiative to forge an EU–Africa–China dialogue on infrastructure (Wissenbach, 2007). No doubt, the EU must have felt strongly that it was tarnished as the former colonizer of Africa and sidetracked by China's resource diplomacy. In 2007 the European Commission gathered together 180 delegates from the three parties at a conference as the first step towards establishing rules of engagement in, and forming a tripartite partnership for, Africa's economic growth and infrastructure development.

5.5.   SUMMING UP: HISTORY REPEATS ITSELF

History does repeat itself, particularly in the context of economic development and growth. The reason is clear: In the history of global growth there have been, and are, always a leader and a group of emulators and laggards in economic growth, innovation, and infrastructure development. Leaders have usually been replaced as others catch up. At any moment, nevertheless, a *hierarchy* of countries prevails, as they are differentiated by per-capita income and stage of growth. Any catching-up country's development is basically a *derived and emulative* process and *cannot be self-contained and autonomous*. Latecomers necessarily *emulate and learn* from early starters, often reaping 'latecomers' advantages' (a phrase introduced by Thorstein Veblen, 1915). It is to be expected, therefore, that latecomers' behavior normally replicates what their earlier starters have done before (Ozawa, 2005). And this process is all the more facilitated by the present IT revolution that substantially diminishes the constraints of time and distance in knowledge diffusion – and by the current trend of trade and investment liberalization that attracts more operations of MNCs as transferors of firm-specific industrial knowledge. All this universal evolutionary development is elaborated upon in the FG theory presented above.

The advanced West went through Stage-II growth early on and carried on the hunt for resources and markets overseas under colonialism. Western MNCs were once engaged in infrastructure development and institution building in their colonies. Extant railways, seaports, administrative institutions, and cultural heritages (including common languages) are the major remnants that still serve their useful purposes in the former colonies, though limited in many respects in modern times. Japan likewise ventured out on a similar path – both before World War II (under its own brand of colonialism) and after the war (under its resource diplomacy during the 1970s). And the necessary infrastructure and institutions were built by the Japanese in those developing countries that were able to supply resources. China's current scramble for resources overseas is understandable and predictable from the FG model, since it is in the midst of Stage-II growth. Its 'no-strings-attached' approach is controversial. But, surely so was colonialism – and though to a lesser extent, so was Japan's resource diplomacy as well. Indeed, history repeats itself, albeit in a modified fashion each time.

In essence, the current mode of economic catch-up in the developing world is basically *pre-programmed* in terms of the growth experiences of the advanced West. The ladder of economic development (as seen in Figure 3.1) has been built by hegemonic countries in the past and is now held up as a model for any aspiring developing country to emulate. Yet this model of growth is embedded in high energy and resource consumption, especially petroleum, and leads to a host of environmental problems, especially when a catching-up country happens to be in Stage-II growth. No wonder, then, that China, which has even been dubbed 'a ravenous dragon',[29] is currently in the spotlight of world attention and criticism. The rapid growth of heavy and chemical industries accompanied by pollution and China's hunt for resources, however, are merely revealing the structural weaknesses of the (hegemon-provided) ladder of economic development. As one study puts it,

> . . . the chief economist of the International Energy Agency predicted in April 2007 that China would become the world's largest emitter of carbon dioxide in 2007 or 2008. Yet at 4.1 tons per year, China's per-capita emissions of carbon dioxide were still vastly lower than those of the United States at 19.6 tons per capita and year. As China is increasingly catching up, these figures demonstrate that *the development model pursued by Western societies is not globally sustainable.* If the consumption patterns of the industrialized world are the model for poorer societies, even the strictest environmental policies of financial institutions will not contain the environmental damage that the resource extraction required for this will cause. (Bosshard, 1970, pp. 18–19, emphasis added)

At the moment, however, the Western development model is the only viable one, if not the first-best. Its alternative option, the Soviet-style centralized-regime model of growth, proved to be a failure. However imperfect it may be, capitalism is highly malleable and capable of constantly evolving in adaptation to the changing socio-politico-economic conditions around the world – yet always with private property and market competition as its distinctive foundations. Capitalism is an amazing machine of innovation (Baumol, 2002); hence it will likely be able to cope with the environmental problems over the long haul. For example, although Japan experienced probably the world's worst case of pollution around the late 1960s, it has since been quite successful in introducing pollution-control innovations to help clean up the environment.

Furthermore, a particular country may be in Stage-II growth, thereby displaying its *stage-specific* attributes (the intensity of resource use and a voracious appetite for overseas resources). As it moves up the ladder of economic development, however, such attributes in their pronounced form will disappear at higher growth stages. China's frantic search for resources is transitory, and its economic behavior will alter as it joins the ranks of the advanced countries. India, too, is presently bent on bolstering heavy and chemical industries and is already active in its resource diplomacy toward Africa, dallying with Sudan in constructing a pipeline linking Khartoum to Port Sudan. This is again understandable, since India is going through the similar stage-delineated experiences on its path to economic development.

NOTES

1. For instance, a city water supply cannot be imported, but a foreign MNC in that business can set up a local operation. As is well known in the Heckscher-Ohlin trade theory, FDI (capital movement) is a substitute for trade (goods movement).
2. Colonialism actually started much earlier with the Portuguese and the Spaniards, but mostly for spices, precious metals, ivory, and slaves: ' . . . an irresistible wave of imperialism spread out through the Atlantic and Indian oceans, and by 1700 the Europeans controlled every current of trade touching Europe, as well as the slave trade from Africa to the West Indies and some flows of gold and ivory from West Africa to the East' (Hohenberg, 1968, p. 49).
3. In the recent past Japanese companies made FDI in Russia, which is eager to build up Stage-III industries. Japan's carmakers (such as Toyota, Nissan, and Honda) set up assembly plants mostly in the St Petersburg area. It now takes 30–40 days for cargo to get from Japan to St Petersburg via Europe. If a Trans-Siberian rail route via Vladivostok (on the Sea of Japan) is developed, it will be able to cut down the time by five to 15 days. Mitsui & Co. is reportedly in talks with Russian Railways to invest in and operate a network of warehouses and other logistics for shipping parts and components, thereby saving on inventories. 'Mitsui Nears Deal to Offer Russia Freight Services', *Nikkei Weekly*, July 23, 2007, p. 6.
4. 'A WiMax Breakthrough in India', *BusinessWeek* (on line), March 15, 2008.
5. As reported in 'Its Creators Call Internet Outdated, Offer Remedies', *Wall Street Journal*, October 2, 2007, p. B1.

6. 'The Unsung Heroes Who Move Products Forward', *New York Times* (on the web), September 30, 2007.
7. Economic Council (1970).
8. MITI, *Tsuho Hakusho*, 1971.
9. MITI, *Tsusho Hakusho*, 1973.
10. This description of the Asahan project is partly based on Stockwin (1976), Ozawa (1979), and 'Asahan Aluminum Project Launched', *Oriental Economist*, August, 1975, pp. 15–17.
11. This section is partly based on Ozawa (1979, pp. 135–6).
12. MITI, Japanese Government (1976).
13. 'Singapore Venture will Start Work on Petrochemical Complex', *Japan Economic Journal*, December 26, 1978.
14. 'Japanese Concerns Study Saudi Project for Petrochemicals', *Wall Street Journal*, January 23, 1979.
15. 'IBJ and Traders Seek Big Oil Deal with Mexico', *Japan Economic Journal*, December 19, 1978.
16. 'Japan Firms Step up India Investment', *Nikkei Weekly*, August 20, 2007, p. 1.
17. Head (1974).
18. As an extension of this author's earlier work, an excellent further analysis of the Japanese government involvement in 'private' overseas investments was made by Solis (2004).
19. 'Experience in Poverty Reduction to be Shared', *China Daily*, June 22, 2006, p. 1.
20. 'China Bolsters Ties with Africa: Beijing's Sway Worries U.S.', *Japan Times*, February 8, 2007, p. 4.
21. 'Energy Partnership Based on Equality', *China Daily*, June 22, 2006, p. 1.
22. 'China in Africa: Never Too Late to Scramble', *Economist*, October 28, 2006, pp. 53–6.
23. 'Feeding China's Oil Thirst: Entrepreneurs Join Hunt for Resources', *Wall Street Journal*, January 2, 2007, p. A10.
24. 'Chugokujin, Sudan de Seiko [Chinese succeed in Sudan]', *Asahi Shimbun*, November 23, 2006, p. 15.
25. 'Africa and China: Wrong Model, Right Continent', *Economist*, October 28, 2006, p. 17.
26. 'In Africa, China's Expansion Begins to Stir Resentment', *Wall Street Journal*, February 2, 2007, p. A1.
27. Ibid., p. A1.
28. 'Africa and China: Wrong Model, Right Continent', *Economist*, October 28, 2006, p. 18.
29. 'A Ravenous Dragon: A Special Report on China's Quest for Resources', *Economist*, March 15, 2008.

6. The Asian model for Latin America? A tale of two regions

6.1. LATIN AMERICAN DRAMA

This chapter discusses the relevance of the Asian experiences for other developing regions by choosing Latin America as an example for comparative analysis. Latin American countries were once strongly influenced by Asia's successful catch-up growth and quickly followed suit by adopting outward-oriented development policies in the late 1980s. Yet they have not really succeeded in sparking regional growth as vibrantly as their Asian counterparts. Chile, which opened up for trade in the late 1970s (much earlier than any others in the region), is clearly an exception in this chronicle. Yet its catch-up growth and industrial transformation have not been quite as stellar as its Asian brethren in the same period, say, South Korea's or Taiwan's. The most recent sudden spurt of Panama's small economy is another outlier that registered a growth rate of 11 percent in 2007 (comparable to China's), but the country is beset by sharp income inequality, corruption, and widespread poverty (among as much as 40 percent of the population).[1] So is the Dominican Republic despite its relatively fast growth in the 1990s.

Also, the same thing can be said about the region's two largest economies, Mexico and Brazil, though they have no doubt made significant progress by their own past standards in economic development. True, Brazil's $1.3 trillion economy is currently buoyed up by the commodity boom and is fast growing at an annual rate of 5 to 6 percent, which is, nevertheless, a mediocre rate by Asian standards. Furthermore, Latin America as an economic bloc has, on the whole, not turned into a regionally integrated, vigorous growth cluster as in Asia. In recent years, some countries in Latin America even returned to their former anti-capitalist Marxist stance in policy orientation, bogging themselves down in a morass of socialist control and inefficiency.

What is holding back the region from fully benefiting from the global economy, whereas Asia has gained so much? This question prompts us to examine major differences in the two regions' development policies, institutions (especially belief systems), and circumstances, thereby in turn helping us recapitulate the defining features of the Asian model by comparison. This chapter will first briefly review the recent policy experiences of Latin America, and then contrast the persistence of its Marxist ideology with the present zeitgeist of the rapidly growing and regionally agglomerating Asian economy.

6.2.　POLICY SWITCH AND RECIDIVISM

Latin America as a whole was once engaged in an inward-looking import-substitution (IL-IS) policy of economic development after World War II. The powerful theoretical arguments in favor of this development strategy were advanced by, *inter alia*, Prebisch (1950), Singer (1950), Nurkse (1953), and Rosenstein-Rodan (1961). Buttressed by the Marxist 'dependency' theory, IL-IS policy came to be actively pursued across Latin America, starting in the 1950s and lasting towards the end of the 1980s. Those first two decades witnessed considerable success in economic growth but in the end encountered stagnation and serious structural problems. This occurred because the initial investment opportunities for import substitution were quickly exhausted, and protection led to market distortions and resource misallocation.

Interestingly enough, the IL-IS policy was built on a combination of the *export-pulled primary sector* and the *import-replacing manufacturing sector*. As a legacy of colonialism, resource-rich Latin America became overwhelmingly reliant on primary production for export. Hence, IL-IS policy was designed to earn as much foreign exchange as possible from primary exports (grain, food, minerals, oil, and other raw materials) and to channel funds into a manufacturing sector that would supply protected domestic markets. In this process, priority was given to the promotion of the manufacturing (urban) sector at the cost of not fully developing—or even neglecting further investment in, thereby unintentionally crowding out – the resources (rural) sector. This unbalanced dual-sector regime impacted on the political economy of Latin America and trade patterns with their major partners, such as the US, Europe, and Japan.

The protected domestic markets initially did attract FDI but mostly the kind that sought the 'protection rent' created under such inward-focused strategies. Manufacturing, thus fostered, failed to become competitive. This is because it was mainly for their rather small domestic markets and could not exploit scale economies. And the quality of their manufactures did not reach international standards as they were not exposed to the rigor of global competition. Without manufactured exports, their trade balance inevitably remained unstable and unfavorable because of their heavy dependence on primary exports which were subject to both short-term price fluctuations and a secular deterioration in their terms of trade vis-à-vis the industrialized advanced countries.

By the end of the 1960s, Latin America's IL-IS policy had quickly begun to hit diminishing returns in its protected domestic industries, contributing to slow growth. This was also accompanied by a host of politico-economic problems, such as glaring income inequality, public debt, hyperinflation, high unemployment, and grinding poverty. With the exception of Chile, however, Latin American countries on the whole did not discard IL-IS policy right away. For almost two more decades, they continued to stay on the same path under high trade barriers and state interventions.

While Latin America was preoccupied with IL-IS, the US kept its market open, attracting imports of labor-intensive manufactures (mostly consumer goods) from East Asian countries that pursued an outward-looking, export-promotion (OL-EP) policy, as seen in Chapter 4. Inward-oriented Latin American countries could not capitalize on such an opportunity simply because of their lack of export orientation. In fact, East Asia's successful export-driven growth was one important motivation for Latin America's eventual policy switch. In addition, Latin America was hampered by financial crises and the heavy burden of debt servicing throughout the 1980s, which came to be known as the 'lost decade of development'. The price of commodities also came down from the relatively high levels of the 1970s, an unfavorable development for the resource-exporting region. During the same decade, Latin American governments indulged in easy foreign indebtedness as the then-expanding Eurodollar market eagerly made sovereign loans, which would later come back to haunt them with debt crises.

Meanwhile, Chile had already switched from IL-IS to OL-EP in 1976 onwards. How the so-called 'Chicago boys' played a critical role in formulating Chile's OL-EP strategy in 1976–82 is a well-known story. Its rather abrupt policy switch was forcefully carried out under the grip of General Augusto Pinochet. It was, however, Mexico that decisively set the tone for the rest of the region when its civilian government chose a similar open-market model in 1989. Argentina, Brazil, and Venezuela soon followed their policy reformulation, and a wave of economic liberalization began to sweep the region during the 1990s.

A new era thus began. A liberalization frenzy took hold, privatizing nearly everything in sight 'from the Buenos Aires Zoo to Mexico's 18 commercial banks',[2] cutting tariffs to world levels, opening the doors to foreign investment, and signing free-trade pacts, most notably the Southern Cone Common Market, Mercosur (currently involving Argentina, Brazil,

Uruguay, and Paraguay). No doubt, the rise of East Asia had a strong demonstration effect on the region. In addition, US-educated political leaders, such as Mexico's President Carlos Salinas da Gortari and Argentine's Economy Minister Domingo Cavallo, as well as a large cadre of similarly US-trained technocrats in high-ranking positions, were able to communicate with each other across Latin America through old school ties of Harvard, Yale, Chicago, Columbia, Stanford, and other top universities. Inflation soon began to be contained, capital investments soared, and GDP climbed throughout the region. Latin America welcomed the 'Washington Consensus' of trade and investment liberalization, privatization, and deregulation.

Yet the resultant liberalization-triggered growth did not last long. On the heels of the Asian financial crisis of 1997–8, Latin America was shocked with a series of financial crises, starting in Brazil (1998) and then in Argentina (2001). Unemployment rose, and social unrest ensued. Unstable politico-economic conditions cast a heavy shroud of doubt over the appropriateness of the region's open-door policy, thereby laying the ground for another policy change in the battered region. Leftist politicians succeeded in grabbing power. Most dramatically, Hugo Chavez in Venezuela, who instigated a failed coup attempt in 1992, became president. He now advocates a return to a Cuban-style command economy in 'a socialist Venezuela in a socialist Latin America' and calls his political philosophy the 'new 21st socialism'. Argentina's Nestor Kirchner revived Peron-style populist socialism, and 'globaphobia' colored his growth policy. Luiz Inacio Lulu da Silva was elected in Brazil in 2002. Other leftist leaders also won elections: Rafael Correa in Ecuador, Evo Morales in Bolivia, which recently nationalized its energy industry, Daniel Ortega in Nicaragua, and Fernando Lugo in Paraguay. These leaders are turning their economies away from OL-EP and back to IL-IS regimes – and even worse to nationalist socialism. Why this recidivism to Latin American-style socialism?

In the meantime, Mexico and Brazil (though the latter is now governed by da Silva, a moderate socialist), Latin America's two largest economies which still keep their economies outward-oriented, have been doing relatively well in economic performance with growth rates averaging about 5 percent – certainly better since the early 1970s but not quite up to snuff by East Asian standards. Even the much-touted Mercosur has not really evolved into a genuine customs union as it has allowed too many exceptions in removing trade barriers. Why hasn't the open-door policy worked in Latin America as effectively as it has in East Asia? Why does the Marxist ideology still shimmer across the region, and especially in those countries that have recently returned to the leftist camp?

6.3. TWO FUNDAMENTAL IMAGES OF THE WORLD ECONOMY

The two regional economies are operating under their two diametrically opposite ideational tenets. In this regard, it is appropriate to refer to Kenneth Boulding's (1956) concept of the 'image of reality' (how we *perceive* the world around us and how we *interpret* the messages therefrom) that governs our thinking, perspectives, and behavior. Since reality is in a state of constant flux, our images also must change. Our perception, however, often lags behind a sudden alteration in reality. Without exception, economic theories are formulated in accordance with theorists' perception of the global economy; that is, models are built on theorists' images of reality. And over more than a century, two fundamental images of the global economy have been dominating our thinking; one image was perceived and bequeathed by Adam Smith (1723–90) in the tradition of economic liberalism and the other by Karl Marx (1818–83) in that of socialism.

On one hand, Smith developed a sanguine, pro-business view of the world against the backdrop of the buoyant dynamic era of incipient capitalism he witnessed in Glasgow, where merchants, shippers, and bankers all prospered by importing an ever-rising amount of tobacco from Virginia and the West Indies in exchange for Glasgow products such as silk, leather, and iron. 'Glasgow belonged to him; it was his laboratory and its merchants were his teachers'.[3] When he completed his magnum opus, *An Inquiry into the Nature and Causes of the Wealth of Nations* (1776), England was about to enter a new era, the era of the Industrial Revolution – notably with the commercialization of James Watt's steam engine in 1775.[4]

On the other hand, Karl Marx (born 95 years later than Smith) formed a different image as he lived through and observed the turbulent period of unfettered capitalism towards the end of the Industrial Revolution. Income distribution became increasingly polarized into astronomical wealth and abysmal poverty. Marx saw two classes emerge from the unbridled growth of capitalism – the bourgeoisie and the proletariat. Thus the phenomenon of class struggle he perceived came to underline his analysis. Marx no doubt empathized with and championed the have-nots.

Interestingly, the two schools have influenced our thoughts about trade and investment in a rather diametrical fashion. In the main, Smith's economic liberalism (*laissez-faire* principle) has come to dominate the way we think of international trade, as best exemplified by the free-trade doctrine of comparative advantage. In contrast, the Marxist school has so far been very strong in conceptualizing the exploitative role of foreign investment in the developing world, particularly in Latin America where the Marxist 'dependency theory' is buttressed by the region's past experience with colonialism – the legacy of the West's Stage-II growth. This theory has been dominant and popular among local intellectuals partly because it did not encounter any viable and equally persuasive theoretical alternative that is empirically based on some positive relationships between MNCs and economic development in the host countries.

Yet the experiences of the rapidly growing Asian economies with large inflows of FDI, a new Smithian growth model, suddenly presented a whole new image as an attractive alternative – at least during the 1990s. The East Asian experiences have demonstrated that MNCs can serve as a conduit of industrial knowledge – and as a powerful jump-starter for growth. The phenomenal infusion of FDI into East Asia, especially China, has climaxed in *concomitant* explosive growth and trade expansion across the region. The Marxist dependency theory – and its widely held image of capitalism as an exploiter of underdeveloped economies – flies in the face of the symbiotic relationships that came to exist between foreign MNCs and the developing host countries across East Asia. In fact, the Asian experience presents several 'paradoxes' for Marxists: (i) an undreamed-of rise in wages and household incomes (a fast reduction in dire poverty) and even the occurrence of labor shortages in the labor-driven stage of growth, the very stage viewed by radical economists as that of labor exploitation, (ii) the fast accumulation of domestic savings and investable surpluses despite – or rather because of – heavy dependence on foreign MNCs in labor-driven manufacturing and exports, (iii) relatively equitable income distribution or 'shared growth', and (iv) the swift emergence of labor-seeking outward FDI (that is, Third-World MNCs) from the very developing countries that were themselves labor-surplus and low-wage economies only a short time ago. Rapidly catching-up countries – by means of their *own* newly minted MNCs – are thus joining the ranks of multinational employers of job-starved labor in their less-developed brethren, spreading employment opportunities.

All these revelations (facts) are in stark contrast to the visions or images of the Marxist school. The economic achievements in East Asia have thus been flashing new messages that demand a change in the fast-obsolescing images of the global economy still held by radical economists, politicians, and policymakers in Latin America.

6.4.   EMULATION VS. DEPENDENCY

6.4.1.   The Smithian Opportunity-seeking Model: Emulation

The driving mechanism of Asia's tandem growth is *emulative learning* on the part of follower countries. Therefore, the Asian model may alternately be called the 'emulation model'. Indeed, the region has been an *ideal* laboratory – another Glasgow – for theorizing the positive interactions of MNCs and local enterprises in propelling economic development.

Unlike the dependency school that derives its theoretical underpinning from Marxism, the emulative development model draws on the simple idea that *learning from the more advanced countries is the basic step any developing country must take if it is to catch up*. More than 200 years ago, as a matter of fact, Adam Smith zeroed in on this critical idea:

> Private people who want to make a fortune, never think of retiring to the remote and poor provinces of the country, but resort either to the capital, or to some of the great commercial towns. They know that where little wealth circulates, there is little to be gotten; but that where a great deal is in motion, some share of it may fall to them. *The same maxims which would in this manner direct the common sense of [individuals]* . . . *should make a whole nation regard the riches of its neighbours as a probable cause and occasion for itself to acquire riches. A nation that would enrich itself by foreign trade, is certainly most likely to do so when its neighbours are all rich and industrious.* (Smith, 1776/1908, p. 378, emphasis added)

This observation, though deceptively simple and elementary, contains so much truth. Any underdeveloped country, if it is really serious about raising its standard of living most effectively as a member of the global community, should open up its economy judiciously so as to align the direction of its development efforts with the advanced countries. In other words, the country needs to avail itself of opportunities to trade, interact with, and learn from the more advanced countries – that is, to feed on their lush pastures. In other words, opening-up for the outside world should not be a mere resigned exposure to the forces of global competition; it should be done selectively and strategically by targeting the 'rich' markets of the advanced countries – rather than aligning itself with its 'poor' neighbors (under what may be called 'commiserative regionalism'). What Smith stressed was also *dynamic gains* from focusing export activities on higher-income countries with larger markets. Such trade gives developing countries a chance to reap the economies of scale and hierarchical concatenation. Let's identify this development strategy as the 'Smithian opportunity-seeking' model (Ozawa, 2005).

Here it is worth noting that although Adam Smith was a staunch advocate of deregulation, privatization, and trade liberalism, he also emphasized the key role of the government in managing a transition to the free market. He was against an abrupt ('cold-turkey') approach and in favor of a *gradual and judicious* transition so as to avoid the social costs of economic liberalization, especially if a country has long been subject to all sorts of government interventions as was the case with the England of his time, which had gone through a few centuries of mercantilism. Smith clearly warned of the danger of exposing a protected local industry instantly to the rigor of global competition:

> The undertaker of a great manufacture, who, by the home markets *being suddenly laid open to* the competition of foreigners, should be obliged to abandon his trade, would no doubt suffer very considerably. That part of his capital which had usually been employed in purchasing materials and in paying his workmen might, without much difficulty, perhaps, find another employment. But that part of it which was fixed in workhouses, and in the instruments of trade, could scarce be disposed of without considerable loss. *The equitable regard, therefore, to his interest requires that changes of this kind should never be introduced suddenly, but slowly, gradually, and after a very long warning.* (Smith, 1776/1908, pp. 358–9, emphasis added)

Smith did not specify how and in what way trade liberation should proceed 'never . . . suddenly, but slowly, gradually, and after a very long warning'. Nevertheless, he was very much aware of the importance of adjustments that need to be made because of the sunken investments (or existent sector-specific capital) 'fixed in workhouses, and in the instruments of trade' trapped in those industries now suddenly exposed to import competition.

If sufficient time is allowed, there are various ways of coping with the opening of a protected domestic market to foreign competition. For example, the domestic firms may be able to stand on an equal footing with foreign competitors by (i) installing more efficient machinery and equipment, (ii) adopting better production methods, (iii) coming up with a new product, and/or (iv) replacing the present lines of products with new more competitive ones. These are some of the specific possible avenues for survival, but it *takes time* to go through these structural adjustments. A dynamic 'infant-industry' type of protection may indeed be called for, as envisaged in the FG model of economic development.

In addition to the gradualism required for trade liberalization, Smith argued very strongly in *The Theory of Moral Sentiments* (1759/1976) and *The Wealth of Nations* (1776/1908) (i) that the spirit of benevolence tames selfishness and guides man to behave compassionately towards his follows for social harmony, (ii) that the role of the state in national security, justice, and infrastructural provisions (especially, state-funded education in the wake of the demoralizing effects of the division of labor on the working class) needs to expand *pari passu* with economic growth, and (iii) that the spirit of economic equality needs to be maintained to counteract the 'avarice and ambition in the rich'. What Smith visualized was *compassionate liberalism* – that is, shared growth.

This is because capitalism is the most efficient machine to produce wealth, but a poor machine to distribute the fruits of growth equally or equitably among income recipients. It ineluctably rewards the capable and punishes the incompetent. It also favors the already rich who can invest their wealth in financial markets. In essence, capitalism enables *economic* progress at a national level, but not necessarily *social* progress. The attainment of social progress requires public policies – and the compassion of those who are fortunate enough to become better off under capitalism.

In fact, it is against this backdrop that practically all East Asian economies crafted state-guided gradual liberalization and industrial development (or 'industrial policies' which have long been considered 'dirty words' in Washington, DC). But state intervention should be market-supportive and pro-business. Thus, policy and institutions matter – in building market-compatible (if not totally market-dictated) economies.

6.4.2. The Marxist Model of Dependency

What would the Marxist dependency school say to the Smithian opportunity-seeking model of emulative growth? According to their view, the outer-oriented developing economies are subjugating themselves to trade and foreign capital and being left helplessly impoverished as foreign capital siphons off the surpluses (profits) extracted from local labor and natural resources. Such exploitation by capitalists is supposed first to occur at home and then spread overseas. In radical leftists' view, therefore, labor exploitation is borderless and universal.

Furthermore, any international exchange between the advanced and the less developed is considered 'unequal exchange' and a zero-sum game. This is because development and enrichment at one pole (that is, the advanced world) are inextricably coupled with underdevelopment and impoverishment at the other (that is, the developing world). Thus any hierarchical relationship that necessarily exists between the two worlds creates only exploitative opportunities for the advanced, further polarizing their welfare positions. Here, the 'law of uneven development and polarization' governs; instead of a gap-closing scenario (as envisaged in the Smithian principle of emulative growth), a gap-widening scenario prevails.

As far as the hierarchical structure of the world economy is concerned, therefore, the dependency school postulates that only 'dominant versus dependent' (or 'maliciously dominant versus pathetically dependent') relations persist between the two worlds – in sharp contrast to the 'leader versus challenger' (or 'leading with goodwill versus emulating with ardency') relations observable in Pacific Asia. Here lies an enormous perceptive difference in images of the global economy.

True, economic liberalism have come to be more widely accepted than ever in Latin America since the early 1990s. But the Marxist mindset is still retained consciously or subconsciously by many local intellectuals and politicians. Most recently, as mentioned earlier, it has been revived in Venezuela, Argentina, Brazil, Bolivia, and Equador. Their underlying common views of the global economy are clearly expressed by a well-known Latin American economist, Theotonio Dos Santos (1970):

> In analyzing the process of constituting a world economy that integrates the so-called 'national economies' in a world market of commodities, capital, and even of labor power, we see that the relations produced by this market are *unequal and combined* – unequal because *development of parts of the system occurs at the expense of other parts*. Trade relations are based on monopolistic control of the market, which leads to the transfer of surplus generated in the *dependent* countries to the *dominant* countries; financial relations are, from the viewpoint of the dominant powers, based on loans and the export of capital, which permit them to receive interest and profits, thus increasing their domestic surplus and strengthening their control over the economies of the other countries. For the dependent countries these relations represent an export of profits and interest which carries off part of the surplus generated domestically and leads to a loss of control over their productive resources. In order to permit these disadvantageous relations, the dependent countries must generate large surpluses, not in such a way as to create higher levels of technology but rather *superexploited manpower*. The result is to limit the development of their internal market and their technical and cultural capacity, as well as the moral and physical health of their people. We call this *combined development* because it is the combination of *these inequalities* and the *transfer of resources* from the most advanced and dominant ones which explains the inequality, deepens it, and transforms it into a necessary and structural element of the world economy. (p. 231, emphasis added)

Dos Santo's view once epitomized the fusion of ECLAC (the UN Economic Commission on Latin America and the Caribbean) structuralism and Marxist dependency theory that 'became the accepted way to describe Latin American economic relations, not only among radical intellectuals but among commentators, government officials, the military, and politicians' (Sigmund, 1980, p. 35). Indeed, we can find many variants of dependency theory (for example, Baran, 1957; Frank, 1967; Furtado, 1976; and Amin, 1976).

6.5.   THE 'RESOURCE CURSE' OR THE 'INSTITUTIONAL CURSE'?

One dominant explanation of why Latin America has not grown so vigorously is presented in the 'resource curve' theory of hampered economic development. It basically argues that abundant resource endowments are not a boon but rather a bane. This section surveys and interprets the possible causes of this irony.

Latin America as a whole is much more resource-abundant than East Asia, especially Japan and the Asian NIEs, which are geographically limited in size. This is perhaps the major difference between the two regions. Resource-scarce economies are naturally envious of resource-rich ones. Resource abundance is, however, often considered an obstacle for long-term economic development. There are a number of strong theoretical explanations for this phenomenon. In addition, empirical studies do reveal negative correlations of an indicator of natural resource abundance with per-capita income growth – without regard to whatever causal mechanisms are involved (see, *inter alia*, Sala-i-Martin, 1997; Sachs and Warner, 2001). The possible explanations are given in a variety of theories, which are reviewed below.

6.5.1. The Prebisch–Singer Thesis

The well-known Prebisch–Singer thesis of secular deterioration in the terms of trade (Prebisch, 1950; Singer, 1950) looks at trade relations between resource-exporting developing countries and advanced countries that export industrial goods in exchange for resources. Although productivity growth may occur in both groups over the long run, the benefits are usually shared *unequally* due to their different market characteristics. Commodity markets are highly competitive, whereas industrial goods markets are largely oligopolistic with a great deal of market (pricing) power. The gains from productivity growth can be divided by and distributed to three beneficiaries: consumers (via lower prices), workers (via higher wages), and producers (via higher profits). Given the highly competitive nature of commodity markets, the supply price of commodities tends to be low when output rises. This benefits buyers (that is, advanced countries), while the price of industrial goods is kept high by oligopolistic manufacturers who can thus retain higher profits and pay higher wages. As a consequence, resource-exporting countries end up holding the short end of the stick, while advanced countries retain much of the productivity gain at home. This results in a long-term deterioration of the terms of trade against the resource-exporting developing countries. Those resource-abundant countries that trade with the advanced world are consequently destined to be losers in the long run.

6.5.2. The 'Immiserizing Growth' Theory

The 'immiserizing growth' theory (Bhagwati, 1958) is a short-run version of the Prebisch–Singer thesis and focuses on the same type of terms-of-trade deterioration. It is presented in a formalized way in terms of geometry and mathematics. The most notable example is agricultural goods, since they are subject to sharp output fluctuations caused by climatic conditions that are uncontrollable by producers.

A bumper crop of coffee in a particular year, for instance, will lead to a lower price, immediately worsening the terms of trade for coffee-exporting countries such as Brazil. And if the *negative* terms-of-trade effect is stronger than the *positive* output effect, the welfare of coffee-exporting countries declines unless excess coffee beans are destroyed to curtail the supply. This is a case of self-immiserization. But the reverse is also true when a crop failure causes a higher price and welfare suddenly improves with a windfall profit. These alterations in fortune can therefore explain the *instability* of the price of primary goods in the short run (that is, wiggles along the secular price trend line).

Actually, the basis of this theory has long been known and captured in the so-called 'hog cycle' theory that is built on the reactions and expectations of hog producers. When the price of hogs rises steeply, all farmers decide to produce more in expectation of larger profits. But this leads to an oversupply in the next harvest, resulting in a lower price. The 'fallacy of composition' (what is true for individual parts may not be true for the whole) is thus at work. And when the price falls, the exact opposite occurs. In this case, the real cause of price swings is *man-made* unlike the price swings of climate-determined agricultural goods. However, individual producers' price expectations can be added as another explanatory factor to the immiserizing growth theory so as to reinforce its predictive capacity.

6.5.3. The 'Dutch Disease' Theory

Another popular argument for the resource curse is the 'Dutch disease' theory. This model explains the unfavorable effects of a resource export boom on the progress of the manufacturing sector (that is, industrialization) through various causal mechanisms such as a rise in wages, currency appreciation, and a crowding-out of investment.

When the resource sector expands under an export boom, the wages in that sector rise, attracting workers away from the industrial sector. Consequently, the latter's growth slows down and is impeded. The same turn of events occurs when the home currency appreciates due to a resource-export boom, adversely affecting manufactured exports. And when investment capital is poured into the booming resource sector because of higher rates of return, the manufacturing sector is crowded out, and left inadequately funded and deprived of investment. This hinders industrialization.

6.5.4. The 'Feast-Fast' Cycle

Natural resources are usually regarded as something that a nation as a
whole should own and benefit from rather than something that the private
sector exploits for its own advantage. This belief is usually reflected in the
national (or nationalized) ownership and management of natural resources
or in special permissions licensed out for fees or given to the private sector
in exchange for profit sharing by the government. Government involvement is thus normally inescapable – and indeed, more prevalent in the
resource-rich developing countries, especially in those that were once
colonized by the advanced countries.

As noted earlier, commodity markets are more likely to go through wide
fluctuations in prices and output than their manufacturing and service counterparts. When the markets are booming with higher prices and larger output,
therefore, government revenues rise, especially if state ownership is involved.
In the face of rising windfall surpluses, the government increases spending
and locks in newly introduced social welfare (entitlement) programs. This is a
'feast' time. However, such a good time is soon to be reversed to a 'fast' time,
in which revenues decline while ratcheted-up entitlement spending remains
high. The upshot is rising public debt. This 'feast and fast' cycle can thus
explain the fiscal plight of many resource-exporting countries.[5]

In the meantime, state ownership and involvement often result in corruption and wasteful use of revenues from resource exports. One cross-
country study (Sala-i-Martin and Subramanian, 2003) shows that various
indicators of natural resource endowment are negatively correlated with
measures of institutional quality (that is to say, correlated with measures
of the 'soft state', a notion introduced by Myrdal, 1968). An opportunity
for state ownership also means a further enhancement of socialism as leftist
politicians, once they grab power, are prone to manipulate their incumbent
positions for their own political ends. Measures of institutional quality are
also likely to be associated with indicators of leftist tilt.

6.5.5. Diminishing Returns, Lack of Skill Formation, and Poor Labor Absorption: Foresights of the Australian School

Any economic activity tends to succumb to the law of diminishing returns.
However, resource extraction (and farming) is, in general, even more susceptible to this law than are manufacturing and services, especially when
a catching-up country is in the early stages of development. In the latter,
positive externalities and agglomeration economies in the forms of technological progress, skill formation, and interactive growth normally occur
more rapidly and more extensively, contributing to sectoral dynamism, as

the underdeveloped countries begin to industrialize. After all, mining and agriculture do not really require technically trained or educated workers (say, university graduates), who can, however, find employment in manufacturing (for example, management, product development, engineering, and marketing) and services (for example, R&D, banking, finance, accounting, health, and education). Hence, more opportunities for high quality jobs exist in the latter two (secondary and tertiary) industries.

In this connection, it is worth noting that in the 1920s Australian policymakers rebelled against David Ricardo's doctrine of comparative advantage, arguing that specialization in primary goods would be detrimental to their long-term national interest. To build a nation, Australia needed and encouraged inflows of immigrants (new man power), but its primary sector (prone to diminishing returns) alone would not be able to provide decent jobs. It had to develop manufacturing industries (amenable to dynamic increasing returns) under protection and promotional measures. Hence, unbridled free trade was not good for Australia. Their well-thought-out theoretical argument came to be known as the 'Australian' case for protection. Irwin (1996) succinctly explains:

> Ricardo and the classical school favored free trade as a means of relieving diminishing returns in agriculture by substituting imported goods for domestic production, while shifting factors of production to manufacturing where output could be more easily expanded. But what about other countries that also faced diminishing returns in agriculture, but which instead *exported* those goods? (p. 172, original emphasis)

In the early days of industrialization the US, Germany, and other European nations that initially exported primary goods – as well as Japan whose early exports were silk and marine products – all resorted to the 'infant-industry' rationale for protectionism to build up national industries. In other words, *all these successfully advanced economies did not plunge into the cold-turkey treatment of free trade to kick off their industrialization.* Their approach was more or less in line with Adam Smith's advocacy of gradual and cautious liberalization and institutional preparation, though strongly oriented to international trade. In other words, IL-IS policy – or rather IS-EP policy as seen in the MPX sequence – was appropriate for starting off industrialization.

6.6.   RESOURCE ABUNDANCE AS A BLESSING

The various theories of the resource curse outlined above are all logical and make sense. Some scholars, however, question the validity of such a curse on long-term growth. In fact, the reality is that resource exports, particularly at the time of a commodity boom, provide much-needed foreign exchange that resource-producing countries can use to purchase the necessary capital goods and technologies for industrialization from the advanced world. It all depends on using the export earnings for useful purposes without squandering them.

Indeed, a World Bank report (2002) focuses on this point, stressing that 'natural resources are not a curse but an asset for development', and observes that 'it is impossible to argue that Australia, Canada, Finland, Sweden, and the United States did not base their development on their natural resources. In fact, even today they are net exporters of natural resource-based products' (p. 6). The report urges developing countries to 'play to your strengths' and concludes:

> We must reiterate that rich endowments of natural resources, combined with the aggressive pursuit and adoption of new technologies, are a proven growth recipe. Further, the evidence strongly indicates that their development does not preclude the development of manufacturing or other activities in the 'knowledge' economy. In short, countries that have 'played to their strengths' have done well.
>
> An equally important lesson is that what is important is not so much *what* is produced, but *how* it is produced. Taking advantage of global technological progress is essential in every field, and it cannot be done cheaply. The recurrent lesson of the successful natural resource developers, and of contemporary theory, is the necessity of engendering a high level of human capital and developing a capacity for 'national' learning and innovation. (p. 11, original emphasis)

In other words, the policy prescription offered is *nothing other than* adoption of the Smithian opportunity-seeking model of emulative growth. The *key* to a successful catch-up is knowledge absorption through emulation and learning by interacting with the advanced world. And to this end, appropriate domestic institutions need to be established as the crucial prerequisite.

More specifically, therefore, the report gives three major recommendations: (i) foster openness to trade, market access, and FDI flows, (ii) build new endowments in human capital, knowledge, better institutions, and public infrastructure (by way of general education and lifelong learning, R&D incentives and innovation systems, the adoption of information and communications technology, and building good public infrastructure and institutions), and (iii) don't turn your back on your natural advantages (that is, play to your strengths) (World Bank, 2002, pp. 2–4).

All these recommendations are well-thought-out as a set of measures for climbing the ladder of economic development from the initial resource-based rung to the subsequent higher rungs that are all progressively knowledge-based, as stipulated in the FG paradigm of structural upgrading (Chapter 3). However, Latin America has more immediate needs, such as solving the severe social problems of high unemployment, income inequality, and pervasive poverty.

6.7. TOWARDS 'SHARED GROWTH': REMOVAL OF THE 'INSTITUTIONAL CURSE'

One of the key features of East Asian growth is the 'principle of shared growth', which by contrast is lacking or only weakly put to work in Latin America. The World Bank (1993) explains the East Asian experiences as follows:

> To establish their legitimacy and win the support of the society at large, East Asian leaders established the principle of shared growth, promising that as the economy expanded all groups would benefit. But sharing growth raised complex coordination problems. First, leaders had to convince economic elites to support *pro-growth* policies. Then they had to persuade the elites to *share* the benefits of growth with *the middle class and the poor*. Finally, to win the cooperation of the middle class and the poor, the leaders had to show them that they would indeed benefit from future growth. (p. 13, emphasis added)

To be more specific, East Asian countries carried out, for example, drastic land reform programs to help peasants (Japan, South Korea, Taiwan, and China); price controls on rice, fertilizer, and energy (Indonesia); the *bumiputra* program for ethnic Malays to counter the better-off ethnic Chinese (Malaysia); massive public housing (Hong Kong and Singapore); and small and medium-size business promotion (practically in all East Asian countries) – all these policy measures intended to demonstrate the governments' commitment to shared growth (World Bank, 1993). In addition, 'more rapid output and productivity growth in agriculture', 'earlier and steeper declines in fertility [which helps raise per-capita income]', and 'higher growth rates of physical capital [inclusive of physical infrastructure], supported by higher rates of domestic savings' (ibid., p. 27).

Besides, productivity growth in the primary sector is something Latin America has not promoted in earnest, especially during the IL-IS policy period, and fertility declines have not taken place so steeply in the region – mostly for religious reasons. Increases in population, unemployment, and poverty in Latin America have hindered savings.

Be that as it may, *the principle of shared growth needs to be adopted at a policy level across the region* if Latin America is to prevent recidivism to IL-IS policy, worse still to radical socialism, though this has already started. OL-EP policy or free-market capitalism has come to be blamed for rampant poverty, high unemployment, and income inequality. The cold-turkey imposition of free-market capitalism under the Washington Consensus basically deserves the blame for the widening income gap between the rich and the poor.

As to high rates of savings in East Asia, cultural factors may play a critical role. Frugality is often a tradition in the region. However, it may be an outcome of shared growth, since more evenly distributed incomes lead to a higher rate of savings than a highly skewed income distribution when the rich display 'conspicuous consumption' – and when incomes rise very rapidly and unexpectedly for the masses. And a rise in expected rates of return on investment in education in general and higher education in particular because of the rapid growth of the manufacturing and services sectors also leads to the people's eagerness to save. Most fundamentally, nevertheless, savings come out of workers' incomes. And workers must find employment opportunities in the first place.

6.8.   LABOR ACTIVATION AS A GROWTH STARTER

Although less well-known, Adam Smith stressed the importance of a proper sequencing of industrial development. What he called 'a natural course of things' means that any labor-abundant (hence capital-scarce) country needs at first to make the best use of its most abundant resource, labor, if it is to industrialize successfully. This applies even to resource-rich developing countries because the development of human resources is critical for long-term growth.

As witnessed throughout East Asia, labor-driven development can bring hitherto unemployed and unskilled people into the labor force (Chapter 4). Even at low wages household incomes are expected to rise, satisfying basic needs. Given the importance of an extended family as the household unit in the developing world, what matters is not so much per-capita income per se but family income. Labor-focused policy creates female jobs in particular that did not exist before, supplementing male incomes. In fact, female jobs become more abundant than male jobs in labor-intensive industries. Rural households are particularly dependent on remittances from those (mostly migrant laborers) who are now employed in urban factories. This makes them afford – and eager – to send their children to school. Labor-driven rapid growth improves their prospects for returns on education. And investment in human resources at primary and lower secondary schools (basic human capital formation) thus begins. Besides, wages are not likely to remain low under the labor-focused approach. As amply proven by the East Asian experiences, labor shortages normally occur and wages are destined to rise. In fact, this is the first sign of successful labor-driven development, a sign that also demonstrates *the paradox of labor shortages in labor-abundant developing countries*.

As stressed in Chapter 4, labor-driven growth is thus the most effective measure to alleviate poverty. East Asia's shared growth policies, too, have been no doubt instrumental in reducing dire poverty and bringing about social stability. Nevertheless, the initial priority placed by development policymakers on labor activation through the market mechanism – and its successful result – proved to be more fundamental in lifting the living standards of the have-nots and mobilizing them as vital participants in market-based economic development.

But why hasn't Latin America been able to initiate labor-driven development as a jump-starter for sustainable growth and as an effective measure for poverty reduction? True, Mexico's *maquiladora* program was intended to attract FDI in labor-intensive manufacturing, but it has not really helped spark as much growth and structural transformation in the Mexican economy as seen in East Asia. Perhaps when the program was set up in the 1960s, Mexico's overall wage level (including minimum wage) was already much higher than those prevailing in East Asia (except Japan). And Mexico was hindered from attracting truly low-wage-seeking FDI in clothing, toys, and consumer electronics, and simply could not compete with Asian labor.

Furthermore, at the moment Mexico's true advantage in low-wage activity seems to lie in farming – rather than in manufacturing. Yet America's farm sector with which Mexico has to compete has long been protected. As a consequence Mexican farm workers illegally migrate to the US instead of producing at home and supplying farm exports. It is a well-known economic theory that when trade is impeded, a factor movement (labor migration) occurs as a substitute for trade.[6] According to the US Department of Labor, 53 percent of the 2.5 million farm workers are illegal immigrants, but growers and labor unions put the figure much higher – as much as 70 percent of younger field hands are said to be illegal.[7] It is only in recent years that large agribusiness began to shift their farming operations south of the border in fresh vegetables such as lettuce and broccoli. If this latest trend continues, unskilled labor in Mexico's farm sector will benefit, triggering labor-driven growth.

There is also another encouraging sign that the manufacturing sector of Latin America, especially if near to the US, may increasingly host FDI as American MNCs bring back jobs closer to home because of soaring transportation costs due to high oil prices instead of offshoring to China and other far-away locations. Even IT-related services have begun to be 'near sourced' – instead of being outsourced to Bangalore, India, where costs of doing business have risen due to high employee turnover, inadequate infra- structure, and the appreciation of the rupee against the US dollar. Latin America certainly has a time-zone advantage.[8] And the MNCs from other regions are likewise increasingly interested in relocating production closer to the US and Canada. Mexico and the Central American economies are thus poised to gain from this new trend in international business activity.

6.9. SUMMING UP

The United States is the world's richest market and the wellspring of inno- vations. It is, indeed, rather a shame that Latin America has effectively missed out on exploiting its *locational* advantages of being adjacent to the US. True, the region has been hampered by the burden of colonial history and the persistence of leftist ideologies that are anti-market and anti-private-business. Yet, what really matters for economic development is not whether an incumbent government is controlled by socialists or neo- Marxists but whether the government is burdened with business-unfriendly overregulation, cumbersome legal systems – and corruption. China is a telling example. As pointed out in Chapter 5, it separates business from ideology. In fact, capitalism itself seems unconcerned about the ideologi- cal dogma of the government so long as private property is respected, the legal system works, and profit-seeking business can be conducted without heavy-handed government interference.

There are two key features that characterize East Asia most distinctly but that are lacking in Latin America. These are the existence of strong second-goose economies and an appropriate alignment of countries at different stages of growth, a hierarchical structure that can produce the phenomenon of comparative advantage recycling on a regional basis. In East Asia, Japan and the NIEs have proved to be the powerful second geese that have succeeded in rapid industrial upgrading, thereby handing over comparatively disadvantaged activities down the regional hierarchy of countries.

Globalization may aggravate or alleviate poverty. It has these opposing impacts. Its desirable force needs to be unleashed. The outcome, therefore, depends on a developing country's growth policy and strategy. The driver of poverty reduction in Asia is growth and not distribution change (Chapter 4). A larger pie to share – that is, 'shared growth' – is the Asian goal. By contrast, Latin America is, on the whole, bent on distribution, sacrificing growth itself (that is, a small pie to be distributed equally – supposedly in favor of the poor). Whether the Latin American orientation is good or bad can be judged by comparing the revealed changes in the standards of living in the two regions.

NOTES

1. 'Glitter and Graft', *Economist*, July 21, 2007, p. 39.
2. 'Latin America: The Big Move to Free Markets', *Business Week*, June 15, 1992, pp. 50–62.
3. Sir Alexander Gray, *Adam Smith*, the Historical Association, General Series, G. 10: London, 1948, p. 5, as quoted in Bell (1953, p. 156).
4. 'The year 1775, in fact, marks more clearly than most dates selected as boundary-stones the end of one economic period and the beginning of another. For it was in this year that [James] Watt pushed his invention from the experimental to the commercial stage, and began to supply steam-engines for the market under a patent' (Ashton, 1968, p. 60).
5. The 'feast-and-fast' theory of fiscal crisis is credited to Arthur B. Laffer, who explained the dire financial quagmire of the State of California in the 1990s.
6. For a case of perfect substitutability between free trade and factor movement, see Mundell (1957).
7. As reported in 'Short on Labor, Farmers in U.S. Shift to Mexico', *New York Times*, www. nytimes.com., September 5, 2007.
8. 'The New Economics of Outsourcing', *BusinessWeek* (online), April 14, 2008.

PART III

Money/finance dimension

7. Borrowed growth: balance of payments, capital flows, and development finance

7.1. THE ROLE OF FINANCE IN ECONOMIC DEVELOPMENT

How a catching-up country may climb the ladder of economic development is examined in earlier chapters. Asian countries have been capitalizing on the growth opportunities created by global capitalism, and in turn boosting the forces of globalization as they themselves further integrate into, and shape, the world economy. Yet, so far we have looked only at real-sector catch-up growth (though we did briefly touch on the role of exchange rates as a prompter of industrial upgrading). It is time to take account of the financial dimension of growth. How has the catch-up in the real economy been financed? What sorts of financial markets and products have been brought into existence as Asian economies climbed onto the higher stages of growth? What is the role of the government in financial development at different stages? In other words, we need a financial-sector model of growth comparable to and consistent with its real-sector counterpart.

The purpose of this chapter is to introduce the money-side story of the FG model of growth. We will first consider the notion of 'borrowed growth' as the critical feature of US-led growth clustering, and will conceptually explore the 'business-cycle-magnification' effect of the current account-(CA)-deficit-based financing of economic growth. That is, the danger of 'externally originated (via the financial account) balance-of-payments (BOP) imbalance' is analyzed so as to relate to the currency and financial crises of Asian countries during the late 1990s, America's recent longest boom with its record high CA deficits, and the nature of the US-led co-growth regime.

7.2. BORROWED GROWTH

Any developing country at the start of industrialization must cope with a situation in which internal savings (S) tend to be exceeded by domestic investment (I). Hence, how to cover this inherent deficiency of savings is a critical issue in formulating an effective strategy for economic growth. Any open economy that invests more than it saves at home will end up with a well-known Keynesian disequilibrium in which the CA becomes negative (namely, $CA = S - I$, assuming a balanced government budget). And this CA deficit needs to be financed by capital inflows (that is, external borrowing), since CA necessarily equals the financial account (FA). The FA keeps track of capital inflows and outflows. In other words, rapid growth is financed by a surplus on the FA or a net capital inflow (foreign savings). This type of CA-deficit-based growth finance may be called 'borrowed growth'.

Borrowed growth is a double-edged sword for borrowing countries. Helped by capital inflows, 'input-driven' industrialization à la Krugman (1994) is made possible, and in fact, *accelerated*. Such growth leads to super-economic growth (a boom), which itself in turn attracts more capital inflows, stimulating further growth in a virtuous circle. At the same time, however, once foreign investors sense some danger of weakness in the borrowing country's performance, a herd mentality takes over. This causes an abrupt and exaggerated reversal in capital flows – and a sudden slump (a bust). All this corresponds to the familiar pattern of 'manias, panics and crashes' à la Kindleberger (1996).

The 'East Asian miracle' and the 'East Asian débâcle' of 1997–8, which occurred in tandem, are nothing but the results of excessive debts created through liberalized financial markets by way of hot money inflows. This exaggerated swing from miracle (super-growth) to débâcle (super-crisis) represents the perils of borrowed growth. Indeed, a string of currency and financial crises that East Asia, Latin America, and Russia experienced in the 1980s and 1990s was due to the mismanagement (or 'non-management') of borrowed growth – and due to institutional inadequacy and inappropriate policy responses. Some advanced and mature economies would likewise experience the similar phenomenon of borrowed growth.

7.2.1. Stages of Growth and Balance-of-payments

Borrowed growth, which occurs in developing and advanced countries alike, can be best understood in terms of the stages theory of the balance of payments (BOP). Rapidly growing developing countries are likely to experience CA deficits at the start. Once they succeed in building a strong industrial base, CA (especially merchandise trade) surpluses become their BOP characteristic. In contrast, fully developed and mature countries are prone to CA deficits (largely because of merchandise trade deficits, if not yet CA deficits because invisible trade and investment incomes may be in surplus). In other words, BOP conditions can be interpreted as a matter of how advanced a country is in economic growth – that is, they depend on growth stages. Management of BOP, therefore, requires *different policy responses along the path of industrialization.*

The idea that secular changes in BOP are fundamentally a function of growth is nothing new; it is said to go back at least to J.E. Cairnes (1874), who describes how an initial trade deficit (financed by borrowing) turns to a trade surplus, which then results in repayment of debts and lending abroad (as pointed out in Halevi, 1971). A similar theory (Kindleberger, 1963) posits, in terms of a three-stage construct, that a developing country that opts for the open-economy path of development initially experiences a growing CA deficit in its early stages but soon experiences steady improvements and eventually a CA surplus as it succeeds in building up manufacturing and trade competitiveness at later stages. Other economists present many more stages: five in Meier and Baldwin (1957), six in Crowther (1957), seven in Enke and Salera (1947), and even twelve in Halevi (1971).

More specifically, for example, Crowther (1957) classifies such a long-term trend in growth-driven BOP conditions into six stages: (i) 'immature debtor-borrower' (a deepening CA deficit) → (ii) 'mature debtor-borrower' (a declining CA deficit) → (iii) 'debtor-lender and debtor-repayer' (a rising CA surplus) → (iv) 'immature creditor-lender'(a record-high CA surplus) → (v) 'mature creditor-lender' (a declining CA deficit) → (vi) 'creditor-drawer and borrower' (a rising CA deficit). This six-stage model gives us a starting point for our own analysis.

When an underdeveloped economy opens up for trade and investment at the start of economic development, its CA registers a growing deficit, especially if it is left to free market forces without any restrictions on cross-border transactions. This corresponds to the transition period from the 'take-off' to the 'sustained growth' stage (in the words of Rostow, 1960). During such a transitional period, capital goods, technologies, modern business services, and hitherto unavailable consumer goods are all necessarily imported from the advanced world to develop the country's industrial base and domestic markets. Whatever it can produce (normally primary goods) is exported, but this may not be sufficient to cover the costs of imports. A resultant CA deficit needs to be financed by borrowing from abroad. As the economy succeeds in industrialization, however, this deficit is eventually reversed and eliminated.

Stated in terms of Crowther's theory of BOP, the above-described situation matches the first two stages of 'debtor-borrower'. These early stages represent the most critical, danger-laden period for a developing country, since its rising CA deficits require more and more foreign borrowing unless otherwise controlled – and it plunges deeper and deeper into debts with ballooning interest payments. (This kind of situation is still prevalent in many

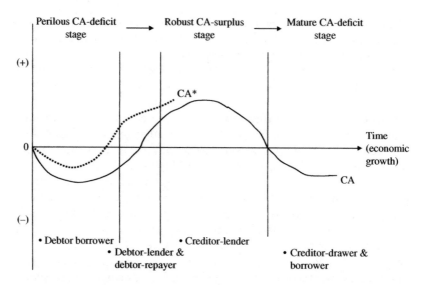

Figure 7.1   A stages model of balance of payments and growth

developing African countries.) This tendency is all the more pronounced if
exchange rates are fixed, since domestic borrowers are falsely assured that
their debts specified in foreign currencies are the same as home-currency
debts. Yet an 'unexpected' devaluation of home currency, which may be
triggered by sudden capital withdrawals by foreign lenders and investors,
would wreak havoc for debtors (as happened in the Asian crisis of 1997–8).
This period can, therefore, be identified as the '*perilous CA-deficit phase*'
(see Figure 7.1).

On the other hand, the subsequent two stages of 'creditor-lender' are
accompanied by CA surpluses (first rising and then declining), the phase
that can be called the '*robust CA-surplus phase*'. Those countries that have
reached this phase are at the height of their industrialization drive, in which
the secondary sector (manufacturing and construction) dominates, serving
as the primary engine of growth – with a shrinking share of the primary
sector and a rising share of the tertiary (service) sector (Clark, 1935). They
are heavily specialized in 'making goods' and their rising incomes derive
from investment-driven growth (that is, investing in productive capacity)
– and from export revenues. In particular, domestic output and exports
in manufacturing industry are mutually reinforcing, making the logic of
cumulative causation (or virtuous cycle) work (Smith, 1776/1908; Kaldor,
1985; Eatwell, 1982; Cantwell, 1987).

In fact, the rapidly catching-up Asian countries have been able to swiftly
leave behind the perilous phase and enter the robust CA phase through a

variety of policy measures. Moreover, a massive inflow of capital, especially in the form of FDI by MNCs that bring advanced technology, leads to a substantial CA surplus – as best witnessed in China's and Vietnam's export booms. Effective policy can expedite a transition into the robust phase, as depicted by the dotted line in Figure 7.1. (This has some interesting theoretical implications for the way we look at BOP, as discussed in Section 7.3 below.)

Finally, the last two stages of 'creditor-drawer and borrower' may be labeled the '*mature CA-deficit phase*'. As a secular trend, the mature advanced countries are likely to stay in this phase, though they may temporarily record surpluses. How, then, can these deficit-prone countries cope with the deficit? In the first place, they can live off their past overseas investments abroad – that is, their investment incomes may be substantially large enough to minimize and keep the deficit at a manageable level. In addition, they are normally capable of attracting capital inflows easily because they enjoy high credit-rating and offer an attractive business environment for foreign MNCs. Some enjoy the privilege of having their currencies used as reserves by other countries. They are thus able to reap seigniorage by 'exporting' their own currencies as financial assets. Their CA deficits can thus be maintained so long as the rest of the world is willing to hold their currencies. All these situations may combine to create favorable conditions in which some advanced countries enjoy an unusually *prolonged* period of borrowed growth, as has been the case with the US.

7.2.1. Financial/Money vs. Industrial/Real Sectors: Interaction

The CA and the FA represent the two sectors of an open economy – the former the 'industrial/real' sector, and the latter the 'financial/money' sector, respectively. They necessarily interact closely in the course of economic development. Real-sector transactions require money-sector transactions for finance and settlement of trade accounts, but the latter often becomes 'autonomous' (no longer 'accommodating') in this age of fast capital flows, compelling CA instead to accommodate.

In this connection, the so-called 'intertemporal theory of production and trade' à la Fisher (Fisher, 1930; Krugman and Obstfeld, 2003), which is within the framework of conventional neoclassical trade theory (typically presented in terms of a product transformation curve and indifference curves), provides a good starting point in analyzing the interface between the industrial and financial sectors. The intertemporal theory predicts that any swiftly developing country imports 'present spending or purchasing power' (to invest in domestic capital formation) by exporting 'future spending or purchasing power'. This means a low relative value (preference) for future spending – that is to say, a high relative value (preference) for present spending. This indicates a high rate of interest reflecting highly productive investment opportunities (high marginal returns to investment) at the present.

Put differently, such a borrowing country has an *intertemporal* comparative advantage in present spending; it borrows from overseas to finance productive investment. Thus, cross-border finance satisfies the needs of its industrial/real sector. As a consequence, domestic capital formation takes place through a CA deficit (= a FA surplus). This model of intertemporal comparative advantage describes an *ideal* growth situation for an international payments equilibrium to be maintained *over time* – ideal, so long as all imports are only investment goods that would yield output surpluses in the future. The financial side of BOP is satisfied by capital inflows which foreign investors are willing to provide. And what is borrowed today will be paid back out of what the country can overproduce tomorrow. There is thus no BOP problem in the long run.

The reality, however, is more complicated, of course. What is borrowed (today's debt) may not be used to build up a debtor country's productive capacity. If borrowed money is squandered on consumption (instead of investment), the country will not be able to pay off debt out of future output. A currency/financial crisis will then occur. This points up how important it is to manage FA transactions judiciously and to use borrowed capital for productive domestic investment. The financial sector (via FA) thus critically interacts with the industrial sector in the process of economic development.

In short, an open economy (S = I + CA) has a *higher* degree of freedom in development finance than a closed economy (S = I), because the former can avail itself of its external balance (CA [= FA]). For a closed economy, domestic savings are the only source of finance, and if domestic savings are not sufficient, it is constrained from growth. An open economy can rely on borrowing from overseas to supplement its domestic savings in order to grow. In this case, CA transactions are autonomous – or *masters*, so to speak, while FA transactions are accommodating – or *servants*. This means that *the more open a growing economy is to capital inflows into its productive capacity-building investment, the higher the rate of growth.* Borrowed growth, however, is accompanied by high risks of excessive capital inflows. A sudden surge in capital inflows may not be properly channeled into productive capital formation, spilling into unproductive, purely speculative types of investment – hence into a greater CA deficit. The domestic need for capital formation may thus be overwhelmed by unnecessarily huge capital inflows. The upshot is a *role reversal*; FA transactions become 'masters', whereas CA transactions become 'servants'.

Moreover, in the context of borrowed growth with unfettered capital flows across borders, rapid growth exposes a developing country to the forces of 'cumulative causation', upward as well as downward, which are generated in both the industrial and the financial sectors simultaneously. These forces would cause both 'super-growth' and 'super-crisis' (magnified boom-and-bust cycles) as explained in the following scenario: (a) high domestic investment (initially accompanied by high savings) → (b) high growth → (c) capital inflows → (d) *super-growth* (acceleration) → (e) more capital inflows → (f) a danger of inflation (due to a rise in money supply caused by capital inflows) and diminished investment opportunities in the industrial sector → (g) speculative and excessive investment in the financial sector (resulting in the rising price of securities, commodities, and real estate) → (h) signs of a collapse (busting) of a bubble → (i) defaults on domestic debts → (j) hot global money to the exits → (k) depletion of official reserves (under fixed exchange rates) → (l) currency crisis (home currency meltdown) → (m) defaults on foreign debts → (n) *super-currency/ financial crisis*.

The boom (super-growth) period is covered by the first-half sequence of (a) through (g), while the bust (super-crisis) is represented by the second-half sequence of (h) through (n). The whole sequence involves *spiraling* interactions (initially complementary and augmenting but later on deleterious and subversive) between the industrial and the financial sectors.

7.2.3. The Financial Account: Three Types of Capital Inflows

Private capital inflows comprise three major types: (i) FDI by multinational corporations, (ii) portfolio investment by securities firms and investment funds, and (iii) bank loans. FDI is the most stable type – not so easily reversible in flows. It involves not only FDI-specific *financial capital* but also, and more importantly, *human and intellectual capital* (industrial knowledge) and *physical capital* (machinery, equipment, and intermediate inputs). Portfolio investment is speculative by nature, hence footloose and susceptible to herd mentality. It is a source of instability in BOP, since it is easily 'cashable' and instantly reversible (Gray, 1999). In fact, it is portfolio investment that triggers a crisis when it is suddenly pulled out of host financial markets. But it is also the kind that comes back quickly as soon as the host countries show any promising signs of economic recovery, thereby boosting a rebound in the host country. Thus it is ironically *both* crisis-triggering and rebound-assisting through its flow mechanism. In contrast, bank loans are relatively stable because of their medium-term nature. Nevertheless, they tend to be overextended in good times, especially under the 'moral hazard' of probable bailouts by both the debtor nation's central bank and the IMF. In addition, they are slow in returning to once-stricken host markets even when the latter show signs of recovery.[1]

It is now widely recognized that FDI is the type of capital inflow that is most desirable for developing countries, since it brings with it advanced technology, managerial and organizational knowledge, and access to export markets – and above all, a long-term commitment to local production. Also, it is generally posited that an appropriate sequence of capital inflows into a developing country is first to liberalize long-term capital inflows (particularly FDI) ahead of short-term capital inflows (Eichengreen et al., 1999). And above all, necessary institutional preparations are called for prior to financial liberalization (Mishken, 2006). And there is increasing opinion that short-term capital inflows, especially hot money for foreign exchange speculations, need to be controlled as a makeshift measure to avert disruptive consequences.

7.2.4.   Two Genres of BOP Imbalances: 'CA-pulled' vs. 'FA-pushed'

As mentioned above, there has recently been a role reversal between CA transactions and FA transactions. The former used to be 'masters', and the latter 'servants', in the sense that trade is financed and settled by accompanying financial transactions. The latter merely facilitate the former. When the Bretton Woods system of pegged exchange rates early on permitted discretionary controls on short-term capital flows, trade, and foreign exchanges, CA transactions used to be the primary/autonomous part of international economic activities, whereas their FA counterparts merely played the secondary/accommodating role by financing CA transactions. These were the standard characterizations of CA and FA that were accepted and taught in international economics (see, for example, Meade's (1951) definitive tome on the theory of BOP).

7.2.4.1.   CA-pulled type: internally originated deficits
In those days, CA deficits, when they appeared, were the result of an *internal* disequilibrium caused by an excess of aggregate demand over aggregate supply (output) at home, as best stipulated in the Keynesian 'absorption' theory of BOP (Alexander, 1953). CA deficits were regarded as the consequence of a country 'living beyond its means' (since CA = Y – absorption (C + I + G)). To correct a serious CA deficit, therefore, tight macroeconomic policies (monetary as well as fiscal) were called for and applied to reduce domestic expenditures. The best way for an economy to grow was then to raise domestic savings to finance domestic investment, since capital flows were 'imperfect' due to restrictions under the Bretton Woods system.

Indeed, the BOP served as a strict guidepost for macroeconomic stabilization. Those countries that could not manage BOP had to seek a bailout from the IMF. The IMF, however, imposed so-called 'conditionalities' or an austerity program on borrowing governments to solve *internal* disequilibrium (excessive spending). The governments thus had to implement IMF-prescribed deflationary policies to force themselves to live 'within their means'. If an austerity diet was judged unworkable, the IMF allowed a devaluation of the currency in the face of 'fundamental disequilibrium'. These IMF prescriptions – the austerity program and devaluation – were considered appropriate and effective to deal with internally originated (CA-caused) BOP crises, since capital flows (FA transactions) remained largely controlled.

7.2.4.2. FA-pushed type: externally caused deficits
With liberalization of cross-border capital movements and rising liquidity sloshing around the global economy, however, the whole situation began to change. Pure financial transactions have grown ever larger in volume as an autonomous type of capital flows (especially, hot money) and have risen in importance, overwhelming CA transactions. Here, most capital flows go through the foreign exchange markets: as Kasa (1999, p. 1) once put it colorfully, 'On a typical day in the foreign exchange market roughly $1.5 billion change hands. This means that in less than a week foreign exchange transactions have exceeded the annual value of world trade'. When other types of capital flows which are not transacted through the foreign exchange markets (for example, physical flows of hard currencies such as the US dollar and the Euro to be used as a store of value outside of the US and the Eurozone – and illegal transactions) are included, the volume of capital flows is even greater. Besides, Kasa's observation is now nearly a decade old. Financial flows must since then have grown even larger with a rapid rise in the growth of the global economy.

Be that as it may, most capital flows (especially portfolio investments and bank loans) are primary and autonomous – and no longer secondary and accommodating in the traditional sense. When a country is flooded with capital inflows (hence, a huge surplus on its FA), it is compelled either to let its currency appreciate (under flexible exchange rates) or to inflate its economy (under fixed exchange rates). This expansionary pressure caused by imported liquidity in turn leads to a CA deficit *for the very purpose of relieving such pressure via increased imports*. Even if the country's CA deficit rises, it is still possible that its currency will remain overvalued. This outcome may be called 'a continuous CA deficit but still a strong currency' paradox, as experienced by the US for many decades. This type of

CA deficits is an *externally originated (FA-pushed)* BOP imbalance where FA transactions become masters (causes) and CA transactions servants (effects), an imbalance that is diametrically opposite to the traditional *internally originated (CA-pulled)* BOP imbalance where the CA is still the master and the FA is the servant (Ozawa, 1998).

7.2.4.3. Asian financial crisis

At the time of the Asian financial crisis of 1997–8 the IMF was severely criticized for its continued imposition of outdated austerity programs on the bailed-out Asian governments. Those stricken Asian countries had been maintaining fundamentally sound macroeconomic conditions: relatively well-balanced budgets, stable money supplies, and price stability. In the case of the Asian crisis, the debtors were mostly the private banks which borrowed from overseas in foreign currencies (mostly the US dollar) and lent to domestic firms in local currencies. When the links of their currencies to the dollar were broken as a consequence of depleted international reserves, the debtors were no longer able to repay. Consequently, the IMF's conventional prescriptions made things worse. The bailed-out economies were driven into a severe slump by high interest rates and tight fiscal conditions. Businesses collapsed, causing even more bad loans, thereby sparking a banking crisis. Banks contracted loans and precipitated a credit crunch. The conventional IMF remedies that were once developed to cope with internally originated (CA-pulled) BOP imbalances proved to be not a medicine but rather a poison for those countries with externally originated (FA-pushed) BOP imbalances.

It can be generalized, therefore, that when an economy is still under-industrialized and its financial sector underdeveloped (that is, still in the early stages of development), it is prone to internally originated BOP imbalances, and that as the economy successfully scales the ladder of economic development, attracting capital inflows into its financial markets, it tends increasingly to succumb to externally originated BOP imbalances. In the recent booming commodities markets, for example, the resource-exporting countries have registered suddenly ballooning CA surpluses, which result in inflationary pressures at home. This phenomenon is particularly pronounced among the Middle Eastern oil-exporting countries (in their resource-based Stage-I growth), which are compelled to consider depegging their currencies from the US dollar. For them, their CA transactions (largely oil and natural gas exports) are predominantly autonomous (that is, masters), while their FA transactions are secondary/accommodating (that is, servants). In other words, their BOP imbalances are fundamentally caused in the real sector, not in the financial sector. We will look at country-specific experiences below.

7.3.   ASIA'S BOP EXPERIENCES

How effectively have the Asian countries managed the perils of borrowed growth? First of all, Japan was lucky, since its catch-up growth occurred during the period of the original IMF regime of fixed exchange rates that permitted controls on capital flows. In order to maintain an official rate (Y360 to the US dollar), the Japanese government pursued a BOP-guided monetary policy for growth. Exports were initially encouraged to earn as much foreign exchange as possible to accumulate reserves. Economic growth was stimulated so long as its deficit-creating effect on the BOP remained manageable. However, once the BOP started to show a deficit that could no longer be financed by official reserves, tight monetary policy was immediately applied to slow down the pace of growth (so as to reduce imports). As soon as the BOP conditions improved, Japan then quickly went back to expansionary monetary policy and resumed high growth. This 'stop and go' cycle was then repeated many times until Japan escaped from the perilous CA-deficit phase and moved into the robust CA-surplus phase (for this well-known BOP-guided monetary policy, see Wallich and Wallich, 1976).

Since in those days FA transactions were closely controlled, the BOP imbalances Japan faced were *only* of the internally originated type. Japan was 'protected' from unstable capital flows by the IMF's then legitimate capital controls. Its financial sector, particularly the banking industry, was strategically used as a vital instrument of high catch-up growth in the form of a central-bank-guided 'main-bank' system (Aoki and Patrick, 1994). Japan adopted what may be called 'bank-loan capitalism', in which 'central-bank-based finance of development' was actively used for the purpose of avoiding external dependence, namely borrowed growth (Ozawa, 1999b). The role central banks can play as the major financier of economic development is not well recognized. They have the power to pump liquidity into the economy, which can be used as loanable funds for productive investment. Of course, this power, when abused, entails high risks of fueling inflation or even hyperinflation, as often seen in many developing countries. Yet, as emphasized by Joseph Schumpeter (1934), the availability of bank loans is critical in financing entrepreneurs' business activities, and monetary ease does not necessarily spur inflation so long as loans are not used for consumptive purposes. This is exactly the mechanism early postwar Japan actively made use of with the help of the Bank of Japan under the central-bank-piloted main-bank system.

In sum, Japan in effect enjoyed 'infant BOP protection', so to speak – thanks to the original IMF system which gave immunity to capital and foreign exchange controls in those days. Thus, Japan was able not only to escape from the dangers of externally originated BOP imbalances but also to resort to its reinforced main-bank system for industrial catch-up – reinforced by its central bank, which lent its power of credit creation to corporate Japan.

Furthermore, not only did Japan minimize external borrowing but it discouraged inward FDI. Japan, instead, eagerly purchased technology via licensing agreements from the West, thereby acquiring the technological assets possessed by Western MNCs in an unbundled fashion (Ozawa, 1974a). Licensing served as an effective substitute for inward FDI, since Japan already had a well-developed capacity to absorb foreign technology. (Actually this may be considered a form of 'borrowed growth' observable in the industrial/real sector, since Japan borrowed advanced knowledge from the West.) When FA transactions began to be liberalized in the mid-1970s, Japan had already been sufficiently structurally developed to withstand any major currency fluctuations in foreign exchange rates. Short-term capital flows thus caused no serious disruption to the real sector.

True, Japan's experience is peculiar to its early postwar economic environment and obviously not comparable with the present-day world. However, it is perhaps worthwhile for developing countries to pay attention to Japan's conservative and cautious approach to CA management and learn from it. In this respect, China's cautious approach to CA management and FA liberalization is in line with, and comes closest to, the Japanese model, though China is far more open to inward FDI and far more export-driven. As to China's exchange controls, even a mainstream neoliberal economist, such as Paul Krugman (1998, p. 77), approvingly notes:

> Why hasn't China been nearly so badly hit as its neighbors [during the Asian currency crisis]? Because it has been able to cut, not raise, interest rates in this crisis, despite maintaining a fixed exchange rate; and the reason it is able to do that is that it has an inconvertible currency, a.k.a. exchange controls. Those controls are often evaded, and they are the sources of lots of corruption, but they still give China a degree of policy leeway that the rest of Asia desperately wishes it had.

In the meantime, China has been steadily accumulating trade surpluses since the start of the 1990s because of its strong export performance (except for 1993 when its CA temporarily registered a deficit of $11.9 billion). Its official reserves now stand at over $2 trillion (at the time of writing). Given its unwillingness to quickly revalue the yuan, China's official reserves are ever on the rise, and its money supply has been accordingly expanding with a resulting high rate of inflation. It has been issuing government bonds to mop up excess supplies of money (that is, sterilization policy), has raised the reserve requirements for banks, and has most recently begun to require exporters to park revenues in special accounts while the funds are verified as genuine earnings from trade (to curb hot money inflows). On the whole, nonetheless, it has opted for inflation rather than letting the yuan rise sharply.

Taiwan's fiscal conservatism is likewise an approach akin to the Japanese strategy. Taiwan has been managing its New Taiwan dollar quite effectively at both economy and company levels. Its CA has stayed in the black ever since the start of the 1980s – that is, in the robust CA-surplus stage. Whenever exports dropped, it has introduced temporary exchange control measures such as a ban on Taiwanese firms' forward contracts and a reporting requirement on foreign exchange remittances to the central bank, all designed to discourage speculation. Taiwanese businesses are traditionally conservative in corporate finance, since many are owned by families, and external borrowing is normally kept to a minimum. As a whole they had very low debt-to-equity ratios in the neighborhood of 30 percent in the 1990s, and this is a major reason why Taiwan escaped the contagion of the Asian crisis.

Singapore is similarly in the robust CA-surplus phase. Even during the Asian crisis it ran CA surpluses – for example, $14.6 billion in 1997. The Hong Kong government, too, was able to maintain its currency-board exchange system without any difficulty. In August 1998, it even supported local stock prices by investing $15.2 billion in Hong Kong's 33 biggest companies to fend off currency speculation.[2]

In contrast, all those troubled economies in East Asia during the Asian crisis exhibited two common characteristics that were opposite to the approaches taken by Japan, China, Taiwan, Singapore, and Hong Kong. The stricken countries were all hooked on footloose global money and allowed borrowed growth to take its own course. They permitted unfavorable CA conditions to develop and prematurely liberalized capital inflows. Thailand, the birthplace of the Asian crisis of 1997, had continually run CA deficits from the mid-1960s onward (except in 1986 when it had a small surplus). Its CA deficit had hovered around 8 percent of GDP prior to the crisis. In 1987, Thailand began a series of deregulations on interest rates and banking transactions and opened the Bangkok International Banking facilities, which served as a conduit for capital inflows when rising local interest rates widened the rate differential vis-à-vis the outside world. Capital inflows from overseas were then funneled by poorly supervised and inexperienced local bankers into speculative real estate and stock markets, which sparked a bubble. The upshot was a currency and banking crisis as foreign investors rushed to the exits at the first signs of an unwinding asset boom.

Indonesia and Malaysia were similarly caught in the trap of the perilous CA-deficit phase. (Indonesia went from a $1.9 billion deficit in 1985 to a \$7.8 billion deficit in 1996; Malaysia from a \$613 million deficit in 1985 to a \$4.9 billion deficit in 1996.) Both instituted swift capital liberalization, which made them dependent on foreign capital inflows. Indonesia's financial liberalization measures introduced in 1983 and 1988 had resulted in large interest differentials (5 to 10 percent), attracting capital inflows.

South Korea had closely followed Japan's self-reliant financial approach to industrialization until the late 1980s when it encountered a ballooning CA deficit. In fact, it once used central-bank-based development finance via 'policy loans' in a top-down micro-managed fashion (Ozawa, 1999a). To finance the deficits, the Korean government took advantage of the favorable climate in international credit markets rather than drawing down foreign reserves. FA liberalization was implemented in the latter half of the 1980s to prepare for the opening of capital markets in the early 1990s (Park, 1994). Up to the currency crisis in 1997, Korea had been able to maintain a stable market exchange rate for the won against the US dollar, though its real exchange rate remained overvalued (Lee, 1998). *Chaebols* competed with each other in expanding industrial capacities by borrowing short-term capital from abroad. Overcapacity, an export slump (hence, a high CA deficit), and a rising ratio of short-term debt to foreign reserves, and recession-triggered business bankruptcies in the late 1990s all coalesced into the inevitable conditions for the currency and financial crisis that occurred in November 1997.

It is clear that those Asian countries that fell victim to the financial crisis were all entrapped in the snare of 'externally originated BOP imbalances', as they prematurely liberalized their financial markets – prematurely in the sense that they were not quite ready institutionally to deal effectively with massive inflows of short-term capital. The excessive capital inflows reinforced an underlying business cycle that was then in the making, magnifying a fragile boom that was unavoidably destined for its bust. These capital inflows were not really needed for a healthy economic expansion in Korea.

In fact, some argue that high domestic savings alone in Korea, as well as all other afflicted countries, were sufficient to finance respectable rates of economic growth *without* borrowing foreign capital. A study made by the Nomura Research Institute (Kan, 1999) demonstrates that during the period of 1991–6, even without external borrowings, Thailand would still have grown at an annual rate of 6.7 percent (instead of the actual rate of 8.2 percent), Malaysia at 7.5 percent (instead of 9.0 percent), Indonesia at 7.2 percent (instead of 7.8 percent), the Philippines at 2.4 percent (instead of 2.8 percent), Korea at 7.1 percent (instead of 7.4 percent), and China at 11.7 percent (instead of 11.5 percent) (Table 7.1).

Table 7.1   Growth rates without capital inflows, 1991–2006

	S: Saving* (domestic)	F: Capital* inflow	I: Investment* = S + F	G: Annual Growth rate (actual)	ICOR	S-based growth rate = S/ICOR
ASEAN						
Thailand	34.9	7.7	42.6	8.2	5.2	6.7
Malaysia	35.0	6.5	41.5	9.0	4.6	7.5
Indonesia	32.1	2.6	34.7	7.8	4.4	7.2
Philippines	19.0	3.2	22.2	2.8	8.1	2.4
South Korea	35.4	1.5	36.9	7.4	5.0	7.1
China	40.1	–1.0	39.2	11.5	3.4	11.7

Notes: * As percentage of GDP.
ICOR: Incremental capital-output ratio.

Source: A study made by the Nomura Research Institute cited by Kan (1999, p. 17).

This hypothetical scenario, however, assumes that *all* domestic savings – and they alone – are channeled entirely into domestic capital formation without any CA imbalance. The assumption of a balanced CA means that a developing country is restricted from importing all necessary capital goods (including advanced technology) for fast catch-up growth and that it therefore may not be able to grow at a brisk rate – that is to say, the incremental capital-output ratio (ICOR) will increase under import restrictions. Despite these unrealistic assumptions, nevertheless, the study does point to rather small net contributions of capital inflows to total growth in those high-saving countries when the risks of externally originated (FA-pushed) BOP imbalances are taken into account.

7.4. AMERICA'S BORROWED GROWTH

The US economy has been operating in a mode of borrowed growth. It is in the mature CA-deficit stage. Its economic expansion has been supported by large capital inflows that can supplement or rather substitute for domestic savings. Its CA deficit has been escalating toward nearly $1 trillion in 2008 – say, from about $300 billion at the end of the 1990s. It has recently hovered at around 6.5 percent of GDP. Combined with the banking crisis in the wake of the subprime mortgage débâcle, America's borrowed growth has finally begun to cause a sharp fall of the US dollar against the British pound and the Euro in particular, starting in early 2008. The dollar then rebounded as the credit crisis spread to Europe, and investors sought a safe haven in US Treasury securities.

The US has long enjoyed this unique status as a safe haven despite its heavy debt to the rest of the world. First of all, it is not so much US borrowers but foreign investors who bring money to America's financial markets. The US is not really 'borrowing' in the real sense of the term in order to finance its CA deficit – that is, a situation of *internally* originated BOP imbalances. Excepting some political opposition to foreign interests' attempts to buy out America's 'strategic' companies, America allows free capital inflows to fuel its economic growth. Such inflows of foreign savings result in an ever-growing CA deficit – that is, a situation of externally originated (FA-pushed) BOP imbalances.

Ever since the end of World War II, the US has arguably been a safe haven for many foreign investors. It is one of the most politically stable countries where reliable securities (most of all, Treasury securities) and sophisticated (often high risk but high return) private financial instruments are in abundant supply. In contrast, those export-driven developing countries that rapidly accumulate large hoards of exchange reserves lack such well-developed financial markets at home for the very simple reason that they are not fully developed yet (as will be set out in detail in terms of a stages model of financial development in Chapter 8). In this sense, they are engaged not so much in interest arbitrage as in 'institutional arbitrage'.

In addition, the US dollar, despite its fall, has been the world's dominant currency, allowing a high level of tolerance of a CA deficit. In a sense, the US dollar itself can be looked upon as America's most important *export*. For most of the time the dollar has been a good (even superior) substitute for gold (which Keynes even called 'barbaric'), and the global economy has come to operate effectively on a *dollar* standard.

Yet America's borrowed growth cannot go on without encountering financial problems. In September 2008, it hit a snag, causing a serious financial market crisis. And the government had to intervene with an unprecedented $700 billion bailout.

7.4.1. US-led Co-growth Regime

Following in the footsteps of the UK, the US established another hegemon-led growth cluster (that is, Pax Americana), and has been spreading market democracy as its ultimate objective. America's efforts have gained traction, especially since the collapse of the Soviet Union. The IT revolution that originated in the US has accelerated this trend. Growth clustering has developed – and fed on – a hierarchy of closely interacting economies, especially on the Pacific Rim, a hierarchy that is highly conducive to rapid growth in both the hegemon country and follower countries. The United States is basically in the advanced 'post-industrial' stage of growth where value-added activities are concentrated on services or the tertiary sector (notably finance, R&D, higher education, and healthcare). On the other hand, Asia as a whole is in the 'lower-tier' stages where the primary sector is still dominant in China, India, and the ASEAN countries and the second-ary sector accounts for a relatively significant portion of economic activity in the NIEs – and even in Japan.[3]

And what is unique about US-led growth clustering in Asia is that these differences in growth stages have become complementary with – and supportive of – each other, mutually augmenting and reinforcing structural transformation through trade and investment. As predicted by the real-sector model of industrial upgrading (Chapter 3), this cluster has grown increasingly energy-intensive – especially oil-intensive – in both industrial and consumptive activities, deepening its dependence on, and its involvement in terms of FDI operations with, energy-producing countries, notably in the Middle East. This US-led co-growth regime is schematically illustrated in Figure 7.2.[4]

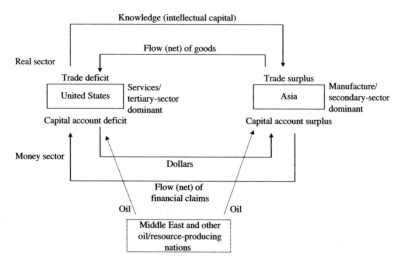

Figure 7.2   The US-led co-growth regime

Basically, the US has been a major (initially *the* major) final demand
provider (via importing Asian goods and services) and the leading financial
manager of the regime, while Asia serves as the workshop of the world.
As the lead goose, the US disseminates knowledge (intellectual capital) to
Asia – via FDI, licensing, exports of capital goods (knowledge-embodied
goods), and education and training of Asian students. And Asian countries
then produce and export back goods to the US, Europe, and each other
across Asia. The US in particular has, on the whole, willingly tolerated
huge trade deficits, year after year, in its own interests – that is, to keep
domestic prices under control by satisfying excess demand with imports.

These features represent cross-Pacific transactions on the real-sector side
of the Pacific-Rim economy. And high mass-consumerism is accompanied
by heavy dependence on oil as the major fuel. This hallmark of US-led
global capitalism is imprinted on Asia, as well. As a result, it has ineluctably compelled the oil-producing world to be inserted ever deeper in the
capitalist expansion in the global economy – with the consequence of a new
geopolitics across the globe, involving a mélange of religious, cultural, and
institutional diversity across oil-producing regions.

On the money-sector side, the US runs huge *twin* deficits: a government
debt of about $1 trillion (and soon much more) and a continuous trade
deficit in the neighborhood of $800 billion annually. Together they have
been inundating the world with dollars. To cover its enormous trade gap,
the US has to 'borrow' nearly $2 billion a day. Asia – and the oil-producing

regions – recycles accumulated dollars (the outcome of huge trade sur-pluses) back to the US so that the latter's trade deficit is adequately funded and its growth can be further stimulated without inflation. This provides a parking place for developing countries' foreign reserves.

Dollar recycling also helps prevent Asian currencies from appreciating so that the value of Asian financial investments in the US remains pro-tected – and Asian exports maintain price competitiveness. And overall, the US-led growth cluster has so far been functioning quite well to benefit its constituent countries in a virtuous circle, despite many dire warnings about its imminent collapse (such as a sudden withdrawal of foreign-held money from the US and a rise in protectionism) – that is, the possibility of this co-growth regime turning into a co-stagnation structure exists.[5]

In fact, the US-led growth cluster used to be much smaller in size when Japan was initially the only Asian economy benefiting from US-led global capitalism in the early postwar period. But the NIEs soon joined, replicat-ing the Japanese experience. And now, China, Vietnam, and India are in the midst of participating in the co-growth cluster. Because of their sheer size, China and India's participation in the system has culminated in a far larger phenomenon of regionalized agglomeration in Asia. Consequently, *the greater the cluster becomes and the more increasingly it is dominated by vigorous follower geese, the greater the risks for trade deficits.* After all, this cluster originally started out basically as a geopolitical system at the begin-ning of the Cold War but has evolved – and morphed – into a more market-coordinated system ever since the fall of the Soviet Union. Nevertheless, it is still a political economy – not a pure market – system with a host of political issues on both the part of the US and other advanced countries and the part of the catching-up world.

7.4.2. Sovereign Wealth Funds: Creatures of America's Borrowed Growth

Why the recent sudden emergence of sovereign wealth funds (SWFs), and why are they so controversial – controversial in the advanced West? These questions can be easily answered in terms of our model of US-led growth clustering as above presented, since SWFs are the creatures of America's borrowed growth. As seen above, the world operates practically under a dollar standard. America's rising CA deficits mean an ever-bulging stock of international reserves in the hands of surplus countries. Understandably, they are now justifiably interested in earning as high a rate of return as possible on their reserve assets – higher than that on the US Treasury securities they have so far mostly held. They also symbolize a *wealth shift* from the advanced countries to resource-producing (notably oil-exporting) countries. And this shift has speeded up now that rapidly catching-up countries such as China and India are in Stage-II growth where their heavy and chemical industrialization and their rising incomes increase demand for natural resources, especially oil, as seen in Chapter 5.

SWFs or government-controlled investment funds are created by export-driven countries out of the massive foreign exchange reserves they accumulate. The world's largest SWF is the Abu Dhabi Investment Authority with more than $900 billion in assets, and the second largest are the Government Pension Fund of Norway and the Government Investment Corporation of Singapore with their respective assets worth $300–350 billion. They are followed by other SWFs such as various Saudi Arabian funds (totaling about $300 billion in assets), the Reserve Fund for Future Generations of Kuwait ($250 billion), China Investment Corporation ($200–300 billion), and Temasek Holdings of Singapore (above $150 billion). Together they control nearly $3 trillion in assets (at the time of writing) but are expected to raise their stakes to $12 trillion or even more by 2015, depending on oil prices and US trade deficits.[6]

There will be many more SWFs in the future so long as America's borrowed growth continues with its continuous trade deficit, and so long as global capitalism is hooked on high energy and resource consumption. In fact, for example, China actually has two more funds, the National Social Security Fund and the China–Africa Development Fund. Interestingly, moreover, China's State Administration of Foreign Exchange (SAFE), which manages China's $1.7 trillion in bulging foreign exchange reserves, the world's largest, which continue to rise by an average of $1.7 billion a day, reportedly bought a 1.6 percent stake in France's biggest corporation, Total, as well as a 1 percent stake in British energy giant BP, in April 2008. SAFE began to act just like any other SWF. Also, resource-rich Latin American countries are setting up government-run funds. Most recently, for instance, Chile decided to invest $5.9 billion in two such funds, and its investment strategy is modeled after the Norwegian Government Pension Fund. Iceland, too, is mulling over setting up a wealth fund to better manage its foreign exchange earnings from exports of marine products (which account for 31 percent of its total exports) and aluminum (accounting for 20 percent).[7] Even India, a country with current account deficits, is considering launching a SWF which can manage part of what few foreign reserves it has for higher returns – instead of just for safety and liquidity.

SWFs are deliberately set up in order to channel trade surpluses or public fund into high-yield investments instead of merely into US Treasury securities, other government bonds, and bank deposits, all of which are risk-free but low-yielding. In this respect, SWFs are quite akin to America's state pension funds devoted to managing state employees' retirement funds – and for that matter, no different from any other countries' public retirement funds (like South Korea's National Pension Service with $220 billion in assets, which decided to shift its investments away from US government debt in March 2008). Yet national pension funds operate in retirees' financial interests and seek only reliable returns. By comparison, SWFs may easily use their investment power not so much for higher returns but solely for strategic national interests as well. This is one important reason why the Committee on Foreign Investment in the US now requires potential foreign investors to submit personal information about previous military and government service. Furthermore, SWFs' state ownership enables them to avoid public scrutiny, since they are not subject to the normal standards of transparency and governance imposed on private investors.

Here lie their potential conflicts with the core tenet of market capitalism, since investments are supposed to be commercially profit-motivated and not politically guided for strategic national interests. Yet, SWFs are now the providers of vital liquidity to world financial markets. To allay these fears and avert a potential backlash, in March 2008 the US joined with Abu Dhabi and Singapore in laying out two sets of guidelines, one for SWFs and the second for host countries. SWFs would make a formal declaration that 'investment decisions should be based on commercial grounds, rather than to advance directly or indirectly, the geopolitical goals of the controlling government'. In turn, the host countries forsake protectionism and discrimination against SWFs. The IMF and Organisation for Economic Co-operation and Development (OECD), too, are similarly developing a set of best practices for both the state-run funds and the host countries.

So far, SWFs are, indeed, behaving just like any other investment fund, and have seized the opportunity to buy minority stakes in some of the world's biggest commercial and investment banks, such as Citigroup, Merrill Lynch, UBS, and Barclays as a credit crunch spread in the aftermath of the subprime mortgage crisis. SWFs are similar in investment horizons to private equity firms, and interestingly, close relationships have developed between the two.

7.5. SUMMING UP

Borrowed growth is the defining feature of US-led global capitalism. Developing countries are urged to open up not only for trade in goods and services but also for cross-border financial flows – and for FDI in banking, insurance, and related businesses. Open economies can enjoy many more growth opportunities than closed ones, though the risks associated with financial liberalization are equally larger. Financial markets are inevitably subject to 'manias, panics, and crashes'. Although there have been a number of crises and backlashes, financial liberalization has been the order of the day across the globe.

The flying-geese stages model of development finance is introduced to analyze recent Asian experiences. For East Asia, which is characterized by a high rate of savings, borrowed growth might have had a high cost, though temporarily. Some countries were not institutionally protected from – nor prepared for – financial crises. They tended to be carried away by borrowed growth.

The US has been able to gain much from its borrowed growth largely because of the special status of the dollar as the dominant international currency and its highly innovative financial markets that are capable of attracting and retaining investment from abroad (more on this in Chapter 8). Sovereign wealth funds are the creatures of America's borrowed growth – and of the oil-*driven* economic structure of production and consumption it has pioneered on the heels of what Pax Britannica had innovated. The US-led co-growth regime most recently has been beset by the subprime mortgage débâcle and the subsequent credit crunch that brought about an implosion of Wall Street and one of the largest-ever government bailouts. Borrowed growth (CA-deficit-based growth) is the underlying cause of America's financial market turmoil – just as it was the culprit in the Asian financial crisis of 1997.

NOTES

1. Technically speaking, these different characteristics are reflected in the coefficient of variation in statistical analysis. In general, it is much higher for portfolio investment than for FDI. According to UNCTAD (1998, pp. 14–15), interestingly, bank loans exhibited a much larger volatility coefficient than either FDI or portfolio investment in 12 selected countries over the period of 1992–7.
2. 'Hong Kong Spent some $15.2 Billion to Buy up Stocks', *Wall Street Journal*, October 21, 1998, p. A15.
3. These stage-differentiated characteristics are well predicted in the Clark model of growth (1935).
4. This type of co-growth regime has so far developed most effectively on the Pacific Rim and not so much in other parts of the world. Asia's success was owing, at least initially, to a near perfect FG formation, an ideal hierarchy of countries that has been conducive to industrial agglomeration at a regional level, as explored in earlier chapters.
5. Needless to say, this possibility needs to be carefully explored – a topic for future research. It should be noted in passing, however, that the Asian currency crises of 1997 occurred due to the integration of financial markets across the Pacific Rim, but that they did not cause a collapse of the regime nor weaken the forces of US-led growth clustering – thanks in large measure to the IT revolution in the US which revitalized the global economy. For the immediate post-crisis financial conditions in East Asia, see Zhan and Ozawa (2001).
6. 'Ascent of Sovereign-wealth Funds Illustrates New World Order', *Wall Street Journal*, January 28, 2008, p. A2.
7. 'Iceland Wealth Fund is Proposed', *Financial Times*, April 25, 2008, p. 7.

8. Creating the world in America's own image?

8.1. INTRODUCTION

This chapter looks at the US as the first lead goose in global financial markets by focusing on the recent phenomenal growth of one particular American innovation, private equity. It involves both venture capital and buyout funds. Its stellar appearance has had an immediate impact on the rest of the world, especially in those fast-developing countries that have opened up their financial markets. Asian countries in particular had their first encounter with America's buyout firms that sought fire-sale assets in the aftermath of the Asian financial crisis of 1997–8 (and they came to be despised as 'vulture funds'). Elsewhere, they have been also given the opprobrious nicknames of 'gluttons', 'barbarians at the gate', and 'locusts', reflecting the controversial nature of their operations.

What is private equity? Why has there been such a swift growth of private equity worldwide? What are the undesirable attributes of private equity? What is good about it? How can we make sense of this new financial development that first appeared in the US, and that has spread so quickly to other countries? What does this mean for the fast-growing Asian countries (especially China and India) whose financial markets are increasingly integrated into the global economy?

The purpose of this chapter is three-fold: (i) to explore the rise of private equity (venture capital and buyout funds) as a financial innovation (a new business model) in the US and its spread to other countries, (ii) to introduce an analytical framework within which to understand the basic nature of financial development in terms of a flying-geese stages model, and (iii) to briefly discuss how the model can shed light on the so-called 'Lucas–Schultz' paradox of capital flows that move in a perverse direction – namely, from poor to rich countries despite a higher marginal productivity of capital in the former.

8.2. AMERICA THE INNOVATOR

The US is no doubt the world's foremost leader in introducing numerous new-fangled goods, services, financial products, and business models, the innovations that eventually spread to other countries. Private equity is one of America's financial innovations. The US is usually ranked number one – or is always at least among the top five in innovation.[1] This trend-setting activity earlier occurred most dramatically in the manufacturing and distribution sectors. It is, however, now taking place more frequently in financial markets. Ever since 1999, when the US Supreme Court formally ruled that financial business methods were patentable, US financial institutions have been leading the world in obtaining patents for financial products. As the US loses competitiveness in manufacturing as a result of economic growth and structural change, its innovative activities are focusing more than before on services, especially financial services.

Before we examine private equity, it is worth briefly reviewing what sorts of financial innovations have been introduced in the US. Historically speaking, America's most significant (though not widely known) financial innovation is probably the checking account (demand deposits) that was introduced in the mid-19th century. This 'do-it-yourself' device (that is, to write out your own money) was originally intended to avoid a tax imposed by the National Bank Act of 1863 on the issuance of then-prevalent private-bank notes.

A number of other innovations likewise took place in response to regulations. Regulation Q (ceilings on deposit rates) of 1933, for example, eventually led to the fast growth of the Eurodollar market[2] during the 1960s and 1970s. American banks transferred their customers' deposits overseas so as to pay higher (unregulated) interest rates. And Eurodollar deposits in turn became a money market instrument (an 'overnight sweep' account). Also, money market mutual funds (shares on which investors can write checks) were born on Wall Street in 1971 and grew phenomenally in the late 1970s and early 1980s as market rates exceeded Regulation Q ceilings.

Advances in computer-based information technology prompted the popular use of credit cards in the US ahead of any other countries. Following the success of Diners Club, American Express, and Carte Blanche, Visa (formerly BankAmericard) and MasterCard (previously MasterCharge) were quickly introduced in the late 1960s. All these originally 'made-in-America' cards now dominate the world. The IT revolution similarly gave birth to the automatic teller machine (ATM) and the automated banking machine (ABM) (a 'one-stop service' combination of an ATM, an Internet link to the bank's website, and a direct phone connection to customer service).

In addition, so-called 'derivatives' or future contracts were created by the Chicago Board of Trade in 1975 to reduce financial risks. Trades in derivatives were in turn facilitated and promoted by improvements in computer software. And securitization (converting otherwise illiquid financial assets into tradable securities in the capital market), one of the most significant financial innovations, has come to proliferate in financial markets.[3] Loans began to be securitized in an ever-complex manner into what are commonly referred to as 'collateralized debt obligations (CDOs)'. All these, and many other, new financial products and services paved the way for the emergence of innovative business models and financial engineering in the US, notably hedge funds and private equity.

And innovations, especially in their formative stages, naturally invite high-risk and speculative investments, which have actually ended up in bubbles and busts, as witnessed in the junk bonds bust of 1989 and most recently, the subprime mortgage meltdown that began in 2007. Indeed, subprime mortgages were another innovation just like junk bonds. The former created a *new* market for low-creditworthy individuals (hence, 'junk mortgages'), while the latter a new market for less-than-investment-grade bonds (hence, 'junk bonds'). Fannie Mae (Federal National Mortgage Association) and Freddie Mac (Federal Home Loan Mortgage Corporation), the government-created mortgage-supporting organizations in the secondary market, pushed their liberal political mandate for 'affordable' housing for low-income families under the banner of 'the American dream'. What made things worse is that the subprime mortgage innovation was combined with many layers of securitization and derivatives ('collateralized-debt obligations' and 'credit-default swaps' and all that) – and accommodated by the easy monetary policy of the Federal Reserve that was in turn facilitated by the anti-inflationary effect of low-priced imports (as discussed in Chapter 7). Mortgage securitization itself was innovated and promoted by Fannie Mae. The outcome was a house of cards built on Wall Street that finally collapsed in September 2008.

Financial innovations originating in the US (and for that matter, in any other country) are, at least at the start, often controversial because of their very explosive nature (a 'vortex of change' in Schumpeter's words), as they dramatically and inexorably impact on the existing financial market structure and regulatory regime, heightening levels of uncertainty and risk. They need to be, therefore, closely monitored by regulators and policymakers not only in the US but also in other countries to which innovations are sooner or later to be disseminated in this age of globalization. Yet these innovative finances often fail to receive proper oversight. But more fundamentally, financial innovations often occur as a regulation-skirting arrangement or in less-regulated areas, catching the government off-guard.

8.3. PRIVATE EQUITY

8.3.1. Origin

Private equity in its present form is another financial innovation born in America. Two types of private equity exist: buyout funds and venture capital. To begin with buyout firms, especially those engaged in leveraged buyout (LBO), they in particular have recently seen explosive growth. This financial business model was conceived on Wall Street by investors like Jerome Kohlberg, Jr., Henry Kravis, and George Roberts, who all once worked at Bear Stearns in the 1960s. Their firm, Kohlberg, Kravis and Roberts & Co. (KKR), set up in 1976, is the pioneer and original architect of the new industry. As Kravis put it,

> In 1976 there was no such thing as private equity . . . [At first] We cobbled together the $400 thousand from eight people. The first full year, 1977, we bought three companies. Today [2008], over the last year and a half, we've raised $31 billion of new equity capital for private equity, all over the world. What has changed is the enormous availability of capital . . .
> I remember in 1979, going to Europe, because Paul Volcker put on credit controls. We had announced that we were going to buy McKesson, and we couldn't raise any money here because there was no acquisition lending. I flew to talk to people, and I just got blank stares from these institutions. How can three guys and a broom buy companies? We couldn't raise any money.[4]

No doubt, the private-equity industry has ever since been riding the rising waves of global capital produced by America's borrowed growth (as seen in Chapter 7). KKR was the beginning of this innovatory business model introduced in the US.

Given the birthplace of private equity, most of the world's largest private-equity funds are American (in addition to KKR, Blackstone Group, Bain Capital, Carlyle Group, Lone Star Funds, TPG (formerly Texas Pacific Group), Bear Stearns Merchant Banking, and the like). Many are now, however, also British and European (for example, Apax Partners, Bridgepoint Capital, Knightsbridge Capital, PPM Capital, Permira, Terra Firma Capital Partners, and Geutsche Beteilingungs). The US still dominates the industry (approximately 30 percent), though its market share has declined (for example, down from as much as 68 percent in 2000) and continues to decline as other countries began to adopt this American financial innovation.[5] The trend is described as an ongoing phenomenon driven by 'the new kings of capitalism' and 'at the sharp end of capitalism today'.[6]

8.3.2. Leveraged Buyout Funds

In a nutshell, buyout funds are in the business of buying, transforming, and selling companies for profit. When buyout firms rely heavily on debt – in addition to their own equity capital, they are called 'leveraged buyout (LBO)' firms. Accordingly, they have thrived on the recent global financial markets awash with capital (as mentioned above by Henry Kravis). However, LBO firms, and not venture capitalists, are the ones that are often vilified as 'vultures', 'gluttons', 'barbarians at the gate', and 'locusts', all connoting their greediness.

LBO firms acquire and manage undervalued companies, either privately owned or publicly listed, and sell them for profit within a relatively short span of time, normally within three to five years. For this operation, LBO firms borrow large sums of money by issuing bonds or IOUs to other investors and lenders. Their increased leverage (debt) helps reduce the firms' corporate income tax via interest payments. Also, it helps them retain more profits internally (because of comparatively less dividends) and concentrate on management performance with generous equity-based incentives, notably stock options, without much interference from shareholders.

As far as LBO is concerned, there are three ways to create value: (i) *value arbitrage*: buying low and selling high; (ii) *balance-sheet restructuring*: designing value-adding links of equity and debt via financial engineering; and (iii) *income-statement restructuring*: improving business performance to generate cash flows (Blaydon and Wainwright, 2006). These three types of operations may not be separate in a clear-cut way but rather occur simultaneously in combination.

Value arbitrage involves buying weak companies at a low price and selling them at a high price later on. The acquired companies may happen to be merely riding on business cycles or 'boom-bust' cycles, doing poorly in a downswing but rebounding on an upswing. This is no different from the basics of stock-market investment. It is a purely financial transaction without adding any economic substance to companies' real assets. This type of financial deal occurred straight after the Asian financial crises of 1997–8 devastated five East Asian countries (Thailand, Malaysia, Indonesia, the Philippines, and South Korea). Foreign LBO firms, especially from the US, were then vilified as 'vulture funds' and loathed because they were thought to feed on distressed local enterprises. The host governments were concerned that local industries would be bought out by foreign interests at fire-sale prices, adversely affecting their national efforts to develop and build up domestic industries. Most of the buyouts in post-crisis Asia were, however, fortunately done by foreign manufacturers in the same industry, and the foreign acquirers injected capital as well as technology, thereby strengthening, on the whole, those acquired local enterprises (Zhan and Ozawa, 2001).

Balance-sheet restructuring (*financial engineering*) is a controversial operation, since it necessarily raises the liabilities (debts) of the purchased companies. This feature of private equity is the most profitable for the industry, yet the most troublesome for society and policymakers. In fact, as private-equity firms aggressively push for profit maximization by financial engineering, the industry may be harmful to society.

In contrast, *income statement restructuring* means running business more efficiently and more profitably, adding substantive economic value to corporate assets. It is generally believed that LBO firms can serve as a powerful engine of corporate transformation by creating value of economic substance. These firms can strive to make companies run better over a period of five to ten years by injecting not only capital but also new managerial resources. (Interestingly, the private equity group Colony Capital is reportedly getting involved in reviving the pop star Michael Jackson after it bought from a hedge fund a $23 million loan backed by Jackson's Neverland Ranch.[7]) Given the nature of private-equity funds, however, their focus is mainly on financial management, not so much on the technological (R&D) and production ('bricks and mortar') side of companies.

Value arbitrage and financial engineering tend to be often abused. *BusinessWeek* published a cover story article, 'Gluttons at the Gate',[8] and listed four warning signs: (i) 'huge dividends and fees' – record sums of dividends and enormous fees for everything from dispensing advice to covering their taxes; (ii) 'serial charges' – collecting excessive payments from companies several times a year, thereby jeopardizing the companies' financial health; (iii) 'debt bombs' – loading-up of debt on companies to the extent of lowering their credit ratings and even driving them to bankruptcy; (iv) 'quick flips' – taking companies public within a short period of time (in some cases less than a year) after buyout. These signs signal the excessive profit-seeking of financial capitalism. No wonder some call the rise of private equity 'the purest capitalism' (so called by ABC Radio National, November 19, 2006).

Although there is nothing illegal about these transactions, they often border on fraudulent activities. They at least raise ethical and social issues. Buyout firms normally make a profit by extracting fees from both their private-equity investors via management fees (usually 1.5 percent) and the companies in their investment portfolios via a host of large service fees that are unknown to outsiders. In fact, this is probably why such business practices represent the 'wealth-driven' phase of economic growth that may even be considered the stage of 'drift and ultimate decline' for the entire economy (Porter, 1990). Private-equity firms' long-term orientation seems to have vanished considerably, turning into short-term profit making via 'quick flips'. It is said that it took only six months for America's number-one rental car firm, Hertz, to be flipped (that is, bought and sold back to the public stock). In some instances the flip period is even shorter.

8.3.3. High Risks, High Returns

The expected rate of return on private-equity investment is normally high as it reflects high risks and long-term commitments on the part of capital contributors (investors' equity capital being locked up for as long as 10 to 12 years in the funds). Because of the high risks, most private-equity funds are offered only to institutional investors and high net worth individuals, who can afford to have their money tied up for a long period of time and to risk losing their investments in the case of business failures. In the US, for instance, most funds require $2.5 million of net worth (exclusive of primary residence) and at least $200,000 of individual income for two documented years.[9] High risks are correlated with, and compensated by, high returns in the private-equity industry.

Successful funds are said to have reaped annual returns as high as 30 percent in the recent past. In short, private equity is basically a high-income luxury financial product; only those investors that are rich enough to bear substantial financial losses are allowed to participate in the market.[10]

BOX 8.1.   PROCESS ANALYSIS OF VALUE CREATION VIA PRIVATE EQUITY

Value creation for investors occurs in two ways: *stock-market value creation* (stock markets create value for shareholders) and *private-equity value creation* (private-equity funds create value by buying, restructuring, and selling companies). This means that *two* different types of investors have thus emerged: *public-equity holders and private-equity holders.* This development can be explained in terms of a three-period analysis:

Period 1:   'In the beginning there were the stock markets'. Initially (in the *pre*-buyout period), public stock markets register different

---

levels of value creation for the shareholders of listed companies as indicated by stock prices. Stock prices are the gauge of how the listed companies are performing.

Period 2:   Now, suppose that LBO funds are born. They purchase those public companies that they think are undervalued (not maximizing corporate value for investors) and whose management they think can be made better. The existing public-equity holders of original companies must earn satisfactory profits when they sell their shares to LBO funds (otherwise they would not). Hence, any buyout offer makes their stock prices higher than the initially prevailing market prices, an additional charge known as a 'deal premium'.[11] Buyout firms usually target those listed companies that have a large amount of cash (retained earnings) and a stable flow of income earnings. These characteristics enable buyout firms to load up debt on companies. Their cost-cutting efforts to increase profitability may result in laying off workers and shifting production to lower-cost locations (including those overseas), which often causes friction with labor unions and local communities.

Period 3:   A deal, once completed, leads to the post-buyout period, during which private-equity value creation occurs as a result of value arbitrage, balance-sheet restructuring (financial engineering), and/or income-statement restructuring, as seen above, all of which involve higher risks because of the heavy use of debt. In fact, to avoid a default risk, another financial transaction called 'credit-default swaps' usually occurs.[12] And finally, later on, when companies are taken back to the stock market successfully, private-equity value creation is to be reflected in new stock prices, higher than the original ones.[13]

In summary, private-equity value creation equals initial stock-market value creation + additional risk-taking (via value arbitrage, balance-sheet restructuring, and/or income-statement restructuring), which is the post-sellout stock-market value creation. This is why news about buyout deals normally results in higher stock prices in anticipation of companies' improved value creation. While companies are in the hands of private-equity firms, however, the class of equity shares held by private investors is *no longer* the same as that of those equity shares previously publicly traded on stock exchanges. These are two different kinds of shares (as different as apples and oranges, though both are fruits), since *entirely different levels of risk are involved.* In other words, two different classes of shareholders are created in the process: *public equity* versus *private equity* shareholders. And corporate governance may be driven more intensively and more aggressively (notably in terms of financial engineering) for value creation by private equity than by public equity.[14]

8.3.4. Corporate Governance

What does this mean for corporate governance – and shareholder interests? For years, public-equity shareholders were unfamiliar with how much more value could actually be created by private-equity firms. Hence public-equity shareholders used rather passively to hand over companies to LBO firms and corporate chieftains. It is said that deal premiums were actually somewhat smaller than in corporate takeover deals (21 percent versus 25 percent in 2006), and that public-equity shareholders are now rebelling against private-equity firms and company directors, demanding higher deal premiums.[15] In other words, new shareholder activism is in the making. And this is construed as a move to close the return gap between stock-market and private-equity value creations.

If the notion of corporate governance is narrowly interpreted merely as value maximization (higher dividends and higher share prices) for the sole benefit of investors, private-equity value creation is judged more efficient than conventional value creation under public equity (that is, only through the stock markets). Given the fact, however, that private equity is becoming increasingly short term-oriented (that is, 'quick flips'), fee-extractive, and debt-loading, these excesses most likely jeopardize the long-term health and viability of companies. Because of the very nature of private equity, transparency and accountability inevitably decline as equity is removed from public view (stock exchanges and their accompanying regulations) – with the result of greater potential pitfalls for ethical compromise and fraudulent activities. This capital-market transformation away from public equity (whose transparency is required by regulations) and toward private equity (characterized by private secrecy) may be regarded as a phenomenon in which 'forsaking the sunlit uplands of global finance, the market for capital is plunging into the shadows'.[16] The corporate governance under private equity may be detrimental to the whole economy as it increases the social costs, while raising private gains only for a privileged group of private-equity investors.[17] Interestingly enough, however, the private-equity industry claims

(i) that their purchases of publicly listed companies make management more long-term oriented (usually, three to five years), since management is freed from the pressure of stock prices on a quarterly basis (value creation on stock exchanges), and (ii) that private equity can protect buyout firms' financial engineering skills and secrets from competitors, thereby encouraging them to become even more innovative. It should be noted, however, that although financial products are now patentable, many private-equity firms may prefer to keep their business secrets in-house without applying for a patent.

8.3.5. Venture Capital

In contrast to LBO firms, venture capital (VC) funds are usually recognized as something socially desirable, since they directly foster entrepreneurship and commercialization of new ideas and technologies. VC funds are basically structured to invest in, and nurture, promising business startups and take them public by initial public offerings (IPOs) on the stock exchanges later on when they become successful. Indeed, private-equity firms were originally crafted mostly for this purpose. To be more precise, there is also angel capital (or 'business angels'), which is differentiated from VC. Angel capitalists use their *own* money to invest in embryonic startup companies. In fact, it is said that they stand between 'friends and family' and VCs, investing in 10 to 20 times many more startups than VCs. They normally invest relatively small chunks of capital (anywhere between $25,000 and $1.5 million in each portfolio company) in a diversified group of entrepreneurial ventures.[18] In contrast, VC may be more dependent on other investors' money.

Both angel and venture capitalists foster and assist new ideas to develop into successful sustainable businesses. These funds once played the key role of spawning and helping high-tech companies like Intel and Google grow and prosper on their bright ideas in Silicon Valley. VC business quickly became the envy of the world and has come to be widely adopted in other countries. Up until the late 1970s, just a few wealthy families, such as the Rockefellers and the Whitneys in the US, used to be the most typical investors in private-equity funds, buying and managing young fledgling ventures. These days, however, institutional investors (for example, pension funds, insurance companies, and endowments) and a large number of wealthy individuals (if not as rich as families of the Rockefeller class) are the major capital contributors. Although the absolute amount of money invested by venture capitalists has risen, less than one-fifth of the total money in private equity is nowadays allocated to VC investments, while the rest is spent on buyouts of established companies.[19]

8.4. STAGES OF BUSINESS FINANCE

As we recall, what the original FG theory envisioned are basically (i) the *qualitative evolutionary transformation* of a country's industrial structure over the course of growth and its accompanying necessary changes in institutions (a country's regulatory, incentive, and governance systems), and (ii) a *hierarchy of countries* within which new technology, new ideas, and industry *transmigrate* from the most advanced to the less advanced. It stresses the structural dynamics of the global economy in an ever-integrating environment.

Here, we now apply the idea of structural transformation in the context of a hierarchy of countries specifically to the financial dimension of economic growth – that is, how financial markets in individual countries evolve structurally over time as their real economy grows, interacting with the outside world. Again, we will draw on historical experiences and trace out the typical sequence of financial ('money sector') development that corresponds to the sequence of industrial ('real sector') development.

A historically derived pattern of financial development can be summarized in terms of a stylized three-phase model (as illustrated in Figure 8.1):

Phase 1.   In the early stages of a country's economic development, *family-based and trader-based finances* are most predominant. Family-based finance (often supplemented by friends) is basically motivated to set up and run family-owned businesses so as to provide sustenance and wealth for future generations. It is thus long-term-oriented by nature. This type of business is governed by trust, and ownership interest is protected by blood relations. On the other hand, trader-based finance provides short-to-medium-term funding for specific transactions such as provision of raw materials and sales outlets for farmed-out (commissioned) production, usually in the context of a cottage industry. These traditional sources of fund are soon to be increasingly supplemented by *bank-based finance*, as the banking industry develops. Meanwhile, the capital markets (stocks and bonds) are still in an embryonic state. Stock exchanges, if ever established, still remain inchoate and largely illiquid. Nascent local banks begin to lend to successful founder-owned businesses against the latter's assets as collateral. In this phase, therefore, there is *no* separation of ownership from management. Accordingly, the issue of corporate governance is hardly relevant in the modern sense of the term.

The industries that develop in this early phase are mostly labor-intensive, low-end manufacturing (such as textiles and garments, sundries, and other types of light industry) and localized services (mostly petty trade). The

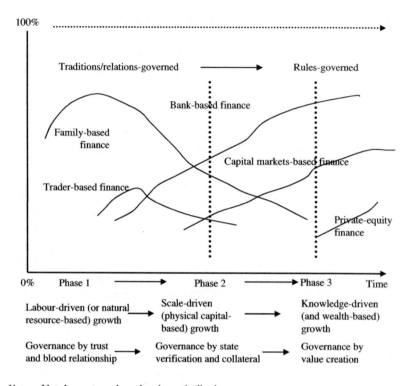

Note: Not drawn to scale, only schematically shown.

*Figure 8.1 Evolutionary financial development and governance structure,
FG style*

amounts of capital required for local businesses are relatively small. This
explains why family-based and trader-based finances are adequate and
prevalent. If a developing country is on track for rapid industrialization,
family businesses are likely to diversify and expand through forward, as
well as backward, business linkages.

In the meantime, the local government normally sets up, runs, and owns
basic infrastructure industries such as transportation, telecommunications,
and utilities – and special-purpose banking (for example, for small business
finance and long-term infrastructure development). On the whole, local
enterprises are intended to serve as essential builders of their community
economy – rather than as profit-maximizers for owners.

Phase 2. The intermediate stages of economic development are typically
characterized by rapid growth (hence rising savings) and more modern,

larger-scale industries (for example, steel, basic chemicals, heavy and electrical machinery). These industries exploit scale economies and are far more intensive in the use of physical capital (machinery and factory facilities) and natural resources (raw materials and fuels) – and the use of increasingly more human capital (educated and skilled workers and technology) than in the previous phase. Thus, the secondary sector (manufacturing and construction) grows rapidly, while the primary sector rapidly contracts as a percentage of GDP, as envisaged in Colin Clark's theory of economic growth (Clark, 1935).

Industry's need for capital, therefore, far exceeds the capacity of families to finance and retain family businesses. Modern businesses are normally incorporated as legal persons and owned by equity investors. As a consequence, family- and trader-based finances start to decline. Instead, bank-based finance rapidly gains importance. The banking sector itself benefits from rising savings as people's income increases. Also, the government usually steps in and creates funds for business development by way of fiscal expenditures (including subsidies and tax breaks) and central banking practices (pumping liquidity into the economy and helping banks make more loans to businesses).

Banks naturally serve as the overseer of borrowers, contributing to better corporate governance. Collateral, as well as relational banking, serves as a key incentive to ameliorate the problem of moral hazard. The people are, on the whole, eager to safeguard whatever amounts they can save by depositing with banks. Banks' role as a financial intermediary (that is, indirect finance) is thus preponderant. In fact, this is the stage at which banks are regarded as 'the headquarters of the capitalist system' (Schumpeter, 1934). The whole economy industrializes at a rapid pace at first and then gradually later on (as it goes through the inflection point of an S-shaped long-term growth curve).

Capital-market-based finance (stocks and bonds) also takes off, particularly when the country's financial markets are institutionally ready for, and capable of attracting, foreign capital inflows. As some industries already developed in the previous phase mature, many small family-owned businesses may go through consolidation via mergers and acquisitions (M&As), and some choose to be listed on local stock exchanges. Investment banking develops as the caretaker of issuing new shares and investing in stocks. The usual *principal-agent* problems arise as a result of the gradual separation of ownership and management.

Depending on a country's culture and traditions, however, the multi-stakeholder model is likely to be adopted rather than the shareholder model at this stage of economic development. In many developing countries, business enterprises are still regarded, by and large, as the social organizations responsible and accountable for the welfare of their local communities in terms of employment creation and national economic development – rather than as the pure economic organizations devoted solely to the maximization of profits and shareholder value. Shareholder activism is, therefore, not likely to be socially respected and accepted. If the notion of corporate governance (value creation) is accepted, it is not so much for the purpose of earning high returns solely for shareholders but in the interests of multi-stakeholders (employees, retirees, suppliers, creditors, and communities – in addition to shareholders).

Phase 3.   In the most advanced stages of capitalist development, as seen in the first lead-goose country (formerly the UK and currently the US), the capital markets become strategically crucial and complex for corporate finance, though bank loans still remain overall more significant in financing businesses. The tertiary sector in the advanced economy grows dominant, accounting for easily more than three-fourths of GDP, and the entire economy is increasingly driven by intellectual capital (knowledge, ideas, and talent). Both the primary and secondary sectors sharply decline as a percentage of GDP. That is, the New Economy gains on the Old Economy. The former is driven by a synergy of technology and finance, as aptly described by Mandel (2000): 'If technology is the engine for the New Economy, then finance is the fuel'.

New financial products (such as options, futures, swaps, securitized products, and other derivatives) are innovated one after another. And new financial business models (such as hedge funds and LBO funds) are tried and adopted as mainstream financial practices – especially in the lead-goose country. That is, in a mature capitalist economy higher-risk, higher-return financial activities are relentlessly introduced and pursued. M&As increase in frequency, as corporations *themselves* become 'tradables', no different from shares traded on the stock market. Demand for such financial products is basically high-income-elastic; it is the type of product suitable for high-income countries. High-income countries can afford risk-taking in speculative financial investments, and many financial transactions practically border on pure gambling in nature, so much so that the epithet 'casino capitalism' applies (Strange, 1997).

As the financial industry in the most advanced capitalist economy continues to evolve, the capital markets (shares and bonds) themselves go through a radical makeover away from public equity and toward private equity. Thus, this development involves two different groups of equity investors: public-equity shareholders and private-equity shareholders (the latter with a much higher degree of tolerance and acceptance of higher risks). Furthermore, the debt market simultaneously and likewise shifts away from public debt (that is, issuing bonds and borrowing from commercial banks) towards private debt (that is, borrowing from hedge funds and private investment banks).

Financial markets are more susceptible to the problems of asymmetric information (that is, adverse selection and moral hazard) and a boom-bust cycle than in manufacturing industries. Hence, a higher level of institutional adaptation and adequacy – especially in terms of regulatory controls and ethical standards – is required. This is the very reason why the financial markets are more heavily regulated than others. Any lead-goose country in financial development needs to cope with this institutional challenge. (This is best illustrated by the legislation of the controversial Sarbanes–Oxley Act of 2002 in the US – controversial because of its onerous regulatory control on internal accounting, which, many argue, weakens the competitiveness of US financial markets and drives investors from public equity into private equity.)

It should be kept in mind that the above stages model is, on purpose, highly stylized to delineate the underlying *historical* patterns of evolving financial markets. These historical traces do not mean that latecomers necessarily follow in the footsteps of first-comers in exactly the way the latter have trail-blazed. On the contrary, latecomers have the unique advantage of adopting any of those vehicles of finance already in existence and well-tested in the advanced world. In other words, the catching-up sequence is necessarily *time-compressed and stages-co-mingled.*

Financial market development, as it evolves over time, is normally accompanied by a shift of corporate – as well as political/social – governance from relation-based to rule-based (Oman et al., 2003). The pace of such a shift, however, differs across countries. Each country's financial development has its own historical trajectory and momentum of institutional building, which are differentiated in evolutionary characteristics. For example, in some countries family-owned businesses still remain preponderant even at fairly advanced stages of economic development largely because of the lack of institutional adequacy and the rule of law.

Here, therefore, it is worth stressing two caveats over copying the advanced countries' financial innovations: First, business governance can take a *variety* of forms, each of which differs in effectiveness depending on the particular stage of economic development in which a country happens to be. Such stages-adaptive forms of financial governance are illustrated in Figure 8.1 in terms of three types: 'governance by trust and blood relationship', 'governance by costly state verification and collateral,' and 'governance by value creation'. Second, the Anglo-American style corporate governance under public equity – and now increasingly under private equity – (both centered on value creation for shareholders) is *just* one of them and may be *neither necessarily superior nor always most desirable for long-term economic growth.*

Given the present flood of new financial products, services, and engineering techniques from the US, it makes perfect sense for catching-up countries to liberalize their financial markets most cautiously. Different markets need to be liberalized separately in accordance with their respective institutional capacity to cope with the disruptive forces of integration into global capitalism. An appropriate sequence of liberalization is called for.

8.5. PRIVATE-EQUITY FIRMS AS NEW FINANCIAL MULTINATIONALS

How has the private equity originating in the US impacted on the rest of the world? Economic growth is accompanied by *both* financial market development and related institutional arrangements, and private-equity investment as one of the latest innovations requires the most advanced and sophisticated institutional infrastructure.

Since private equity is a high-income financial product, it is mostly irrelevant to Phase-1 countries that have a relatively low level of per-capita income and savings. In this phase, as seen above, family-owned businesses are prevalent and dominant. Interestingly, they themselves can be regarded as a 'crude' class of private-equity investors in their own right. Financial institutions still remain largely decrepit in Phase-1 countries. (Here, a 'micro-private-equity' model – analogous to 'micro-banking' – in the form of 'micro-angel capital' may be conceivable.)

As might be expected, as soon as a catching-up country moves into Phase 2, it becomes structurally more compatible with private-equity investment. In fact, venture capitalists from the advanced countries are eager to take high risks because of the potentially high rewards in rapidly catching-up countries, such as China and India (which epitomize successful Phase-2 countries). As China and India's earlier-developed (lower-tier, traditional) industries (such as textiles, food, and retail) mature and consolidate, some family-owned businesses are anxious to be acquired or merged with others or are ready to be bought by private-equity firms. Furthermore, startups in the newer high-tech industries (especially Internet-enabled industries) are popping up. All these developments create new profitable opportunities for financial services. Here, venture capital can play an important role and may be in great demand, offering a favorable environment for private-equity firms.

In fact, India is drawing many more American and European private-equity firms than any other newly emerging country – because of its phenomenal growth, its liquid and transparent stock markets, its abundance of family-owned companies, its well-functioning legal system (to protect private property), and its democratic government, along with all the other institutional legacies it received as a member of the British Commonwealth. Major private-equity players are already operating, with offices in Mumbai, Bangalore, and Delhi. They are reportedly making deals at a furious pace:

> In the first nine months of 2006, India saw 329 venture capital and private-equity investments worth a total of $5.9 billion – more than double the tally for 2005 – with some 60% coming from foreign players . . . The size of deals is growing, too: from around $8 million four years ago to an average of $25 million today. The record for 2006 was set by Idea Cellular, which in November received $950 million from a clutch of investors including Providence Equity Partners, ChrysCapital, Citigroup, and Spinnaker Capital. A new benchmark may be on the horizon: Reliance Communications is in talks with private-equity players such as Blackstone, Texas Pacific, and KKR to fund its $10 billion bid for cellular carrier Hutchison Essar.[20]

It is said that at the start of 2007, Indian companies offered the highest rate of return on equity in Asia, approximately 21 percent – compared, for example, with 9 percent for China. This induced Western private-equity firms to expand their investments. Over the previous few years, New York-based Warburg Pincus sold for a total of $1.6 billion its stake in Bharti Airtel, a regional carrier, which it had bought for $300 million in 1999. Telecoms and outsourcing were the first industries that attracted the interest of Western private-equity companies. Private-equity firms, however, started to diversify away from these areas into others such as healthcare, food, real estate, travel, and hotels[21] – and even infrastructure. 3i Group, the UK-based private equity firm, set up one of the largest infrastructure funds in India, having raised a total of $1.2 billion, as India's government made a plan to spend about $500 billion to overhaul its dilapidated infrastructure such as ports, roads, and power plants.[22] It is reported that, so far, as much as $8 billion of fund raising is in the pipeline, a fund that targets Indian infrastructure facilities.[23] Blackstone Group, Carlyle Group, 3i Group, Morgan Stanley, and others are eagerly building business in private equity.

China, too, has displayed its uniquely attractive features that are conducive to foreign private-equity investments. It adopted market capitalism by opening its doors in 1978, while retaining its communist (yet actively pro-business) government. A combination of economic freedom, political stability (though 'politically forced'), and a relatively open market has sparked heady economic growth. State enterprises began to be rapidly privatized, and entrepreneurs started new businesses in the private sector. As a result, new stocks and bonds began to be offered in large numbers on the local stock and bond markets. Consequently, 'a record 21% of funding for Chinese companies will have come through the country's share and debt markets', and 'funding from outside the banking system will have grown sixfold since 2002, to 8.6 billion yuan ($1.3 billion) [by the end of 2006]'.[24] In other words, *state* equity and debt have been converted into *public* equity and debt.

Although China is still a communist country, it makes the most active use of the stock markets. Three of its largest state-owned banks – the Industrial and Commercial Bank of China, the China Construction Bank, and the Bank of China – have been successfully privatized by initial public offerings (IPOs). The Industrial and Commercial Bank of China's IPO that raised about $21.6 billion, was the largest IPO in history. Some of the world's largest financial institutions such as Citigroup, UBS, HSBC, Goldman Sachs, and Merrill Lynch, the major chieftains of financial capitalism, all acquired minority stakes in these big Chinese state banks ahead of public listings, and earned huge profits.[25]

Against the backdrop of this favorable trend toward privatization, many American and European private-equity firms have been venturing into China. They are eager to help convert public equity and debt into their private counterparts. Open to foreign investors are a great variety of industries ranging from pharmaceuticals and electronics to food and beverage to real estate to private equity itself. Intel's venture-capital unit is known to be a key player on China's private-equity scene, having invested more than $200 million in local startups since as early as 1998.[26] During the first half of 2005, consumer electronics was the number one industry, drawing the largest amount ($50 million out of a total of $323 million in all industries) of investment from foreign private-equity firms. Real estate, however, came to rank first ($105.9 million out of a total of $687.3 million) during the same period of 2006. Since foreign investors are known to have a tendency to pay more than locals, Beijing was worried that inflation would be fueled and that many local Chinese might be priced out of the housing market. This concern apparently prompted the implementation of new rules to curb accelerating foreign investment in real estate in July 2006.[27]

In addition, there is a growing backlash against the acquisition of state-owned enterprises by foreign private-equity funds at what are perceived to be bargain prices. Carlyle's failed attempt to take control of Xugong, one of China's biggest manufacturers of construction machinery, reflects such social pressures. Nevertheless, China sees an important role for private-equity funds in its financial markets but likes to nurture its own home-grown funds.

At present, China is in the midst of heavy and chemical industrialization, increasing demand for energy and causing environmental problems (as is typical with Stage-II growth). Venture capitalists are finding new businesses in energy-related industry; 'from June 2005 to June 2006, American venture capitalists put $100 million into China-based start-ups focused on alternative energy, double the investment in the period a year earlier'.[28] All in all, China received $12.8 billion in private equity investment in 2007, a jump from only $5 billion in 2005, creating a hot market for private equity – and is even expected to register 30 percent-plus annual growth for the next three years.[29] China's fast-growing small-to-medium firms that need expertise and capital to expand internationally are said to be eager for deals with foreign private equity funds.

There are also some strong signs that other developing economies, such as South Africa and Latin America, are now targeted as the new frontiers of private-equity capital. Surprisingly, South Africa ranked third as a host after North America and Israel when the stock of private-equity investment was measured as a percentage of GDP (at the end of 2005). Blackstone Group, Bain Capital, and KKR are reportedly bidding for a big retail chain Edcon (Edgars Consolidated Stores) that has over 900 stores across southern Africa and a market value of about $2.6 billion (at the time of writing). *The Economist* describes these private-equity investors in South Africa as 'far-flung barbarians'.[30] This may not be a surprise. After all, South Africa is a nation of the British Commonwealth, with well-developed financial markets and capitalist institutions. Private-equity multinationals are thus strongly drawn to Anglo-American countries. Israel, too, is closely aligned with the Anglo-American world.

It should be noted in passing that *it is Phase-2 countries – not Phase-1 countries – that are likely to experience financial crises*, as was the case with East Asia in 1997–8 and Russia and Latin America in the 1980s, particularly when some Phase-2 countries are still in their early/immature stage of financial integration into global capitalism and not well equipped with strong capitalist institutions.

By contrast, Phase-3 countries are in a good position to host foreign private-equity firms as well as to set up their own counterparts. The US and the UK lead the world, along with other advanced Anglo-American countries (Canada, Australia, New Zealand).[31] On the other hand, Germany and Japan have been somewhat less enthusiastic about the arrival of buyout funds. Their financial markets and corporate governance systems have long been dominated by banks (universal banking in Germany and the main-bank system or more recently, close-relational banking in Japan).

However, they, too, are nevertheless increasingly entering the private-equity industry.

A recent episode in Germany illustrates this trend. In April 2005, Franz Muntefering, then the chairman of the governing Social Democratic Party, branded private-equity investors as 'locusts'. His remark, however, ironically served to educate local investors about this new financial business and to help it catch up and grow. In August, Angela Merkel's cabinet approved Germany's first law to promote private-equity investment, which made private-equity funds qualify as limited partnerships with a lower tax rate instead of as investment funds. Indeed, the locust incident appears to have popularized private equity in Germany: 'In the first half of [2006], the number of private equity transactions in Germany nearly doubled from a year earlier, to 106 from 54. The value of the deals was 20.8 billion euros, or $26.3 billion, up 51 percent from a year earlier'.[32]

Japan was once known for its protectionism against outside capital. It is now more open, however. Even some major banks (albeit once bankrupt) have been acquired by foreign private equity funds. Shinsei Bank (once bought out and taken for IPO by Ripplewood Holdings of US), Aozora Bank (45.5 percent owned by Cerberus of US) and Tokyo Star Bank (acquired by Lone Star Funds of US) are the primary examples. In fact, M&A deals are booming with an eye to promoting management reforms and exploiting scale economies. Companies with undervalued shares feel threatened by hostile takeovers, and even seek the help of buyout funds. As a result, the domestic and foreign buyout funds targeting Japanese companies have increased. Their capital is estimated to stand at more than Y2 trillion ($17 billion). TPG (formerly Texas Pacific Group), for example, expects that as many owner-managers who built their businesses during the high-growth period from humble beginnings will be retiring soon, good M&A opportunities are emerging in the consumer-related, electric machinery and financial industries. This American private-equity firm sets aside $1 billion annually for its investment chest in Japan.[33]

Indeed, the opportunities for foreign private-equity funds to make deals in Japan seem abundant, now that *keiretsu* (postwar industrial conglomerates) have started to break up. Corporate reforms are in progress, and the acquisition market has been liberalized, allowing 'triangular mergers' in which the shares of a foreign company that buys a Japanese company as its subsidiary are exchanged for existing shares held by the stockholders of the acquired company. Precisely because of the foreign threat of takeover, however, Japanese companies themselves are consolidating to ward off foreign invasion. The Japanese themselves are quickly learning the tricks of the LBO game. The fears corporate Japan has about buyout funds is their short-termism (that is, quick flips). This was ostensibly the major reason why the Japanese government blocked a bid by a UK fund, TCI, to increase its stake in J-Power (Japan's major electricity wholesaler) to 20 percent from 9.9 percent in April 2008. Such opposition was said to be in the interests of long-term (20–25 years ahead) planning and commitment to power-grids and nuclear power development, which might be jeopardized by proactive shareholders who were simply after quick profits.

Japan's neighbor, South Korea, is even more wary of foreign control of its industries, especially by private-equity funds. For example, Lone Star Funds of the US acquired Korea Exchange Bank, the country's number four bank by assets in the aftermath of the financial crisis of 1998. Although it was initially welcomed, Lone Star struggled to sell the bank as it faced public criticism for having bought the bank at a fire-sale price. Like Japan, Korea is ambivalent about foreign ownership – largely for cultural reasons.

Yet, younger Asian countries such as China and India are nurturing their own innovation systems suitable for Stage-III and IV growth that is more knowledge-based. Consequently, venture capital funds are likely to expand in Asia. Indeed, large multinational corporations in electronics, pharmaceuticals, and other science-intensive industries are increasingly engaged in what Ernst (2006) calls 'innovation offshoring' by hiring low-cost Asian scientists and engineers at their newly opened R&D centers, notably in China and India. New discoveries and inventions that are expected to come on stream from these research facilities will need to be commercialized and developed into marketable products and services. Here, private equity, particularly venture capital, will be in increasing demand.

8.6. SOVEREIGN WEALTH FUNDS AND PRIVATE EQUITY

As examined in Chapter 7, SWFs are state-run investment funds set up mostly by oil-exporting countries and export-driven Asian countries, and are the creatures of America's borrowed growth. Interestingly enough, there are some close resemblances – and increasingly closer ties – between the two. Some even argue that SWFs are comparable to private equity on a long-term investment horizon:

> Unlike investment vehicles such as mutual funds, pension funds, and insurance companies, petrodollar sovereign wealth funds have no urgent need for either income from their investments or liquidity. They typically do not have external investors who may withdraw capital at short notice, nor do they have liabilities that they are obligated to pay out in the future. The same is true for private

petrodollar investors. They consequently have the leeway to take a very long view in their investments – and could potentially take higher levels of risk than traditional investors can, in the hope of securing larger returns. (Farrell et al., 2007, p. 60)

Given an increasing shift toward short-term investments, as reflected in 'quick flipping', buyout firms may not, after all, be so long-term in their investment horizon. Besides, LBO funds depend heavily on debt capital and are subject to possible withdrawal claims by lenders. The above quote perhaps applies better to venture capital, since it is surely long-term-oriented as it nurtures and transforms innovative ideas into promising new businesses. It is true, nevertheless, that SWFs and private equity firms are both largely free from equity holders' myopic demand for quick dividends – and can take higher risk more flexibly without worrying about stock prices, since they are not publicly listed.

Some SWFs have already developed alliances with private equity firms. For example, China Investment Corporation paid $3 billion for a stake in Blackstone, America's private equity group, which listed its shares in June 2007, thereby undermining its own business model and whose share price went down by more than 40 percent by the end of the year (consequently, the Chinese company was naturally castigated in Beijing). Interestingly, SWFs themselves have begun to mimic private equity firms in their investment strategies by setting up funds to invest directly in companies. They are quickly learning the ropes from private equity. Abu Dhabi's Mubadala fund and Dubai International Capital are good examples. The latter is even expected to grow larger than most existing private equity funds (Farrell et al., 2007, p. 61). In short, SWFs and private equity funds are likely to deepen their partnership in global capital markets.

8.7. SUMMING UP

Venture capital and LBO funds took root first in the US, and have spread to the rest of the world. Private equity is one of the latest business innovations in the arena of global corporate finance and governance, along with hedge funds, which have increasingly allied with private-equity firms for the purpose of risk dispersion. Venture capitalists helped push the frontier of high-tech entrepreneurship in the IT-based industries, first in America's Silicon Valley during the dot.com boom of the 1990s. Private equity has created an entirely new class of investors who are willing to make higher-risk, higher-return investments than public equity.

Demand for such investment opportunities has risen particularly from wealthy individuals and institutional investors (most recently, SWFs), who are no longer satisfied by low yields on conventional securities – and who can afford to take higher risks and potential large losses. Private equity has set a new standard of value creation for investors by compelling management to perform more efficiently, hence more profitably, for business owners. At the same time, however, there is a clear danger that because of the very nature of leveraged financial engineering, the companies acquired are exposed to greater risks of default and potential bankruptcy than ever before, information about which is shielded from public scrutiny.

This chapter has considered how private equity, one of the latest financial innovations in the US, has been spreading to the rest of the world. In the process, US – and European – private-equity firms have thus turned into the new financial multinationals. They are venturing out from advanced to less-advanced countries. Private equity has therefore emerged as a *new* format of international capital flow – just like, and in addition to, the conventional formats such as conventional FDI, portfolio investment, bank loans, and intra-company finance. These capital flows are distinctly differentiated in terms of formats. This is, indeed, quite contrary to the assumption widely accepted in neoclassical economics that capital flows 'unpacked' and smoothly – without any specific formats.

No wonder, then, that neoclassical economists are accordingly puzzled by a relatively small flow of capital from rich to poor countries despite the latter's supposedly much higher marginal productivity of capital. This puzzle is known as the 'Lucas–Schultz' paradox (Lucas, 1990; Schultz, 1964). One explanation for the paradox is given in terms of institutional factors, particularly in terms of government policies and private property protection (Harberger, 1998; North, 1999; De Soto, 2000). Lothian (2006) empirically – in terms of econometrics – found that policies such as 'pursuit of price stability, fewer direct interventions and sound institutional structures' are the key determinants of capital flows from poor countries. True, policies do matter. After all, financial transactions entail many more complex problems of asymmetric information ('adverse selection' and 'moral hazard') than trade in tangible commodities, problems that can be alleviated only by appropriate policies and institutional arrangements.

However, another factor – and perhaps an even more fundamental reason – exists. It involves differences in structural market characteristics that are inherent in, and specific to, the different stages of financial development as a country grows, the stages that can explain a path of institutional development. In this regard, the new 'flying-geese' theory of financial (money-sector) development introduced in this chapter explicitly recognizes these structural differences in stages of financial development and treats them as its primary explanatory variable. It demonstrates that developing countries at lower stages of financial development have structural incompatibilities with certain forms of capital (such as private-equity buyout funds and hedge funds) that have been earlier innovated in advanced countries, especially in the US – incompatibilities that cannot be rectified by policies alone.

In sum, (i) cross-border capital flows in differentiated formats, and (ii) structural differences within the existing hierarchy of countries reflect their different stages of financial and institutional development. And these facts can go a long way to explaining why capital (say, private equity's buyout capital) does not flow as smoothly from advanced to less developed countries as posited by neoclassical economics; on the contrary, it flows uphill. SWFs are a prime example. They are active recyclers of wealth mostly from export-driven countries back to the financial markets of advanced countries. Thus, the new FG model of financial development introduced in this chapter can shed additional light on the 'Lucas–Schultz' paradox.

NOTES

1. Most recently, for example, Isead, a prominent French business school, chose the US as 'the top country in generating new ideas, adapting them quickly and profiting from them'. 'U.S. is Ranked Leader in Business Innovation', *Wall Street Journal*, January 16, 2007, p. A19.
2. The birth of the Eurodollar itself is, however, generally attributed to the Soviet Union's action in the early 1950s to move its deposits in the US to Europe and keep them in dollars. This was done because of fears that the US would freeze the deposits if left there.
3. Many of these financial innovations are touched upon in any standard college textbook on money and banking. But Mishkin's textbook (see, for example, the eighth edition, 2007) does a good job at explaining them via a classification into three types: (i) responses to changes in demand conditions, (ii) responses to changes in supply conditions, and (iii) avoidance of regulations.
4. 'Private Equity: In the Midst of Change, Reflections on Private Equity's Past', *Hermes* (Columbia Business School's alumni magazine), winter 2008, pp. 22–28.
5. In 2006, US private-equity firms (322 funds) alone raised a record amount of money, $215.4 billion. The global private-equity industry was estimated to have over $710 billion in assets at the end of 2006. 'Private-Equity Firms Raked in Record Amounts Last Year', *Wall Street Journal*, January 11, 2007, p. C6.
6. 'The New Kings of Capitalism', *Economist*, November 25, 2004.
7. 'Michael Jackson: The Next Elvis?', *Wall Street Journal*, June 13, 2008, w1.
8. 'Gluttons at the Gate', *BusinessWeek*, October 30, 2006, pp. 58–66.
9. Or at least $300,000 of joint income (with spouse) (Wikipedia, 2007).
10. With high windfall profits reaped from the ever-rising prices of oil, many royal families in oil-producing Arab countries are among those eager to contribute capital to private equity firms. For example, the Qatari royal family backs the investment fund Delta (Two) of England, which recently launched an attempt to buy out J Sainsbury, a British supermarket chain.
11. This is also known as a 'spread', the difference between a seller's current stock price and the price that a buyer has agreed to pay. This has created a new financial market in which

takeover speculators bet on the direction of changes in the spreads on pending deals. If the spreads narrow, the speculators profit.

12. These risk-dispersing derivatives increased seven-fold to as much as $26 trillion in September 2006 over 2003. 'The Dark Side of Debt', *Economist*, September 23, 2006, p. 11.

13. Along with high deal premiums resulting from active buyout activity, value creation by private-equity firms will contribute significantly to a bull stock market. They are no doubt one of the major shakers and movers of stock prices. They prop up, in general, share prices for small and medium-size companies, since those companies are normally buyout targets. Options are also used to speculate. When Hilton Hotels were bought out by Blackstone Group in early July 2007, reportedly the stock surged 26 percent, the August $40 calls jumped from 85 cents to $5.90, giving a huge single-day return of close to 600 percent.

14. This does not necessarily mean that private equity always yields higher returns than public equity, however. For example, comparing private equity funds with the public-equity market in average annual net returns to investors, 1986–2003, the overall average for European private equity was 19.0 percent, as opposed to 12.3 percent for European public equity. The same comparison for American private equity was 12.4 percent, as opposed to 17.1 percent. Harper and Schneider (2004).

15. 'The New Activist Investors: More Shareholders Fight Buyout Firms, Management for Bigger Deal Premiums', *Wall Street Journal*, January 24, 2007, p. C16.

16. 'The Dark Side of Debt', *Economist*, September 23, 2006, p. 11.

17. UK and US lawmakers are now scrutinizing the private-equity industry amid growing public concern that it pays too little taxes (a lower tax rate as partnerships rather than as corporations) and is too quick to lay off employees.

18. See Wainwright (2003).

19. 'The New Kings of Capitalism', *Economist*, November 25, 2004.

20. 'Private Equity Invades India', *BusinessWeek* online, January 8, 2007.

21. Ibid.

22. '3i Group Closes India Fund at $1.2bn', *Financial Times*, April 17, 2008, p. 18.

23. 'Morgan Stanley Seeks Piece of Indian Growth', *Wall Street Journal*, April 24, 2008, p. C3.

24. 'Chinese Capital Markets: Out of the Shadows', *Economist*, December 16, 2006, p.78.

25. Ibid.

26. 'To China, With Venture Capital', *BusinessWeek online*, July 24, 2006.

27. 'Foreign Investors Weigh Property Curbs in China', *Wall Street Journal*, July 26, 2006, p. B6.

28. 'A Light Bulb Goes on, and China Starts Thinking Alternative Energy', *New York Times*, January 19, 2007,

29. 'China's Private Equity Boom', *BusinessWeek* (on the web), July 16, 2008.

30. 'Private Equity: New Gates to Storm', *Economist*, January 20, 2007, pp. 84–5.

31. Australia, for instance, seems wholeheartedly to be embracing private equity. In fact, Australia pioneered a new privatization form of investment in infrastructure (such as highways and airports) between state and local governments and pension funds, which soon involved private investors. The practice has recently spread to the United States where some states and cities were able to lease public properties to private investors. Infrastructure investing is attracting private-equity groups because of 'the predictable cash flows, the limited competition, high barriers to entry and regulatory protection'. ('The Popularity of Infrastructure Investing', *Economist*, January 20, 2007, p. 83.)

32. 'The Buzz on German Private Equity', *International Herald Tribune*, October 21–2, 2006, p.11.

33. 'Rush of M&As Reflects New Dangers, Opportunities', *Nikkei Weekly*, November 20, 2006, pp. 1, 3.

Bibliography

ABC Radio National (2006), 'Private Equity – the Purest Capitalism', an ABC program broadcast in Australia on November 19, transcript, www. abc.net.au.

Abramovitz, Moses (1986), 'Catching Up, Forging Ahead, and Falling Behind', *Journal of Economic History*, **46** (2), 385–406.

Akamatsu, Kaname (1935), 'Wagakuni Yomokogyohin no Boeki Suisei [The Trend of Japan's Trade in Woolen Goods]', *Shogyo Keizai Ronso*, **13**, 129–212.

Akamatsu, Kaname (1937), 'Wagakuni Keizai Hatten no Sogo Benshoho [Synthetic Dialectics of Japan's Economic Advance]', *Shogyo Keizai Ronso*, **15**, 173 ff.

Akamatsu, Kaname (1961), 'A Theory of Unbalanced Growth in the World Economy', *Weltwirtschaftliches Archiv*, **86**, 196–215.

Akamatsu, Kaname (1962), 'A Historical Pattern of Economic Growth in Developing Countries', *Developing Economies*, preliminary issue No. 1 (March–August), 1–23.

Alexander, Sydney S. (1953), 'Effects of a Devaluation on a Trade Balance', *IMF Staff Papers*, **2** (April), 263–78.

Amin, Samir (1976), *Unequal Development: An Essay on the Social Formations of Peripheral Capitalism*, New York: Monthly Review Press.

Amsden, Alice H. (1989), *Asia's Next Giant: South Korea and Late Industrialization*, Oxford: Oxford University Press.

Amsden, Alice H. (2001), *The Rise of 'The Rest': Challenges to the West from Late Industrializing Economies*, New York: Oxford University Press.

Aoki, Masahiko, Hyung-Ki Kim, and Masahiro Okuno-Fujiwara (eds) (1997), *The Role of Government in East Asian Economic Development: Comparative Institutional Analysis*, Oxford: Clarendon Press.

Aoki, Masahiko and Hugh Patrick (1994), *The Japanese Main Bank System: Its Relevance for Developing and Transforming Economies*, Oxford: Oxford University Press.

Arndt, S. and H. Kierzkowski (eds) (2001), *Fragmentation: New Production Patterns in the World Economy*, Oxford: Oxford University Press

Arrighi, Giovanni (1994), *The Long Twentieth Century*, London: Verso.

Ashton, Thomas S. (1968), *Iron and Steel in the Industrial Revolution*, New York: Augustus M. Kelley.

Asian Development Bank (ADB) (2004), *Key Indicators of Developing Asian and Pacific Countries*, Manila: ADB.

Asian Development Bank (ADB) (2005), *An Initial Assessment of the Impact of the Earthquake and Tsunami of December 26, 2004 on South and Southeast Asia* (January), Manila: ADB.

Audretsch, David B. (1987), 'An Empirical Test of the Industry Life Cycle', *Weltwirtschaftliches Archives*, **123** (120), 297–308.

Balassa, Bela (1980), *The Process of Industrial Development and Alternative Development Strategies*, Essays in International Finance, No. 141, Princeton, NJ: International Finance Section, Princeton University

Balassa, Bela (1989), *Comparative Advantage, Trade Policy and Economic Development*, New York: New York University Press.

Baran, Paul (1957), *The Political Economy of Growth*, New York: Monthly Review Press.

Bastable, Charles F. (1887), *The Theory of International Trade*, Dublin: Hodges, Figgis.

Baumol, William J. (2002), *The Free Market Innovation Machine*, Princeton, NJ: Princeton University Press.

Beane, D. (1997), *The Singapore and Malaysia Electronics Industries*, Boca Raton and New York: CRC Press.

Bell, Clive (1987), 'Development Economics', in J. Eatwell, M. Milgate, and P. Newman (eds), *The New Palgrave Economic Development*, New York: Norton.

Bell, John F. (1953), *A History of Economic Thought*, New York: Ronald Press.

Berri, David and Terutomo Ozawa (1997), 'Pax Americana and Asian Exports: Revealed Trends of Comparative Advantage Recycling', *International Trade Journal*, **11** (1), 39–67.

Best, Michael H. (2000), 'Silicon Valley and the Resurgence of Route 128: Systems Integration and Regional Innovation', in John Dunning (ed.), *Regions, Globalization, and the Knowledge-based Economy*, Oxford: Oxford University Press.

Bhagwati, Jagdish (1958), 'Immiserizing Growth: A Geometrical Note', *Review of Economic Studies*, **25**, 201–5.

Bhagwati, Jagdish (1984), 'Why are Services Cheaper in the Poor Countries?', *Economic Journal*, **94**, 279–80.

Bhagwati, Jagdish (2004), *In Defense of Globalization*, New York: Oxford University Press.

Bhalla, A.S. and Shufang Qiu (2004), *The Employment Impact of China's WTO Accession*, London: RoutledgeCurzon.

Blaydon, Colin and Fred Wainwright (2006), 'The Balance between Debt and Added Value', *Financial Times*, September 29, 2006; Tuck School of Business at Dartmouth, http://mba.tuck.dartmouth.edu.

Bosshard, Peter (2007), *China's Role in Financing African Infrastructure*, Berkeley, CA: International Rivers Network.

Bottomore, Tom (1976), 'Introduction', in Joseph A. Schumpeter, *Capitalism, Socialism and Democracy*, edited by Tom Bottomore, London: Allen & Unwin.

Boulding, Kenneth (1956), *The Image, Knowledge in Life and Society*, Ann Arbor, MI: University of Michigan Press.

Cairnes, J.E. (1987), *Some Leading Principles of Political Economy*, New York: Harper & Brothers.

Cantwell, John A. (1987), 'The Reorganization of European Industries after Integration', *Journal of Common Market Studies*, **26**, 127–52.

Cantwell, John A. (1995), 'The Globalization of Technology: What Remains of the Product Cycle Theory?', *Cambridge Journal of Economics*, **19**, 155–74.

Chandler, Alfred D. Jr (2001), *Inventing the Electronic Century: The Epic Story of the Consumer Electronics and Computer Industries*, New York: Free Press.

Cheng, Leonard K. and Henryk Kierzkowski (eds) (2001), *Global Production and Trade in East Asia*, Boston, MA: Kluwer Academic Publishers.

Clark, Colin (1935), *The Conditions of Economic Progress*, London: Macmillan.

Crowther, Geoffrey (1957), *Balance and Imbalances of Payments*, Boston, MA: Graduate School of Business Administration, Harvard University.

Curtis, P.J. (1994), *The Fall of the U.S. Consumer Electronics Industry: An American Trade Tragedy*, Westport, CT: Quorum Books.

Cutler, Harvey, David Berri, and Terutomo Ozawa (2003), 'Market Recycling in Labor-intensive Goods, Flying-geese Style: An Empirical Analysis of East Asian Exports to the U.S.', *Journal of Asian Economies*, **14**, 35–50.

Cutler, Harvey and Terutomo Ozawa (2007), 'The Dynamics of the "Mature" Product Cycle and Market Recycling, Flying-geese Style: An Empirical Examination and Policy Implications', *Contemporary Economic Policy*, **25** (1), 67–78.

Dasgupta, Susmita, Benoit Laplante, Hua Wang, and David Wheeler (2002), 'Confronting the Environmental Kuznets Curve', *Journal of Economic Perspectives*, **16** (1), winter, 147–68.

De Soto, H. (2000), *The Mystery of Capital*, New York: Basic Books.

Dollar, David (1986), 'Technological Innovation, Capital Mobility, and the Product Cycle in North-South Trade', *American Economic Review*, **76** (1), 177–90.

Dollar, David and Kraay, Aart (2001), 'Trade, Growth, and Poverty', Working Paper, Development Research Group, World Bank.

Dollar, David and Kraay, Aart (2002), 'Growth is Good for the Poor', *Journal of Economic Growth*, **7** (3), 195–225.

Dooley, Michael, David Folkerts-Landau, and Peter Garber (2003), 'An Essay on the Revised Bretton Woods System', NBER Working Paper 9971 (September).

Dos Santo, Theotonica (1970), 'The Structure of Dependence', *American Economic Review*, **60** (May), 231–6.

Dowling, M. and C.T. Cheang (2000), 'Shifting Comparative Advantage in Asia: New Tests of the "Flying Geese" Model', *Journal of Asian Economics*, **11**, 443–63.

Dunning, John H. (1993), *Multinational Enterprises and the Global Economy*, Wokingham, UK: Addison-Wesley.

Dunning, John H. (2003), *Making Globalization Good: The Moral Challenges of Global Capitalism*, Oxford: Oxford University Press.

Dutta, Manoranjan (1999), *Economic Regionalization in the Asia-Pacific*, Cheltenham, UK and Northampton, MA, USA: Edward Elgar.

Eatwell, John (1982), *Whatever Happened to Britain? The Economics of Decline*, London: Duckworth.

Economic Council, Resource Study Committee (1970), *Kokusaika Jidai no Shigen Mondai* [Resource Problems in the Era of Internationalization], Tokyo.

Eichengreen, Bary, Michael Mussa, Giovanni Dell'Ariccia, Enrica Detragioache, Gian Maria Milesi-Ferretti, and Andrew Tweedie (1999), *Liberating Capital Movements: Some Analytical Issues*, Washington, DC: IMF.

Elmslie, Bruce T. (1995), 'Retrospectives: The Convergence Debate between David Hume and Josiah Tucker', *Journal of Economic Perspectives*, **9** (4), 207–16.

Engels, F (1872/1940), *Dialectics of Natures*, New York: International Publisher.

Enke, Stephen and Virgil Salera (1947), *International Economics*, New York: Prenctice-Hall.

Ernst, Dieter (1996), 'The Transformation of International Production Networks', paper presented at a seminar, OECD, Paris, February 14.

Ernst, Dieter (2006), *Innovation Offshoring: Asia's Emerging Role in Global Innovation Networks*, East-West Center Special Report No. 10, Honolulu, HI: East-West Center.

Farrell, Diana, Susan Lund, Eva Geriemann, and Peter Seeburger (2007), *The New Power Brokers: How Oil, Asia, Hedge Funds, and Private Equity are Shaping Global Capital Markets*, San Francisco, CA: McKinsey Global Institute.

Fisher, Irving (1930), *The Theory of Interest*, New York: Macmillan.

Frank, Gunder A. (1967), *Capitalism and Underdevelopment in Latin America*, New York: Monthly Review Press.

Furtado, Celso (1964), *Development and Underdevelopment*, translated by R. De Aguiar and E. Drysdale, Berkeley, CA: University of California Press.

Gagnon, J. and A. Rose (1995), 'Dynamic Persistence of Industry Trade Balances: How Pervasive Is the Product Cycle?', *Oxford Economic Papers*, **47** (April), 229–48.

Gerschenkron, Alexander (1962), *Economic Backwardness in Historical Perspective*, Cambridge, MA: Harvard University Press.

Ginzburg, Andrea and Annamaria Simonazzi (2005), 'Patterns of Industrialization and the Flying Geese Model: The Case of Electronics in East Asia', *Journal of Asian Economics*, **15** (6), 1051–78.

Graham, Edward M. (2000), *Fighting the Wrong Enemy: Antiglobal Activists and Multinational Enterprises*, Washington, DC: Institute for International Economics.

Gray, H. Peter (1999), *Global Economic Involvement*, Copenhagen: Copenhagen Business School.

Grossman, Gene and Ann Krueger (1993), 'Environmental Impacts of the North American Free Trade Agreement', in P. Garber (ed.), *The U.S.–Mexico Free Trade Agreement*, Cambridge, MA: MIT Press.

Halevi, Nadav (1971), 'An Empirical Test of the "Balance of Payments Stages" Hypothesis', *Journal of International Economics*, **1**, 103–17.

Harberger, A.C. (1998), 'A Vision of the Growth Process', *American Economic Review*, **88**, 1–32.

Harper, Neil W.C. and Antoon Schneider (2004), 'Private Equity's New Challenge', *McKinsey Quarterly*, web exclusive, August.

Head, Ivan L. (1974), 'Canada's Pacific Perspective', *Pacific Community*, **6**, 16–30.

Hegel, Friedrich W. (1812/1991), *The Science of Logic*, translated by A.V. Miller, Indianapolis, IN: Hacket (1991).

Hicks, John R. (1973), 'The Mainspring of Economic Growth', *Swedish Journal of Economics*, **75**, 336–48.

Hirsch, Seev (1967), *Location of Industry and International Competitiveness*, Oxford: Oxford University Press.

Hirschman, Albert O. (1958), *The Strategy of Economic Development*, New Haven, CT: Yale University Press.

Hohenberg, Paul (1968), *A Primer on the Economic History of Europe*, New York: Random House.

Hook, S. (1958), *From Hegel to Marx: Studies in the Intellectual Development of Karl Marx*, New York: Humanities Press.

Hufbauer, Garry C. (1970), 'The Impact of National Characteristics and Technology on the Commodity Composition of Trade in Manufactured Goods', in R. Vernon (ed.), *The Technology Factor in International Trade*, New York: Columbia University Press, pp. 145–231.

Hume, David (1754/1985), *Essays: Moral, Political and Literary*, edited by Eugene Miller, Indianapolis, IN: Liberty Fund.

Hymer, Stephen (1960/1976), *The International Operations of National Firms*, Ph.D. dissertation, MIT, 1960; published Cambridge, MA: MIT Press, 1976.

Indonesia Development News (1978), 'Japan's Performance Instanced as a Challenge to Other Countries', December, 6–7.

Irwin, Douglas A. (1996), *Against the Tide: An Intellectual History of Free Trade*, Princeton, NJ: Princeton University Press.

JETRO (Japan External Trade Organization) (2003), *Boeki Toshi Hakusho* [White Paper on Trade and Investment], Tokyo: JETRO.

Johansen, S. (1988), 'Statistical Analysis of Cointegration Vectors', *Journal of Economics Dynamics and Control*, **12**, 231–54.

Johansen, S. (1995), *Likelihood-based Inference in Cointegrated Vector Auto-regressive Models*, New York: Oxford University Press.

Kagami, M. and A. Fukunishi (1981), 'Hattentojokoku ni okeru Denki-Denshi Sangyo Hatten [The Growth of the Electric-electronics Industry in Developing Countries]', in M. Kagami, A. Fukunishi, and A. Suehiro (eds), *Hattentojokoku no Denki-Denshi Sangyo* [The Electric-electronics Industry in Developing Countries], Tokyo: Institute of the Developing Economies.

Kahn, Josepha and Jim Yardley (2007), 'As China Roars, Pollution Reaches Deadly Extremes', *New York Times*, August 26, www.nytimes.com.

Kaldor, Nicholas (1972), 'The Irrelevance of Equilibrium Economics', *Economic Journal*, **82** (328), 1237–55.

Kaldor, Nicholas (1985), *Economics without Equilibrium*, Armonk, NY: M.E. Sharp.

Kan, Shu. (1999), 'Asia Tsuhka Kiki to Nihon Keizai eno Eikyo [The Asian Currency Crisis and its Impact on the Japanese Economy]', in S. Urata and T. Kinoshita (eds), *Niju Isseiki no Azia* [Asia in the Twenty-First Century], Tokyo: Toyokeizai Shinposha.

Kanasaki, T. (1982), *Kaden Gyokai* [Household Electric/Electronics Industry], Tokyo: Kyoikusha.

Kapur, Devesh and John McHale (2005), *Give Us Your Best and Brightest: The Global Hunt for Talent and its Impact on the Developing World*, Washington, DC: Center for Global Development.

Kasa, K. (1999), 'Time for a Tobin Tax?', *FRBSF Economic Letter*, April 9, 99–12.

Katzenstein, Peter J. and Takashi Shiraishi (eds), (2006), *Beyond Japan: The Dynamics of East Asian Regionalism*, Ithaca, NY: Cornell University Press.

Keesing, Donald B. (1967), 'Outward-looking Policies and Economic Development', *Economic Journal*, **77** (306), 303–20.

Kierzkowski, Henryk (2001), 'Joining the Global Economy: Experience and Prospects of The Transition Economies', in S. Arndt and H. Kierzkowski (eds), *Fragmentation: New Production Patterns in the World Economy*, Oxford: Oxford University Press.

Kindleberger, Charles P. (1963), *International Economics*, New York: Irwin.

Kindleberger, Charles P. (1996), *Manias, Panics and Crashes: A History of Financial Crises*, New York: Wiley.

Klein, Lawrence W. (2000), 'Can Export-led Growth Continue Indefinitely? An Asian-Pacific Perspective', *Journal of Asian Economics*, **1** (1), 1–12.

Koizumi, H. (1990), *Kaden Gyokai* [Household Electric/Electronics Industry], Tokyo: Kyoikusha.

Kojima, Kiyoshi (1973), 'Reorganization of North-South Trade: Japan's Foreign Economic Policy for the 1970s', *Hitotsubashi Journal of Economics*, **13** (2), 1–28.

Kojima, Kiyoshi (1975a), 'Ganko Keitairon to Purodakuto Saikururon [FG Theory vs. PC Theory]', in Monkasei [his students] (eds), *Gakumon Henro* [Learning as Pilgrimage], Collection of Papers in Memory of Akamatsu Kaname, Tokyo: Sekai Keizai Kenkyu Kyookai.

Kojima, Kiyoshi (1975b), 'International Trade and Foreign Investment: Substitutes or Complements', *Hitotsubashi Journal of Economics*, **16**, 1–12.

Kojima, Kiyoshi (1978), *Direct Foreign Investment: A Japanese Model of Multinational Business Operations*, London: Croom Helm.

Kojima, Kiyoshi (2000), 'The "Flying-geese" Model of Asian Economic Development: Origin, Theoretical Extensions, and Regional Policy Implications', *Journal of Asian Economics*, **11**, 375–401.

Kojima, Kiyoshi, (2003), *Gankokei Keizai Hattenron: Vol. 1, Nihon Keizai, Azia Keizai, Sekai Keizai* [The Flying-geese Theory of Economic Development: Vol. 1, The Japanese Economy, the Asian Economy, and the World Economy], Tokyo: Bunshindo.

Kojima, Kiyoshi (2004), *Gankokei Keizai Hattenron: Vol. 2, Azia to Sekai no Shin Chitsujo* [New Order for Asia and the World], Tokyo: Bunshindo.

Kojima, Kiyoshi (2006), *Gankokei Keizai Hattenron: Vol. 3, Kokusaikeizai to Kinyukiko* [International Economy and Monetary System], Tokyo: Bunshindo.

Kravis, I.B. and R.E. Lipsey (1983), *Toward an Exploration of National Price Levels*, Princeton Studies in International Finance 52, Princeton, NJ: International Finance Section, Princeton University.

Krueger, Ann O. (1985), 'The Experience and Lessons of Asia's Super Exporters', in Vittorio Corbo, Anne Krueger, and Fernando Ossa (eds), *Export-oriented Development Strategies: The Success of Five Newly Industrializing Countries,* Boulder, CO and London: Westview Press.

Krugman, Paul (1979), 'A Model of Innovation, Technology Transfer, and the World Distribution of Income', *Journal of Political Economy*, **87** (2), 253–66.

Krugman, Paul (1984), 'Import Protection as Export Promotion: International Competition in the Presence of Oligopoly and Economies of Scale', in Henryk Kierzkowski (ed.), *Monopolistic Competition and International Trade*, Oxford: Clarendon Press.

Krugman, Paul (1994), 'The Myth of Asia's Miracle', *Foreign Affairs*, **73** (6), 62–93.

Krugman, Paul (1998), 'Saving Asia: It's Time to Get Radical', *Fortune*, **138** (5), 75–80.

Krugman, Paul and Maurice Obstfeld (2005), *International Economics: Theory and Policy*, Sixth edition, New York: Addison Wesley.

Kumra, Gautam (2007), 'Upgrading India's Energy and Transportation Networks: An Interview with a Leading Infrastructure Builder', *McKinsey Quarterly*, web exclusive, November.

Kwan, C.H. (1994), *Economic Interdependence in the Asia-Pacific Region*, London: Routledge.

Landes, David S. (1969), *The Unbound Prometheus*, Cambridge: Cambridge University Press.

Leamer, E. (1984), *Sources of International Comparative Advantage: Theory and Evidence*, Cambridge, MA: MIT Press.

Lee, C.S. and M. Pecht (1997), *The Taiwan Electronics Industry*, Boca Raton and New York: CRC Press.

Lee, Y.-S. (1998), 'A Political Economy Analysis of the Korean Economic Crisis', *Journal of Asian Economics*, **9** (4), 627–36.

Leibenstein, Harvey (1957), *Economic Backwardness and Economic Growth: Studies in the Theory of Economic Development*, New York: Wiley.

Lewis, C. (1938), *America's Stake in International Investment*, Washington, DC: Brookings Institution.

Lothian, James R. (2006), 'Institutions, Capital Flows and Financial Integration', *Journal of International Money and Finance*, **25**, 358–69.

Lucas Jr, R.E. (1990), 'Why Doesn't Capital Flow from Rich to Poor Countries?', *American Economic Review*, **80**, 92–6.

Mandel, Michael J. (2000), *The Coming Internet Depression*, New York: Basic Books.

McKinnon, Ronald I. (2005a), 'Exchange Rates, Wages, and International Adjustment: Japan and China versus the United States', a paper presented at the symposium Revived Bretton Woods System: A New Paradigm for Asian Development?, held at the Federal Reserve Bank of San Francisco, February 4.

McKinnon, Ronald I. (2005b), *Exchange Rates under the East Asian Dollar Standard: Living with Conflicted Virtue*, Cambridge, MA: MIT Press.

McLuhan, Marshall and Quentin Fiore (1967), *The Medium is the Message*, New York: Random House.

McLuhan, Marshall and Bruce R. Powers (1989), *The Global Village: Transformations in World Life and Media in the 21st Century*, New York: Oxford University Press.

McNulty, Paul J. (1972), 'Predecessors of the Multinational Corporation', *Columbia Journal of World Business*, **7**, 73–80.

Meade, James E. (1951), *The Balance of Payments*, Vol. 1, London: Oxford University Press.

Meier, Gerald M. and Robert E. Baldwin (1957), *Economic Development: Theory, History, Policy*, New York: Wiley.

Mill, John Stuart (1848/1909), *Principles of Political Economy*, London: Macmillan.

Ministry of International Trade and Industry (MITI) (1976), *Keizai Kyoryoku no Genjo to Mondaiten* [Present State and Problems of Economic Cooperation], Tokyo: MITI.

Mishkin, Frederic S. (2006), *The Next Great Globalization: How Disadvantaged Nations can Harness their Financial Systems to Get Rich*, Princeton, NJ: Princeton University Press.

Mishkin, Frederic S. (2007), *The Economics of Money, Banking, and Financial Markets*, eighth edition, New York: Pearson-Addison Wesley.

Mundell, Robert (1957), 'International Trade and Factor Mobility', *American Economic Review*, **47**, 321–35.

Myrdal, Gunnar (1957), *Economic Theory and Underdeveloped Regions*, London: Duckworth.

Myrdal, Gunnar (1968), *Asian Drama: An Inquiry into the Poverty of Nations*, New York: Pantheon.

Namayama, W., W. Boulton, and M. Pecht (1999), *The Japanese Electronics Industry*, Boca Raton and New York: Chapman & Hall/ CRC.

Nelson, Richard R. and Sidney G. Winter (1982), *An Evolutionary Theory of Economic Change*, Cambridge, MA: Harvard University Press.

North, Douglass C. (1999), *Understanding the Process of Economic Change*, London: Institute of Economic Affairs.

NSF (National Science Foundation) (2007a), 'Asia's Rising Science and Technology Strength: Comparative Indicators for Asia, the European Union, and the United States', Special Report, NSF 07-319, May.

NSF (National Science Foundation) (2007b), 'Why Did They Come to the United States? A Profile of Immigrant Scientists and Engineers', InfoBrief, NSF 07-324, June.

NSF (2008), Science and Engineering Indicators, www.nsf.gov/statistics/ seindo8, January.

Nurkse, Ragnar (1953), *Problems of Capital Formation in Underdeveloped Countries*, Oxford: Basil Blackwell.

OECD (Organisation for Economic Co-operation and Development), *Series C: Trade by Commodities, Market Summaries, Imports; 1969–1995*, Paris: OECD.

Ohkawa, Kazushi and Henry Rosovsky (1972), *Japanese Economic Growth*, Stanford, CA: Stanford University Press.

Okazaki, Tetsuji (1997), 'Government-firm Relationship in Postwar Japanese Economic Recovery: Resolving the Coordination Failure by Coordination in Industrial Rationalization', in M. Aoki, H.-K. Kim, and M. Okuno-Fujiwara (eds), *The Role of Government in East Asian Economic Development: Comparative Institutional Analysis*, Oxford: Clarendon Press.

Okita, Saburo (1985), 'Special Presentation: Prospect of the Pacific Economies', a speech printed in Report of the Fourth Pacific Economic Cooperation Conference, Seoul, April 29–May 1, Korea Development Institute.

Oman, Charles, Steven Fries, and Willem Buiter (2003), *Corporate Governance in Developing, Transition and Emerging-Market Economies, Policy Brief No. 23*, Paris: OECD Development Centre.

Owens, T. and A. Wood (1997), 'Export-oriented Industrialization through Primary Processing', *World Development*, 25 (9), 1453–70.

Ozawa, Terutomo (1974a), *Japan's Technological Challenge to the West, 1950–1974: Motivation and Accomplishment*, Cambridge, MA: MIT Press.

Ozawa, Terutomo (1974b), 'Japan's Mid-East Economic Diplomacy', *Columbia Journal of World Business*, **9** (3), 38–46.

Ozawa, Terutomo (1979), *Multinationalism, Japanese-style: The Political Economy of Outward Dependency*, Princeton, NJ: Princeton University Press.

Ozawa, Terutomo (1980), 'Japan's New Resource Diplomacy: Government-backed Group Investment', *Journal of World Trade Law*, **14** (1), 3–13.

Ozawa, Terutomo (1992), 'Foreign Direct Investment and Economic Development', *Transnational Corporations*, **1** (1), 27–54.

Ozawa, Terutomo (1993), 'Foreign Direct Investment and Structural Transformation: Japan as a Recycler of Market and Industry', *Business and the Contemporary World*, **5** (2): 129–50.

Ozawa, Terutomo (1995), 'Structural Upgrading and Concatenated Integration: The Vicissitudes of the Pax Americana in Tandem Industrialization of the Pacific Rim', in Denis Simon (ed.), *Corporate Strategies in the Pacific Rim*, London: Routledge.

Ozawa, Terutomo (1996), 'Japan', in J. Dunning (ed.), *Government, Globalization, and International Business*, Oxford: Oxford University Press.

Ozawa Terutomo (1998), 'Tandem Growth and Crisis: Did East Asia Emulate the Japanese Model of Finance?', in A. Nelson and T.-S. Chan (eds), *Proceedings, Vol. 1, Third South China International Business Symposium*, Macao, China: University of Macao.

Ozawa, Terutomo (1999a), 'Bank Loan Capitalism and Financial Crises: Japanese and Korean Experiences', in A. Rugman and G. Boyd (eds), *Deepening Integration in the Pacific Economies: Corporate Alliances, Contestable Markets, and Free Trade*, Cheltenham, UK and Northampton, MA, USA: Edward Elgar.

Ozawa, Terutomo (1999b), 'The Rise and Fall of Bank-loan Capitalism: Institutionally Driven Growth and Crisis in Japan', *Journal of Economic Issues*, **33** (2), 351–8.

Ozawa, Terutomo (2001), 'The "Hidden" Side of the "Flying-Geese" Catch-up Model: Japan's Dirigiste Institutional Setup and a Deepening Financial Morass', *Journal of Asian Economics,* **12**, 471–91.

Ozawa, Terutomo (2003), 'Pax-American-led Macro-clustering and Flying-geese Style Catch-up in East Asia: Mechanisms of Regionalized Endogenous Growth', *Journal of Asian Economics*, **13** (6), 699–713.

Ozawa, Terutomo (2005), *Institutions, Industrial Upgrading, and Economic Performance in Japan: The 'Flying-Geese' Paradigm of Catch-up Growth*, Cheltenham, UK and Northampton, MA, USA: Edward Elgar. Paperback edition (2006).

Ozawa, Terutomo, Moyses Pluciennik, and K. Ngaraja Rao (1976), 'Japanese Direct Investment in Brazil', *Columbia Journal of World Business*, **11**, 107–16.

Park, Y.C. (1994), 'Korea: Development and Structural Change of the Financial System', in H. Patrick and Y.C. Park (eds), *The Financial Development of Japan, Korea, and Taiwan: Growth, Repression, and Liberalization*, New York: Oxford University Press.

Park, Y.C. and W.A. Park (1991), 'Changing Japanese Trade Patterns and the East Asian NIEs', in P. Krugman (ed.), *Trade with Japan: Has the Door Opened Wider?* Chicago, IL: University of Chicago Press.

Patrick, Hugh T. (1967), 'Japan, 1868–1914', in Rondo Cameron (ed.), *Banking in the Early Stages of Industrialization*, New York: Oxford University Press.

Pecht, M., J.B. Bernstein, D. Searls, and M. Peckerar (1997), *The Korean Electronics Industry*, Boca Raton and New York: CRC Press.

Pecht, M., C.S. Lee, Z.X. Fu, J.J. Lu, and W.Y. Wen (1999), *The Chinese Electronics Industry*, Boca and New York: CRC Press.

Pempel, T.J. (1996/7), 'Gulliver in Lilliput: Japan and Asian Economic Regionalism', *World Policy Journal*, **13** (4), 13–26.

Peng, K. and D. Ames (2001), 'Dialectical Thinking, Psychology of', in Neil Smelser and Paul Baltes (eds), *The International Encyclopedia of the Social and Behavioral Sciences*, Amsterdam: Elsevier, pp. 3634–7.

Porter, Michael (1990), *The Competitive Advantage of Nations*, New York: Free Press.

Prebisch, Raul (1950), *The Economic Development of Latin America and its Principal Problems*, New York: United Nations.

Prestowitz, Clyde (2005), *Three Billion New Capitalists: The Greatest Shift of Wealth and Power to the East*, New York: Basic Books.

Radelet, Steven and Jeffrey Sachs (1997), 'Asia's Reemergence', *Foreign Affairs*, **76** (6), 44–59.

Reinhardt, N. (2000), 'Back to Basics in Malaysia and Thailand: The Role of Resource-based Exports in their Export-Led Growth', *World Development*, **28** (1), 57–97.

Rodrik, Dani (1995), 'Getting Interventions Right: How South Korea and Taiwan Grew Rich', *Economic Policy*, **20**, 78–91.

Rosenberg, Nathan (1972), *Technology and American Economic Growth*, New York: Harper & Row.

Rosenstein-Rodan, P.N. (1943), 'Problems of Industrialization of Eastern and Southeastern Europe', *Economic Journal*, **53** (210), 202–11.

Rosenstein-Rodan, P.N. (1961), 'Notes on the Theory of the "Big Push"', in H.S. Ellis and H.C. Wallich (eds), *Economic Development for Latin America*, New York: St. Martin's Press.

Rostow, W.W. (1960), *The Stages of Growth: A Non-Communist Manifesto*, Cambridge: Cambridge University Press.

Rostow, W.W. (1990), *Theorists of Economic Growth from David Hume to the Present*, New York: Oxford University Press.

Rudolph, Karl-Ulrich and Michael Harbach (2007), 'Private Sector Participation in Water and Sanitation for Developing Countries', *CESifo Dice Report: Journal for Institutional Comparisons*, **5** (2), 33–9.

Sachs, Jeffrey D. and Andrew W. Warner (2001), 'The Curse of Natural Resources', *European Economic Review*, **45**, 827–38.

Sala-i-Martin, Xavier X. (1997), 'I Just Ran Two Million Regressions', *American Economic Review*, **87** (2), 178–83.

Sala-i-Martin, Xavier X. and Arvind Subramanian (2003), 'Addressing the Natural Resource Curse: An Illustration from Nigeria', Natural Bureau of Economic Research Working Paper No. 9804.

Schultz, T.W. (1964), *Transforming Traditional Agriculture*, New Haven, CT: Yale University Press.

Schumpeter, Joseph A. (1934), *The Theory of Economic Development*, originally published in Germany, 1911; English translation, New York: Oxford University Press, 1961.

Schumpeter, Joseph A. (1942/1950), *Capitalism, Socialism and Democracy*, New York: Harper & Row.

Science and Technology Agency, Japan (1969), *Kagaku Gijutsu Hakusho* [White Paper on Science and Technology], Tokyo: Finance Ministry Printing Office.

Shinohara, Myohei (1987), 'Patterns and Backgrounds of Dynamics in the Asia-Pacific Economies', in M. Dutta (ed.), *Asia-Pacific Economies: Promises and Challenges*, Greenwich, CT: JAI Press, Part A.

Sigmund, Paul E. (1980), *Multinationals in Latin America: The Politics of Nationalization*, Madison, WI: University of Wisconsin Press.

Singer, Hans W. (1950), 'The Distribution of Gains between Borrowing and Investing Countries', *American Economic Review*, **40**, 473–85.

Smith, Adam (1759/1976), *The Theory of Moral Sentiments*, edited by D.D. Raphael and A.L. Macfie, Oxford: Clarendon Press.

Smith, Adam (1776/1908), *An Inquiry into the Nature and Causes of the Wealth of Nations*, London: Routledge; reproduced: New York: E.P. Dutton, 1908.

Solis, Mireya (2004), *Banking on Multinationals: Public Credit and the Export of Japanese Sunset Industries*, Stanford, CA: Stanford University Press.

Stiglitz, Joseph (2003), 'Towards a New Paradigm of Development', in John Dunning (ed.), *Making Globalization Good: The Moral Challenges of Global Capitalism*, Oxford: Oxford University Press.

Stockwin, Harvey (1976), 'Asahan: Why Japan said Yes', *Far Eastern Economic Review*, **9** (April), 42–3.

Strange, Susan (1997), *Casino Capitalism*, Manchester: Manchester University Press.

Thurow, Lester C. (1985), *The Management Challenge: Japanese Views*, Cambridge, MA: MIT Press.

Tsurumi, H. and Y. Tsurumi (1980), 'A Bayesian Test of the Product Life Cycle Hypothesis as Applied to the U.S. Demand for Color-TV Sets', *International Economic Review*, **21** (3), 583–96.

UNCTAD (1995), *World Investment Report 1995*, Geneva and New York: United Nations

UNCTAD (1997), *World Investment Report 1997*, Geneva and New York: United Nations.

UNCTAD (1998), *World Investment Report 1998*, Geneva and New York: United Nations.

Veblen, Thorstein (1915), 'The Opportunity of Japan', reprinted in *Essays in Our Changing Order*, New York: Viking Press, 1934.

Veblen, Thorstein (1939), *Imperial Germany and the Industrial Revolution*, New York: Viking Press.

Vernon, Raymond (1966), 'International Trade and International Investment in the Product Cycle', *Quarterly Journal of Economics*, **80** (2), 190–207.

Vernon, Raymond (1979), 'The Product Cycle Hypothesis in the New International Environment', *Oxford Bulletin of Economics and Statistics*, **4** (4), 255–68.

Vernon, Raymond (1983), *Two Hungry Giants: The United States and Japan in the Quest for Oil and Ores*, Cambridge, MA: Harvard University Press.

Vogel, Ezra F. (1978), 'Guided Free Enterprises in Japan', *Harvard Business Review*, **56** (3), 161–70.

Wade, Robert (1990), *Governing the Market: Economic Theory and the Role of Government in East Asian Industrialization*, Princeton, NJ: Princeton University Press.

Wainwright, Fred (2003), 'Riding on Angels' Wings', *Financial Times*, August 15.

Wallich, H. and M. Wallich (1976), 'Banking and Finance', in H. Patrick and H. Rosovsky (eds), *Asia's New Giant: How the Japanese Economy Works*, Washington, DC: Brookings Institution.

Williamson, John (1989), 'What Washington Means by Policy Reform', in J. Williamson (ed), *Latin American Readjustment: How Much has Happened*, Washington, DC: Institute for International Economics.

Winter, Alan L. (2004), 'Trade Liberalisation and Economic Performance: An Overview', *Economic Journal*, **114** (February), F4–F21.

Wissenbach, Uwe (2007), 'Partners in Competition? The EU, Africa and China', Conference summary proceedings, Brussels, June 28.

World Bank (1991), *World Development Report*, Washington, DC: World Bank.

World Bank (1993), *The East Asian Miracle: Economic Growth and Public Policy*, New York: Oxford University Press.

World Bank (1994), *World Development Report 1994: Infrastructure for Development*, New York: Oxford University Press.

World Bank (2002), *From Natural Resources to the Knowledge Economy: Trade and Job Quality* (by D. de Ferranti, G. Perry, D. Lederman, and W. Maloney), World Bank Latin American and Caribbean Studies, Washington, DC: World Bank.

Yamazawa, Ippei (1990), *Economic Development and International Trade: The Japanese Model*, Honolulu, HI: East-West Center.

Young, Allyn A. (1928), 'Increasing Returns and Economic Progress', *Economic Journal*, **38** (152), 527–42.

Young, T. and Arrigo, B. (1999), 'Dialectic', in T. Young and B. Arrigo (eds), *The Dictionary of Critical Social Sciences*, Boulder, CO: Westview Press.

Zhan, James and Terutomo Ozawa (2001), *Business Restructuring in Asia: Cross-Border M&As in the Crisis Period*, Copenhagen: Copenhagen Business School Press.

Index